K. Anderson

THE GOSPEL OF LUKE

An Exposition

THE GOSPEL
OF LUKE

An Exposition

by
CHARLES R. ERDMAN

PREFACE BY EARL F. ZEIGLER

THE WESTMINSTER PRESS

PHILADELPHIA

Published by The Westminster Press®
Philadelphia, Pennsylvania

PRINTED IN THE UNITED STATES OF AMERICA

PREFACE

Never has the Gospel of Luke been more needed by the human race than at the present time. We are a sad world that needs good tidings of great joy. This Gospel has those tidings. We are a people who have lost confidence in the spiritual verities of the universe. This Gospel makes no apology for including a number of graphic narratives that can be explained only by belief in the supernatural. For some people, God seems to have no abiding place in a universe that defies our meager comprehension of time and space. Luke's Gospel assures the reader by reliable evidence that the Son of God was incarnate in Jesus of Nazareth, and when he had completed his earthly ministry he returned to the heaven from which he had come. Truly, we need today this sustaining food for our under-nourished souls.

The author of this Gospel is another reason for reader interest. He was a physician, a non-Jew, a convert to Christianity, a travel companion to the apostle Paul on many trips, and was even with Paul for a while during the apostle's imprisonment in Rome. His writing breathes the spirit of a man who was engaged in a labor of love to tell the amazing story of how God had visited this planet in human form; had companied with the people of Palestine in particular; had shown mercy on the poor and the outcast; had compassion on the hungry and the diseased in body and mind; and then had died on a cross to atone for human sin. But on the third day God raised him from the dead. Only a man who knew personally the redeeming love of Christ could write with such passion. Dr. Luke composed a sequel to his Gospel which we know as The Acts of the Apostles. It throws revealing floods of light on the history of the early church.

The volume that you are now reading contains not only the complete text of the Gospel of Luke but also a commentary that explains almost everything that a student wants to learn about and from Luke's Gospel. Each of the seventeen volumes in this series of New Testament commentaries contains the complete text of the book or books included, as well as an exposition of the Scripture passages. In the beginning of the publication of this series it was decided to invite only one writer for the whole list. The choice fell on Dr. Charles R. Erdman, then professor of practical theology at Princeton Theological Seminary. At the rate of about one book per year the series grew. They were purchased and publicized by church school teachers, pastors, college and seminary students, and the laity in general. They have been printed so many times that the plates have worn badly. The reprinting of the entire series in paperback editions required resetting type and creating new plates. All this is warranted, however, by the past popularity of these commentaries, and the conviction of the publisher that this method of the ministry of the Word will be bread cast on the waters that will not return void.

EARL F. ZEIGLER

FOREWORD

The Gospel of Luke is the most beautiful book in the world; at least, so it has been called, and those who know it best are not likely to dispute such praise. The purpose of this little volume is to place the book in convenient form, and by an outline and brief comments to aid in focusing the thought of the reader upon the successive scenes of the Gospel story. These are familiar scenes, but each review of them more vividly reveals the great central Figure as supreme among men in the matchless loveliness of his divine manhood, himself the perfect, the ideal Man.

INTRODUCTION

THE AUTHOR

The surpassing beauty of this book betokens the personal attractiveness of its author and the dignity and importance of its theme. It was written by Luke, "the beloved physician," and it concerns the life and saving work of our Lord. The phrase which describes the writer as "the physician, the beloved one," is full of significance. It was penned by Paul, when a prisoner in Rome, to his friends in distant Colossae. It indicates that Luke was a man of culture and scientific training and that the charm of his character was so conspicuous as to be recognized by the Christian churches of Europe and of Asia. The connection in which this phrase occurs indicates that Luke was not a Jew but a Gentile by birth, and further, that he was a close companion of Paul.

To Luke's authorship is attributed not only this Third Gospel but also The Acts. He was a man of such modesty that he never mentioned his own name even when recording the stirring events in which he played so prominent a part. Nevertheless he revealed himself in every page of his writings and was evidently a man of broad sympathies, an acute observer, a careful historian, and a loyal friend.

The story of his companionship with Paul begins in the record of the apostle's second missionary journey when he was about to sail from Troas on the memorable voyage which resulted in establishing Christianity on a new continent. The two friends journeyed together to Philippi, where a strong church was founded; but while Paul continued his travels through Macedonia and Greece, Luke remained behind, possibly to care for the young converts. Seven years later when Paul was on his third missionary tour he seems to have found Luke at Philippi and to have been accompanied by him on his way to Jerusalem. When Paul was arrested and was confined for two years at Caesarea, Luke was his companion. Later they shared together the perils of the voyage and the shipwreck on the way to Rome, and the imprisonment in the imperial city. Paul appears to have been released and then imprisoned a second time, and when he wrote his last letter, under the shadow of approaching martyrdom, the only friend to remain faithful and to comfort him in his loneliness was Luke.

As might be expected, the narrative composed by such an author is characterized by: (1) unusual literary beauty; it is plainly the product of Greek culture. The divine Spirit chose and equipped a rare instrument in the poetic and refined personality of Luke and through him gave to the world that version of the gospel story which is most exquisite in style and most finished in form.

THE GOSPEL

Yet Luke was not only a man of culture; he was also a Christian physician and thus a man of wide and tender sympathies, and his narrative is therefore characterized by (2) its absorbing human interest. It is a story of real life; it is suffused with emotion; it is full of gladness and sorrow, of songs and of tears; it is vocal with praise and with prayer.

It is the Gospel of childhood. By its tender stories of the birth of John and of Jesus, it places an unfading halo of glory about the brow of infancy, and it alone preserves the precious picture of the boyhood of our Lord. It is the Gospel of womanhood. It sketches for us that immortal group of women associated with the life of Jesus. We see Elisabeth and the virgin mother and the aged Anna, the widow of Nain, the sisters at Bethany, and the repentant sinner, the sufferer bowed down by Satan and the stranger who congratulates Mary, the company that minister to Jesus on his journeys and the "daughters of Jerusalem" weeping on the way to the cross.

It is the Gospel of the home. It gives us glimpses of the family life at Nazareth, of the scene in the house of Simon, of the hospitality of Martha and Mary, of the evening meal with the two disciples at Emmaus and the picture in the parables of the importunate friend at midnight, of the woman searching the room for the lost coin and of the prodigal turning back to his father's house.

It is the Gospel of the poor and the lowly; it warns against the perils of wealth and expresses sympathy and hope for those who are oppressed by poverty and want. This sympathy is sounded in the song of Mary, in the first sermon of the Savior, in the first Beatitude, "Blessed are ye poor." Luke also records the parables of the rich fool and of the rich man and Lazarus, and paints, with Mark, the picture of the widow offering to the Lord her two mites.

It is also the Gospel of praise and of prayer, expressions of the deepest convictions and longings of the human heart. The Gospel opens with a scene in the Temple at the hour of incense and with the Magnificat of Mary and the songs of Zacharias and of the angels. It closes with the benediction of the ascending Lord and the thanksgiving of his joyful disciples.

Luke, however, was not only a man of culture and a beloved physician; he was also a companion of Paul and had traveled with the apostle over a great portion of the Roman world; therefore he naturally wrote a gospel characterized by (3) universal interest. Here no narrow prejudice divides race from race; a despised Samaritan stands as the supreme example of a neighbor, the angels sing of peace among men, and the aged Simeon declares that Jesus is to be a "light for revelation to the Gentiles" as well as the glory of Israel. Luke alone gives the data which link the sacred story to the secular history of the world. His outlook is unlimited. He regards the good news concerning Christ as a message which is vital to the welfare and redemption of the entire human race.

The Portrait of Jesus

1. The Ideal Man

These aspects of his Gospel blend with the picture of his Lord which Luke portrays. The character of Jesus is so subtle and complex as to defy exact analysis, and yet it is evident that certain of its features, common to all, are emphasized successively by each one of the Gospel writers. Matthew depicts its majesty, Mark its strength, and John its sublimity; but Luke reveals its beauty, and paints a picture of the ideal Man, the Savior of the world.

As to all the prime elements of perfect manhood, possibly no two persons may agree; yet none would deny that such was the manhood of Jesus, and none would question that there are two or three moral qualities which he exhibited in a superlative degree, qualities upon which Luke lays special stress.

First of all, Jesus manifested matchless courage. To some interpreters this fearlessness has formed the very essence of the "manliness of Christ." He was not a weak and nerveless preacher of righteousness, but a man of strength, of dauntless resolve, and of courageous action. The mob was eager to destroy him as he began his work in Nazareth, but his enemies quailed before his majestic presence, as "he passing through the midst of them went his way." He was advised to flee from the realm of Herod, but he flung defiance to the king, beginning his message with the words, "Go and say to that fox." The section of ten chapters in this Gospel which describes the last journeys of our Lord opens with a deeply significant phrase, "He stedfastly set his face to go to Jerusalem." Only five chapters devoted to his ministry precede, only five follow.

During all the long period described in the chapters between, Jesus plainly foresaw his coming rejection and suffering and death, but fearlessly and with unfaltering step
he moved onward to the cross. All the heroisms of history
are dwarfed to insignificance by this incomparable courage
of Christ.

More obvious still is the boundless and tender sympathy
of this ideal Man. He declared in his first address that he
had come "to preach good tidings to the poor: . . . to
proclaim release to the captives, and recovering of sight to
the blind, to set at liberty them that are bruised"; and as
we follow in his footsteps we see how his tender heart
yearned over all who suffered and were distressed; he dried
the tears of sorrow; he showed his pity for the outcast and
the impure; he received sinners and was entertained by
publicans; he praised Samaritans and comforted the dying
thief. This world has no other picture of such perfect
compassion, tenderness, and love; and these are essential
to true manhood.

More mysterious, but none the less real, was his constant faith. His life was lived in continual fellowship with
God. In his first recorded saying he declared, "I must be
in my Father's house," and at the last he breathed out his
spirit on the cross with the words, "Father, into thy hands
I commend my spirit." All the intervening days of his life
and ministry were filled with ceaseless prayer. On at least
seven other occasions it is stated that he was praying: at
his baptism, ch. 3:21; after healing the leper, ch. 5:16; before choosing his disciples, ch. 6:12; before Peter's great
confession, ch. 9:18; at his transfiguration, ch. 9:29; before teaching his disciples to pray, ch. 11:1; in the first
agonies of crucifixion, ch. 23:34. So, too, he taught his
disciples to pray with importunity, ch. 11:5-10, with per-
severance, ch. 18:1-7, and with penitence, ch. 18:9-14.
Such trust in God, such sympathy, such bravery, are surely
prominent among the many elements which are blended in
this impressive portrayal of the ideal Man.

2. The Savior of the World

However, Luke has written a version of the gospel and therefore has produced much more than a picture of human perfection or the story of an ideal life. The gospel is the "good news" of salvation secured for us by our Lord; and in the narrative of Luke we behold One who was not only supreme in his manhood but was also the Savior of the world. It was in accomplishing this redeeming work that he revealed such courage and so steadfastly set his face to go to Jerusalem. The salvation he secured is inseparable from the cross.

It was a salvation provided for all, even as his sympathy knew no bounds but was extended to the last and the lowest of men—to the despised publican, to the outcast sinner, to the hated Samaritan, to the crucified thief.

Then, too, as he ever trusted in his Father, so the salvation he secured to us is conditioned upon faith in himself as Redeemer and Lord, a faith which implies repentance and trust and submission and sacrifice. One must be willing to count the cost, to abandon anything which stands between self and the Master. This salvation, however, is wholly of grace, unmerited, free, provided by the Father for all who yield themselves to the loving care of his Son.

This salvation was to be proclaimed to all the nations. Those to whom it became known, and by whom it was accepted, were to become witnesses to the transforming truth. For such testimony they would require courage and wide sympathy and unfaltering faith, and in their courage and sympathy and faith they would be like their Master who by such qualities was manifested as the ideal Man as he was the divine Savior of the world.

THE OUTLINE

VI

I
THE PREFACE
TO THE GOSPEL
Luke 1:1-4

1 Forasmuch as many have taken in hand to draw up a narrative concerning those matters which have been fulfilled among us, 2 even as they delivered them unto us, who from the beginning were eyewitnesses and ministers of the word, 3 it seemed good to me also, having traced the course of all things accurately from the first, to write unto thee in order, most excellent Theophilus; 4 that thou mightest know the certainty concerning the things wherein thou wast instructed.

This preface is a perfect gem of Greek art; even in the English Version it loses little, if anything, of its literary charm. As a prologue it is regarded as unsurpassed for brevity, modesty, and dignity. However, its value lies not in its beauty but in its testimony to the veracity of the writer and to the historic worth and absolute credibility of the gospel story. The fact of inspiration should not blind us to the human means by which the Spirit of God secured accuracy in the communication of truth and in the composition of the Holy Scriptures.

Here we are admitted to the study of a great historian. We see about him his tools and his material; we are informed as to his motives and methods in work, and are told of the qualifications he possesses for his great task. First of all, he has before him many written accounts of the ministry of Christ. He does not reject these as inaccurate but regards any one of them as inadequate. By comparing and combining them he secures valuable outlines for his more complete narrative.

Then, too, he intimates that he is living and writing amid the scenes and in the very atmosphere of the events he is recording; only recently, as he indicates, have these "matters . . . been fulfilled." Again, he has access to the testimony of men who were eyewitnesses of these events and who have been public teachers of the gospel.

Further, he assures us of the absolute accuracy with which he has investigated the incidents of the life and ministry of Christ, even from the earliest scenes; he has sifted his material and weighed the evidence and is to record only established facts.

These facts he is to relate "in order," that is, in the sequence of time, and further still, with the system and the careful regard to proportion and to completeness which should characterize a scientific, historical composition.

Then again he dedicates the book to Theophilus, whose title, "most excellent," indicates that he is a man of rank and official position, one to whom an author would not venture to present hasty, imperfect, and inaccurate work, especially when the one addressed had been instructed already in reference to the matters related.

Thus this preface shows the supreme purpose of Luke was to confirm the belief of Theophilus, who is apparently his patron and friend, and to deepen his conviction of the truth of the gospel story. Surely such an introduction must remind every reader that our Christian faith is based upon an impregnable foundation of historic fact.

II
THE BIRTH AND
CHILDHOOD OF JESUS
Chs. 1:5 to 2:52

A. THE BIRTH OF JOHN FORETOLD

Ch. 1:5-25

5 There was in the days of Herod, king of Judæa, a certain priest named Zacharias, of the course of Abijah: and he had a wife of the daughters of Aaron, and her name was Elisabeth. 6 And they were both righteous before God, walking in all the commandments and ordinances of the Lord blameless. 7 And they had no child, because that Elisabeth was barren, and they both were now well stricken in years.

8 Now it came to pass, while he executed the priest's office before God in the order of his course, 9 according to the custom of the priest's office, his lot was to enter into the temple of the Lord and burn incense. 10 And the whole multitude of the people were praying without at the hour of incense. 11 And there appeared unto him an angel of the Lord standing on the right side of the altar of incense. 12 And Zacharias was troubled when he saw him, and fear fell upon him. 13 But the angel said unto him, Fear not, Zacharias: because thy supplication is heard, and thy wife Elisabeth shall bear thee a son, and thou shalt call his name John. 14 And thou shalt have joy and gladness; and many shall rejoice at his birth. 15 For he shall be great in the sight of the Lord, and he shall drink no wine nor strong drink; and he shall be filled with the Holy Spirit, even from his mother's womb. 16 And many of the children of Israel shall he turn unto the Lord their God. 17 And he shall go before his face in the spirit and power of Elijah, to turn the hearts of the fathers to the children,

*and the disobedient to walk in the wisdom of the just; to
make ready for the Lord a people prepared for him. 18
And Zacharias said unto the angel, Whereby shall I know
this? for I am an old man, and my wife well stricken in
years. 19 And the angel answering said unto him, I am
Gabriel, that stand in the presence of God; and I was sent
to speak unto thee, and to bring thee these good tidings.
20 And behold, thou shalt be silent and not able to speak,
until the day that these things shall come to pass, because
thou believedst not my words, which shall be fulfilled in
their season. 21 And the people were waiting for Zacharias, and they marvelled while he tarried in the temple.
22 And when he came out, he could not speak unto them:
and they perceived that he had seen a vision in the temple:
and he continued making signs unto them, and remained
dumb. 23 And it came to pass, when the days of his min-
istration were fulfilled, he departed unto his house.*

*24 And after these days Elisabeth his wife conceived;
and she hid herself five months, saying, 25 Thus hath the
Lord done unto me in the days wherein he looked upon
me, to take away my reproach among men.*

Luke is the Gospel of gladness, of praise, and of prayer,
of tender, human interest, and of heavenly grace. It is
fitting, therefore, that the narrative should open with a
scene in the Temple at the hour of incense and with a
divine promise which fills a heart with rapturous joy. This
promise concerns the birth of one who is to prepare the
way for the ministry of Christ, and this ministry forms the
sum and substance of the gospel story.

The time was "in the days of Herod," called "the Great,"
a monster of cruelty, a vassal of Rome, who ruled the Jews
with savage tyranny. The political slavery of the people
was only less pitiful than their spiritual decline, for religion
had become an empty form, a mere system of ceremonies
and rites. However, God is never without his witnesses
and his true worshipers. Among these were "a certain
priest named Zacharias" and his wife Elisabeth, who lived
in the hill country of Judea, south of Jerusalem. They

"were both righteous before God," not sinless but without reproach, carefully observing the moral and also the ritual requirements of the law. Yet godliness is no guarantee against sorrow or against the disappointment of human hopes, and these pious souls were saddened because their home was childless. This trial was peculiarly great among a people who regarded childlessness as a sign of divine displeasure, and it was even more distressing to the hearts of the faithful who were yearning for the birth of the promised Messiah.

Twice each year Zacharias went to Jerusalem to perform for a week his sacred tasks. Finally there came to him a privilege which a priest could enjoy only once in his lifetime; the "lot" fell upon him, and he thus was chosen to enter the Holy Place at the hour of prayer and there offer incense upon the golden altar just before the veil in the very presence of God. It was the supreme hour of his life. As the cloud of perfume began to rise, true symbol of accepted petitions, an angel appeared and assured the startled priest that his supplications had been heard. For what had Zacharias then been praying—for a son, or for the salvation of his people? Were not both desires included in that supplication? As the representative of a nation, the priest hardly could have confined his petition to what was purely personal and private. Yet, as he pleaded for the coming of the Messiah, there must have been in his soul the secret yearning of the long years or the memory of that abandoned hope which he had always associated in thought with the salvation of Israel. Many a minister of Christ has a similar experience; in the very performance of his public tasks there rests on his soul the conscious shadow of some private grief.

The angel declared that the prayer for national salvation had been heard, and he gradually unfolded the contents of the divine answer; the Messiah was about to appear, and his coming was to be heralded by a son who was to be born to the aged priest. The angel spoke with great definiteness: the child would be named John; many would rejoice at his birth; he would be a Nazirite, and as such would take the vow of total abstinence from wine and of complete dedication to God; as a consequence of this dedication he would be filled with the divine Spirit and thus enabled to lead his people to repentance. He would labor in the spirit and power of Elijah, calling men to lives of natural affection and justice and preparing them for the salvation which Christ would bring.

So surprising a message was too great to be credited at once by the wondering priest. He had ceased to hope that the longing of his heart could be fulfilled. He therefore asked for a sign by which he might be assured that the blessed promise was true. The angel replied with a statement of his own majestic power and the glory of his mission, and he granted to Zacharias a sign. This sign was at once a rebuke and a blessing. It rebuked the unbelief of the aged priest, yet it strengthened his faith. He was smitten with dumbness which was to continue until the promise of the angel had been realized. Zacharias would not accept the word of the Lord; he would not praise him for his goodness and his grace. Therefore, his tongue was to be silent and he was to be unable to speak until at last his lips were opened in glad thanksgiving. Unbelief is never joyous; infidelity has no songs.

However, the sign suggests supernatural power. The faith of Zacharias and also of Elisabeth will be strengthened by the very silence in their home. So when the people in the court of the Temple waited for the priest to reappear, when as he came they still waited for the usual benediction, when they found that Zacharias had been stricken with dumbness, they concluded he had seen a vision in the Temple, and he himself was assured that the messenger had come from God. In due time the promise was fulfilled; a new life came into being. Meanwhile, until it would be evident that her "reproach" for childlessness had been taken away, Elisabeth lived in strict retirement.

She would not have others, by seeing her, think that she was under divine displeasure at the very time when she secretly knew that she was a special recipient of divine grace. She was jealous for the glory of her God; she delighted in her hidden fellowship with him. From the homes of such priests who can pray, and of such hearts which can trust, there ever have been coming the great prophets of the Lord.

B. THE ANNUNCIATION TO MARY

Ch. 1:26-38

26 Now in the sixth month the angel Gabriel was sent from God unto a city of Galilee, named Nazareth, 27 to a virgin betrothed to a man whose name was Joseph, of the house of David; and the virgin's name was Mary. 28 And he came in unto her, and said, Hail, thou that art highly favored, the Lord is with thee. 29 But she was greatly troubled at the saying, and cast in her mind what manner of salutation this might be. 30 And the angel said unto her, Fear not, Mary: for thou hast found favor with God. 31 And behold, thou shalt conceive in thy womb, and bring forth a son, and shalt call his name JESUS. 32 He shall be great, and shall be called the Son of the Most High: and the Lord God shall give unto him the throne of his father David: 33 and he shall reign over the house of Jacob for ever; and of his kingdom there shall be no end. 34 And Mary said unto the angel, How shall this be, seeing I know not a man? 35 And the angel answered and said unto her, The Holy Spirit shall come upon thee, and the power of the Most High shall overshadow thee: wherefore also the holy thing which is begotten shall be called the Son of God. 36 And behold, Elisabeth thy kinswoman, she also hath conceived a son in her old age; and this is the sixth month with her that was called barren. 37 For no word from God shall be void of power. 38 And Mary said, Behold, the handmaid of the Lord; be it unto me according to thy word. And the angel departed from her.

The prediction to Mary of the birth of Jesus is recorded by Luke with marked dignity, delicacy, and reserve. It is an important record. This prediction is the crown of all prophecy and it reveals the supreme mystery of the Christian faith, namely, the nature of our Lord, at once human and divine.

The same angelic being who had spoken to Zacharias speaks again, not now to an aged and distinguished priest amid the splendors of the Temple in Jerusalem, but to a humble maiden betrothed to a carpenter in an obscure village of Galilee. The angelic salutation, "Hail, thou that art highly favored," has been translated less accurately, "Hail, thou that art full of grace," and it has been misinterpreted to encourage the practice of praying to the virgin as divine. It does not mean, however, that Mary was to be a source but rather a recipient of grace; upon her God was bestowing peculiar favor. She may rightly be regarded as the most blessed among women; but only a woman still.

Mary had been startled by so strange an appearance and greeting; now she was further amazed by the announcement, "Thou shalt . . . bring forth a son, and shalt call his name Jesus." Before her marriage she was to become a mother, and she was to call her child by that significant name which signifies "Savior" or "God is Savior." "He shall be great," continued the angel, both in his person, as "the Son of the Most High," and in his royal power, for "the Lord God shall give unto him the throne of his father David." This throne of David does not refer to the Christian church or to merely heavenly or spiritual influence. It is a rule on earth which here is promised, yet it is not to be limited to one nation nor is it to be confined to one age. It is the Kingdom of the Messiah, which is to bring joy to "the house of Jacob for ever" and also to all the nations of the world—"and of his kingdom there shall be no end."

The exclamation of Mary expressed astonishment but not unbelief: "How shall this be?" Then came the answer

which is unsurpassed as a clear and sublime statement of
the incarnation: "The Holy Spirit shall come upon thee,
and the power of the Most High shall overshadow thee";
the creative power of God was to rest upon Mary as the
cloud of glory had rested upon the tabernacle of Israel,
and as a result the child who would be born should be in
reality, and should be called "the Son of God." Of the
truth of his promise the angel added a sign and proof in
the surprising fact that Elisabeth, the aged kinswoman of
Mary, was soon to be blessed with a son. This was in fulfillment of a promise made by the same angel messenger,
and the marvel in the case of Elisabeth would assure Mary
of the certain accomplishment of the gracious and more
surprising promise to her. The reply of Mary is probably
unequaled in all history as an expression of perfect faith:
"Behold, the handmaid of the Lord; be it unto me according to thy word." Thus she revealed belief in the Word of
God and submission to the will of God. There was no
doubt in her mind as to the truth of the divine promise
with all that it suggested of miracle and of mystery; and
there was no shrinking on her part from all that the fulfillment of this promise possibly might involve of suspicion
and shame and reproach and suffering and even death.
Those who believe most firmly in the promises of God,
submit most patiently to his providences; they see the glory
which surely will succeed the gloom. Mary was to become
the mother of the Messiah, of the Son of Man, of the
Savior of the world.

C. THE MAGNIFICAT Ch. 1:39-56

*39 And Mary arose in these days and went into the hill
country with haste, into a city of Judah; 40 and entered
into the house of Zacharias and saluted Elisabeth. 41 And
it came to pass, when Elisabeth heard the salutation of
Mary, the babe leaped in her womb; and Elisabeth was
filled with the Holy Spirit; 42 and she lifted up her voice*

with a loud cry, and said, Blessed art *thou among women, and blessed* is *the fruit of thy womb.   43 And whence is this to me, that the mother of my Lord should come unto me?   44 For behold, when the voice of thy salutation came into mine ears, the babe leaped in my womb for joy.   45 And blessed* is *she that believed; for there shall be a fulfilment of the things which have been spoken to her from the Lord.   46 And Mary said,*

　　My soul doth magnify the Lord,

47 And my spirit hath rejoiced in God my Saviour.

48 For he hath looked upon the low estate of his handmaid:

　　For behold, from henceforth all generations shall call me blessed.

49 For he that is mighty hath done to me great things;

　　And holy is his name.

50 And his mercy is unto generations and generations

　　On them that fear him.

51 He hath showed strength with his arm;

　　He hath scattered the proud in the imagination of their heart.

52 He hath put down princes from their *thrones,*

　　And hath exalted them of low degree.

53 The hungry he hath filled with good things;

　　And the rich he hath sent empty away.

54 He hath given help to Israel his servant,

　　That he might remember mercy

55 (As he spake unto our fathers)

　　Toward Abraham and his seed for ever.

　56 And Mary abode with her about three months, and returned unto her house.

The Magnificat, the lovely lyric which comes from the lips of Mary, has been sung during many centuries as one of the chief canticles of the Christian church. Its occasion was a visit paid to her kinswoman, Elisabeth, by Mary shortly after she had received the promise of the birth of a son. Elizabeth, on hearing the salutation of Mary, addressed her in high spiritual ecstasy, declaring her supremely blessed among women because of the Son to be born, and wondering at her own honor in being thus visited by the mother of her Lord, by which phrase she means the mother of the Messiah; it is to be noted that the Bible does not contain the phrase "Mother of God." Elisabeth congratulated Mary upon her faith and assured her that the promise upon which Mary relied was certain to be fulfilled.

The name of the song which Mary then sang, the Magnificat, has come from the first line in its Latin form, *Magnificat anima mea Dominum*. The model is that of the ancient hymn sung by Hannah when her heart, like that of Mary, was rejoicing in the promised gift of a son. The verses form a perfect mosaic of Old Testament quotations. The hymn was not addressed to Elisabeth or to the Lord; it is, rather, a meditation upon the mercy and grace of God.

According to the common division the song is composed of four stanzas of four lines each, except the third stanza which contains six lines. The general movement of thought seems to be from the goodness of God to Mary as an individual, to his consequent kindness to Israel as a nation.

The first stanza, or strophe, vs. 46-48, illustrates, as do those which follow, one of the chief features of Hebrew poetry, namely, the expression, in successive lines, of thoughts which are parallel or closely related. In her "soul" or "spirit" or innermost being, Mary praises or magnifies the Lord and rejoices in him as her Savior. This salvation is not only for her people but particularly for herself; it is not only political but also spiritual. It is to be wrought out by the gift God is granting to Mary. He has chosen her, an obscure village maiden betrothed to a poor carpenter, and has bestowed upon her such honor that all future generations will call her "blessed." While realizing the honor, she dwells most upon her unworthiness; while recognizing what it may cost her, she declares her submission as a true "bondmaid" or slave of the Lord. Humility and faith could hardly be more sublime.

The second stanza, vs. 49-50, centers the thought upon the character of God as revealed in his gracious gift. His power, his holiness, his mercy are praised. In his goodness to Mary he had shown his divine power, yet in accordance with the moral perfection of his revealed nature and in order to bring blessings to countless generations who would trust and reverence him.

In the third stanza, vs. 51-53, is an illustration of another feature of Hebrew poetry; not only is there striking parallelism, but here past tenses are used to describe future events; the results of the coming of the Messiah are stated as though already achieved. In contrast with the blessedness of those that fear the Lord, "the proud," the rebellious, and unbelieving are pictured as "scattered" like the hosts of a defeated army; the oppressed are exalted while tyrants are dethroned; the hungry are filled and the rich are sent away "empty." These results are to be regarded as spiritual as well as physical. Such reversals are certain to occur where Christ is accepted, and those who receive blessings from him are the humble who are conscious of their need.

The last strophe, vs. 54-55, emphasizes the faithfulness of God to his ancient promises which Mary sees fulfilled in the birth of her Son. In this saving help given to Israel, God is showing that he has not forgotten the mercy "toward Abraham and his seed" promised to the "fathers" of old. Only in Christ Jesus can be realized all the promises to Israel, all the hopes of the ages.

D. THE BIRTH OF JOHN, AND THE BENEDICTUS Ch. 1:57-80

57 Now Elisabeth's time was fulfilled that she should be delivered; and she brought forth a son. 58 And her neighbors and her kinsfolk heard that the Lord had magnified his mercy towards her; and they rejoiced with her. 59 And it came to pass on the eighth day, that they came to

circumcise the child; and they would have called him
Zacharias, after the name of his father. 60 And his mother
answered and said, Not so; but he shall be called John.
61 And they said unto her, There is none of thy kindred
that is called by this name. 62 And they made signs to
his father, what he would have him called. 63 And he
asked for a writing tablet, and wrote, saying, His name is
John. And they marvelled all. 64 And his mouth was
opened immediately, and his tongue loosed, and he spake,
blessing God. 65 And fear came on all that dwelt round
about them: and all these sayings were noised abroad
throughout all the hill country of Judæa. 66 And all that
heard them laid them up in their heart, saying, What then
shall this child be? For the hand of the Lord was with
him.

67 And his father Zacharias was filled with the Holy
Spirit, and prophesied, saying,

68 Blessed be the Lord, the God of Israel;
    For he hath visited and wrought redemption for his
        people,
69 And hath raised up a horn of salvation for us
    In the house of his servant David
70 (As he spake by the mouth of his holy prophets that
        have been from of old),
71 Salvation from our enemies, and from the hand of all
        that hate us;
72 To show mercy towards our fathers,
    And to remember his holy covenant;
73 The oath which he sware unto Abraham our father,
74 To grant unto us that we being delivered out of the
        hand of our enemies
    Should serve him without fear,
75 In holiness and righteousness before him all our days.
76 Yea and thou, child, shalt be called the prophet of the
        Most High:
    For thou shalt go before the face of the Lord to make
        ready his ways;
77 To give knowledge of salvation unto his people
    In the remission of their sins,
78 Because of the tender mercy of our God,
    Whereby the dayspring from on high shall visit us,

*79 To shine upon them that sit in darkness and the shadow
of death;
To guide our feet into the way of peace.
80 And the child grew, and waxed strong in spirit, and
was in the deserts till the day of his showing unto Israel.*

When the aged priest, Zacharias, had received from an
angel the promise that he was to be given a son who would
be called John and who would be the herald of Christ, and
when he had asked for a sign to attest the truth of the prediction, he was smitten with dumbness as a rebuke for his
unbelief and as a stimulus for his faith. Even when at last
the promise was fulfilled, the sign was not removed and he
was not able to speak until he had given a written expression of his confidence in God. This interesting incident
occurred on the eighth day after the birth of John, when in
the presence of their rejoicing friends the parents were
about to name the child. Many supposed that the name
of the father would be selected. The mother, however,
intimated that the name might be "John." When Zacharias, the father, was consulted, "he asked for a writing
tablet, and wrote, . . . His name is John." There was no
hesitation, no uncertainty, no question in his mind, for this
name had been predicted by the angel, and Zacharias
showed by his decision and firmness that he believed absolutely in the fulfillment of all that the angel had promised
concerning the career of the son who was to be regarded
by his fellowmen as a gift of divine grace and a prophet of
divine appointment. It usually happens that a public confession of faith results in new joy and in wider testimony.
It was surely so in the case of Zacharias: "His mouth was
opened immediately, . . . and he spake, blessing God."
His thanksgiving was voiced in a hymn which, for hun-
dreds of years, has been sung daily in Christian worship.
It is indeed a Christian hymn and a hymn of the Nativity;
for while its occasion was the birth of John, only one
stanza refers to that event; the whole burden of the thanksgiving refers to the approaching birth of Jesus and to the

salvation which he is to bring.

This hymn is named the Benedictus from the first word in the Latin version. It is an ecstatic expression of gratitude to God for his boundless goodness. The poem possibly may be divided into five stanzas of four lines each; but there is a definite pause after the third of these stanzas when the thought turns from the work of Christ to the specific mission of John.

The first strophe, vs. 68-69, speaks of the redemption of Israel as already accomplished in the gift of the Christ who is about to be born and who is described as "a horn of salvation," that is, a manifestation of saving power. He is to appear as a son and heir of David the king.

The second stanza, or strophe, vs. 70-72, indicates that the salvation from all enemies is in fulfillment of the promises made through the prophets and cherished by the ancient fathers and embodied in the holy covenant made with Israel of old.

The third stanza, vs. 73-75, describes the nature of this salvation which was assured by the oath to Abraham; it is to be such a deliverance from political oppression as to make possible for Israel a true, priestly service of God, as a nation holy and righteous before him.

In the fourth stanza, vs. 76-77, the singer turns to address his own son whose birth has given occasion to the song. He declares that John is to be recognized as a prophet of God whose divine mission will be to announce and to define the promised salvation as in its essence not a political but a spiritual redemption consisting in the remission of sin. John was not to be a revolutionist but a reformer. He was to call a nation to repentance that those who obeyed his message might be ready to receive the salvation of Christ.

This mission of John is linked with that of Christ as the description of the latter reaches its climax in the closing strophe, vs. 78-79. The source of all the blessings Christ will bring is found in "the tender mercy of our God"; the essence is a visitation of "the dayspring from on high," when the Sun of righteousness arises upon the helpless, terrified wanderers of the night who are seated "in darkness and the shadow of death"; the result will be "to guide our feet into the way of peace."

Such is the hymn of Zacharias, a hymn of faith, of hope, of gratitude, a song of the salvation provided by the love of God in Jesus Christ our Lord.

E. THE BIRTH OF JESUS Ch. 2:1-20

1 Now it came to pass in those days, there went out a decree from Cæsar Augustus, that all the world should be enrolled. 2 This was the first enrolment made when Quirinius was governor of Syria. 3 And all went to enrol themselves, every one to his own city. 4 And Joseph also went up from Galilee, out of the city of Nazareth, into Judæa, to the city of David, which is called Bethlehem, because he was of the house and family of David; 5 to enrol himself with Mary, who was betrothed to him, being great with child. 6 And it came to pass, while they were there, the days were fulfilled that she should be delivered. 7 And she brought forth her first-born son; and she wrapped him in swaddling clothes, and laid him in a manger, because there was no room for them in the inn.

8 And there were shepherds in the same country abiding in the field, and keeping watch by night over their flock. 9 And an angel of the Lord stood by them, and the glory of the Lord shone round about them: and they were sore afraid. 10 And the angel said unto them, Be not afraid; for behold, I bring you good tidings of great joy which shall be to all the people: 11 for there is born to you this day in the city of David a Saviour, who is Christ the Lord. 12 And this is the sign unto you: Ye shall find a babe wrapped in swaddling clothes, and lying in a manger. 13 And suddenly there was with the angel a multitude of the heavenly host praising God, and saying,

14 Glory to God in the highest,

> *And on earth peace among men in whom he is well pleased.*

15 And it came to pass, when the angels went away from them into heaven, the shepherds said one to another, Let us now go even unto Bethlehem, and see this thing that is come to pass, which the Lord hath made known unto us. 16 And they came with haste, and found both Mary and Joseph, and the babe lying in the manger. 17 And when they saw it, they made known concerning the saying which was spoken to them about this child. 18 And all that heard it wondered at the things which were spoken unto them by the shepherds. 19 But Mary kept all these sayings, pondering them in her heart. 20 And the shepherds returned, glorifying and praising God for all the things that they had heard and seen, even as it was spoken unto them.

The story of the birth of Jesus as related by Matthew is in striking contrast with that of Luke. Matthew depicts Jesus as a King and at his birth the reigning Herod trembles on his throne and the Magi adore him, offering regal gifts. Luke represents Jesus as the ideal Man, and the story is full of human interest. It describes two obscure peasants journeying from their northern home in Nazareth to Bethlehem and there, excluded from the inn, placing in a manger their newborn babe, while the first to visit them are humble shepherds from the neighboring plain. Human interests, however, are not merely earthly interests; the story is vocal with heavenly melodies and inwoven with messages of divine meaning and grace.

Only the most recent scholarship has vindicated the historic accuracy of Luke in connecting the event with the decree of Augustus and with the enrollment under Quirinius. However, these facts are mentioned by Luke not so much to fix the date of the birth of Christ as to explain how this occurred in Bethlehem when the home of his parents was in Nazareth. Only a legal necessity would have made them willing to take such a journey at such a time, but thus it appears that the emperor of the world was concerned unconsciously in the fulfillment of divine prophecy concerning the Savior of the world. According to the imperial decree, Joseph left Nazareth and with Mary, to whom according to Matthew he was not only "betrothed" but married, journeyed to Bethlehem, five miles south of Jerusalem, to be enrolled in his ancestral city. There is born their promised Son. Their exclusion from the inn was not due to any lack of hospitality; much less did it express hostility to Jesus; it was due simply to the crowded condition of the town. However, it is suggestive of the obscurity and discomfort and poverty of Joseph and Mary.

In view of his evident appreciation of the supreme importance of the birth of Jesus, the account of Luke is almost startling in its brevity and simplicity. However, with consummate art, after his own short statement of fact, he allows divine messengers to give the interpretation and to express the significance of the event. These messengers were angels. They appeared to a group of shepherds who were "abiding in the field, and keeping watch by night over their flock." Out of a blaze of heavenly glory came the tidings of great joy to Israel: "There is born to you this day in the city of David a Saviour, who is Christ the Lord." The angel did not then disclose the larger truth, that this Christ was to be the redeemer of all men or that he was a divine Lord. However, a sign was given whereby the shepherds might be able to distinguish the child and to be assured that he was the Christ: "Ye shall find a babe wrapped in swaddling clothes, and lying in a manger." A strange sign it was; yet for us it has become a symbol full of meaning; a Redeemer who was cradled in a manger has known what it is to endure poverty and suffering and neglect, and now he can sympathize with the lowly and distressed even as he is abundantly able to save.

When the good news had been given, there suddenly swelled forth an angel chorus, singing that great hymn of the Nativity which, as subsequently expanded by Christian worshipers, is named from its Latin version, the Gloria in Excelsis. As sung by the angels, it is composed of two verses, each containing three corresponding notes, "glory" and "peace," "in the highest" (heaven) and "on earth," "God," and "men." This is a hymn of praise to God, who in the gift of a Savior manifests in heaven his excellence and on earth reveals his grace to men, the recipients of his favor. The result of this, however, is declared to be "peace"; in Christ alone can peace be secured—peace with God, peace for the human heart, peace between men, peace for the world.

The astonished shepherds hastened to verify the good news, and they became in a real sense the first witnesses for Christ as "they made known concerning the saying which was spoken to them about this child." It is not strange that all who heard wondered, or that Mary treasured in her heart the heavenly messages, or that the shepherds returned to their tasks with gratitude and praise, for there lingered in their memories a song which expresses still the hope of all mankind.

F. THE PRESENTATION OF JESUS, AND THE NUNC DIMITTIS Ch. 2:21-40

21 And when eight days were fulfilled for circumcising him, his name was called JESUS, *which was so called by the angel before he was conceived in the womb.*

22 And when the days of their purification according to the law of Moses were fulfilled, they brought him up to Jerusalem, to present him to the Lord 23 (as it is written in the law of the Lord, Every male that openeth the womb shall be called holy to the Lord), 24 and to offer a sacrifice according to that which is said in the law of the Lord, A pair of turtledoves, or two young pigeons. 25 And behold, there was a man in Jerusalem, whose name was Simeon; and this man was righteous and devout, looking for the consolation of Israel: and the Holy Spirit was upon him. 26 And it had been revealed unto him by the Holy Spirit, that he should not see death, before he had seen the Lord's Christ. 27 And he came in the Spirit into the

*temple: and when the parents brought in the child Jesus,
that they might do concerning him after the custom of the
law, 28 then he received him into his arms, and blessed
God, and said,*

29 Now lettest thou thy servant depart, Lord,
    According to thy word, in peace;
30 For mine eyes have seen thy salvation,
*31 Which thou hast prepared before the face of all peo-
    ples;*
32 A light for revelation to the Gentiles,
    And the glory of thy people Israel.

*33 And his father and his mother were marvelling at the
things which were spoken concerning him;   34 and Simeon
blessed them, and said unto Mary his mother, Behold, this
child is set for the falling and the rising of many in Israel;
and for a sign which is spoken against;   35 yea and a
sword shall pierce through thine own soul; that thoughts
out of many hearts may be revealed.   36 And there was
one Anna, a prophetess, the daughter of Phanuel, of the
tribe of Asher (she was of a great age, having lived with
a husband seven years from her virginity, 37 and she had
been a widow even unto fourscore and four years), who
departed not from the temple, worshipping with fastings
and supplications night and day.   38 And coming up at
that very hour she gave thanks unto God, and spake of
him to all them that were looking for the redemption of
Jerusalem.   39 And when they had accomplished all things
that were according to the law of the Lord, they returned
into Galilee, to their own city Nazareth.*

*40 And the child grew, and waxed strong, filled with
wisdom: and the grace of God was upon him.*

The incidents of the infancy of Jesus recorded by Luke
not only add human interest to the story but they interpret
the future career and the saving work of our Lord.   Thus
when on the eighth day he was named "Jesus," a name
often given to Jewish boys, it was because he was destined
to fulfill all that the name implies, for he was to be the
"Salvation of the Lord."

So, too, when five weeks later he was presented in the

Temple, when his mother offered for herself a sacrifice
which indicated lack of wealth but not abject poverty, the
real significance of the scene is set forth in the prophetic
utterances of the saintly Simeon and Anna.   The first of
these utterances was the song of Simeon, called from the
Latin form of its opening words the Nunc Dimittis ("Now
Lettest Thou Depart").   To this devout soul it had been
revealed that he should not die until he had seen the Messiah, "the Lord's Christ."   Led by the Spirit to the Temple while the parents of Jesus are there presenting their
Son before the Lord, he took the little babe in his arms
and sang the sweetest and most solemn song of the nativity, which, unlike the Magnificat or the Benedictus, promises redemption not only to Israel but to all the world.

"Now lettest thou thy servant depart . . . in peace";
the figure of speech is full of beauty; it is the word of a
faithful watchman who welcomes with joy the hour of his
dismissal, for he has caught the vision of the coming One;
now he is about to be sent away in the peace of an accomplished task, in the peace of fulfilled hope; for his eyes
have seen the Savior according to the promise of the Lord.
The redemption which the Messiah brings, as the song continues to declare, is for all peoples; it is a light to reveal the
way of salvation to the Gentiles; it is to be the true glory
of the favored people, Israel.

While this salvation is provided for all, it will not be accepted by all.   To the wondering mother, Simeon uttered
a dark word of prophecy.   The ministry of Jesus will be
the occasion for the fall and the rise of many.   Their attitude toward him will be a revelation of character; some
will reject him and thus condemn themselves; some will
speak against him, even though he is the very token and
instrument of divine salvation; this opposition will reach
its climax at the cross, when bitter anguish like a sword
will pierce the soul of Mary.   Jesus is to be the touchstone
of character; wherever he is known, by accepting or by rejecting him, men will disclose their true nature; the

"thoughts out of many hearts" will be "revealed."

While Mary and Joseph were still wondering at these sublime words, there appeared an aged prophetess whose long years of widowhood had been spent in continual worship; she, too, praised God for the salvation to be accomplished by the Child of Mary and she went forth to speak of him to all who like her "were looking for the redemption of Jerusalem."

Mary and Joseph, however, returned to their home in Nazareth, where Jesus was to spend his infancy and early childhood. During those years of obscurity his development was normal, but unique in its symmetry and its perfection; he "grew, and waxed strong" in body, but there was just as true a growth in mind and spirit; he was "filled with wisdom: and the grace of God was upon him." The Savior of the world was to be the ideal Man.

G. THE BOY JESUS AT JERUSALEM
Ch. 2:41-52

41 And his parents went every year to Jerusalem at the feast of the passover. 42 And when he was twelve years old, they went up after the custom of the feast; 43 and when they had fulfilled the days, as they were returning, the boy Jesus tarried behind in Jerusalem; and his parents knew it not; 44 but supposing him to be in the company, they went a day's journey; and they sought for him among their kinsfolk and acquaintance: 45 and when they found him not, they returned to Jerusalem, seeking for him. 46 And it came to pass, after three days they found him in the temple, sitting in the midst of the teachers, both hearing them, and asking them questions: 47 and all that heard him were amazed at his understanding and his answers. 48 And when they saw him, they were astonished; and his mother said unto him, Son, why hast thou thus dealt with us? behold, thy father and I sought thee sorrowing. 49 And he said unto them, How is it that ye sought me? knew ye not that I must be in my Father's house?

50 And they understood not the saying which he spake unto them. 51 And he went down with them, and came to Nazareth; and he was subject unto them: and his mother kept all these sayings in her heart.

52 And Jesus advanced in wisdom and stature, and in favor with God and men.

It has been said that the boyhood of Jesus is like a walled garden from which we have been given but a single flower, but this is so fragrant as to fill our hearts with a longing to enter within the secret enclosure. We have but a single incident of his boyhood days; it is recorded for us only by Luke, a visit to Jerusalem paid by Jesus when he was twelve years old. At about this age a young Jew became a "son of the law" and began to observe its requirements, among which were the pilgrimages to the Holy City to observe the sacred feasts. On this first visit to Jerusalem, Jesus was unintentionally left behind by his parents as they started on their return journey to Nazareth. At the end of the first day they failed to find him in the long caravan which was moving northward toward Galilee. The day following, Mary and Joseph returned to Jerusalem, and on the third day they discovered Jesus in the Temple in the midst of the teachers who were surprised at his knowledge of the sacred Scriptures. There was an implied rebuke in the words of Mary, "Son, why hast thou thus dealt with us? behold, thy father and I sought thee sorrowing." In the reply of Jesus there was something of surprise and also of reproof, yet there were deep undertones of love, of spiritual vision, and of solemn resolve: "How is it that ye sought me? knew ye not that I must be in my Father's house?"

These are the first recorded words of Jesus and they are an index and an explanation of his entire career; for their preservation this story was recorded by Luke. If they contained a rebuke for Mary, it must have been conveyed in accents of reverence and affection; and was there not in-

volved a delicate compliment?   Jesus does not reprove his
parents for seeking him, but for not seeking him in the
Temple first of all; and does he not seem to have implied
that his parents had taught him to love the house of God
and to delight in the law of God?   He was saying in effect:
"Why thus did you seek me?   Why did you not remember
that the Temple is the very place where I should be
found?"

These words are thus a revelation of the life in the home
at Nazareth.   It was not by a miracle or due to some divine attribute, but because of the training he had received
from his pious parents, that Jesus at the age of twelve was
a master of the Scriptures, and had learned to reverence
and adore all that was related to them and to the worship
of God.   Is it not possible for parents today to awaken in
the hearts of their children a love for the house and the
Word and the will of God?

These words, further, were a revelation of the consciousness of divine sonship.   Jesus already realized that in a
unique sense God was his own Father, the true source of
his being.   He instantly corrected the words of Mary, "thy
father," which referred to Joseph, with his own words "my
Father," which referred to God.   Luke depicts Jesus as the
ideal Man, but always as one conscious that he was the
Son of God.

Our children should learn to regard God as their Father,
not in the unique sense employed by Jesus as the eternal
Son, nor yet in the sense which can apply to all created
beings, but as denoting that intimate relationship with God
made possible for believers through Jesus Christ our Lord.

Most important of all, these words are the revelation of
a firm resolve, of a great molding purpose; Jesus perceived
that it was his duty to be in the house of his Father—not
merely in the literal Temple, but in the sphere of life and
activity of which the Temple was the great expression and
symbol and sign.   He had determined, that is, to devote all
his thoughts and energies and powers to the definite service

of God. At the age of twelve are not most children sufficiently mature to form a somewhat similar purpose and to
recognize in the service of God the supreme and compre-
hensive duty of every life?

With this definite ideal in mind Jesus returned to Nazareth and continued to live in submission to his parents,
toiling for eighteen years as a carpenter and in the quiet
retirement of an obscure village receiving a training for his
public career which would have been impossible amid the
formalism and the distractions of Jerusalem. His development was as natural as it was perfect; he "advanced in
wisdom and stature, and in favor with God and men"; his
bodily and mental growth were no more marked than his
increasing charm and spiritual power. Such development
is possible in the humblest sphere for those whose lives
are yielded to the will of God.

III
THE PREPARATION
Chs. 3:1 to 4:13

A. THE PREACHING OF JOHN Ch. 3:1-20

1 Now in the fifteenth year of the reign of Tiberius Cæsar, Pontius Pilate being governor of Judæa, and Herod being tetrarch of Galilee, and his brother Philip tetrarch of the region of Ituræa and Trachonitis, and Lysanias tetrarch of Abilene, 2 in the high-priesthood of Annas and Caiaphas, the word of God came unto John the son of Zacharias in the wilderness. 3 And he came into all the region round about the Jordan, preaching the baptism of repentance unto remission of sins; 4 as it is written in the book of the words of Isaiah the prophet,

The voice of one crying in the wilderness,
Make ye ready the way of the Lord,
Make his paths straight.
5 Every valley shall be filled,
And every mountain and hill shall be brought low;
And the crooked shall become straight,
And the rough ways smooth;
6 And all flesh shall see the salvation of God.

7 He said therefore to the multitudes that went out to be baptized of him, Ye offspring of vipers, who warned you to flee from the wrath to come? 8 Bring forth therefore fruits worthy of repentance, and begin not to say within yourselves, We have Abraham to our father: for I say unto you, that God is able of these stones to raise up children unto Abraham. 9 And even now the axe also lieth at the root of the trees: every tree therefore that bringeth not forth good fruit is hewn down, and cast into the fire. 10 And the multitudes asked him, saying, What then must we do? 11 And he answered and said unto them, He that hath two coats, let him impart to him that hath none; and he that hath food, let him do likewise. 12

*And there came also publicans to be baptized, and they
said unto him, Teacher, what must we do?   13 And he
said unto them, Extort no more than that which is appointed you.   14 And soldiers also asked him, saying, And
we, what must we do?   And he said unto them, Extort
from no man by violence, neither accuse any one wrongfully; and be content with your wages.*

*15 And as the people were in expectation, and all men
reasoned in their hearts concerning John, whether haply
he were the Christ;   16 John answered, saying unto them
all, I indeed baptize you with water; but there cometh he
that is mightier than I, the latchet of whose shoes I am not
worthy to unloose: he shall baptize you in the Holy Spirit
and in fire: 17 whose fan is in his hand, thoroughly to
cleanse his threshing-floor, and to gather the wheat into his
garner; but the chaff he will burn up with unquenchable
fire.*

*18 With many other exhortations therefore preached he
good tidings unto the people;   19 but Herod the tetrarch,
being reproved by him for Herodias his brother's wife, and
for all the evil things which Herod had done, 20 added this
also to them all, that he shut up John in prison.*

John the Baptist was the first inspired prophet to break
the silence of the centuries which had elapsed since the
days of Malachi.   The importance of his ministry is indicated by Luke in the minute exactness with which he fixes
its date.   By naming the civil and religious rulers, he gives
a sixfold designation of the time; then, too, it accords with
the universal aspect of his Gospel, and with the genius of
Luke as a historian, to link his story with secular events.
Naturally he mentions first the reigning emperor, Tiberius
Caesar; he next names Pilate, the governor of Judea who
attained an immortality of shame for condemning Jesus to
the cross; Herod Antipas, a seducer and murderer, son of
Herod the Great, is designated as ruler of Galilee; Philip
and Lysanias are said to be governing neighboring prov-
inces; as ecclesiastical rulers, Annas and Caiaphas are
mentioned; while the former had been deposed some years

before, he continued to share with his son-in-law the actual duties of the high priesthood, and he also shared the infamy in which their names are united. Such a list of leading spirits indicates the absolute moral and religious degeneracy of the times and the need of someone to call Israel back to the service and worship of God.

Such a messenger appeared in the person of John the Baptist, who after his long discipline in the wilderness came with a definite message from God and drew out great throngs to the Jordan Valley to attend his preaching and to accept his baptism as a sign and seal of their repentance. The nature of his ministry is declared to have been a fulfillment of the prediction of Isaiah who described "one crying in the wilderness," one sent of God to prepare the way for the coming of Christ. This preparation is pictured in terms of Oriental imagery. When a monarch was about to make a journey, a servant was sent before him to prepare the highway. Valleys needed to be filled, hills lowered, crooked places made straight, rough ways made smooth. Thus, before men would be ready to receive Christ, moral obstacles must be removed; men must repent of their sins and turn from them. Luke closes his quotation from Isaiah with the line, "And all flesh shall see the salvation of God," which is in accord with the universal character of his Gospel.

The burden of the message preached by John was that which in all ages has awakened a response in the hearts of men: he preached sin and judgment, repentance and pardon. The tone of his message as recorded by Luke, however, was particularly severe; here he is said to have addressed the multitudes as the "offspring of vipers" and to have asked them why they were pretending to have heard a warning of wrath to come. The reason for such severity was that, while wishing to escape the impending judgment, the people were unwilling to forsake their sins. They regarded the baptism of John as a magical rite which could make impenitent men safe in the hour of judgment. John

bade them show their repentance by their works and not
to trust in their descent from Abraham as securing their
salvation.   He declared that judgment was upon them; the
ax was already lying at the root of the trees and every
fruitless tree was about to be "hewn down, and cast into
the fire."

To the question of the people John made it perfectly
plain that by repentance he meant no mere form or ceremony, nor was the word merely an abstract theological
term; the thing he demanded was plain and practical, that
each man should turn from his besetting sin and should
show love to his fellowman.   Clothing and food were to be
given to those in need, for repentance meant to turn from
the sin of selfishness.   Publicans or taxgatherers, who were
everywhere detested because of their dishonesty and greed,
were told to demand no more tribute than was appointed
and lawful.   Soldiers, or more exactly "men on military
service," possibly acting as local police, were told to extort
no money by violence and to seek for none by false
charges, and to be content with their wages.   All who are
to receive Christ in any age must turn from their sins.   Repentance is not a mystical experience; it is plain and simple
and practical.   It consists in turning from greed and dishonesty and unkindness and violence and discontent, and
from all that is contrary to the revealed will of God.

The coming of Christ was very definitely predicted by
John.   While some imagined that the prophet himself was
the Messiah, John declared that the mission of Christ was
so much greater than his own that he would be unworthy
as a slave, to loose the latchet of his shoes.   While John
baptized with water, Christ would baptize with the Holy
Spirit and with fire.   Water was a material element, and
merely symbolized an inward change; Jesus would bring
them into fellowship with a divine Person, and would exert
upon their souls cleansing and transforming power.   He
would come, however, to punish the impenitent; he would
separate the wheat from the chaff; the former he would

gather into his garner, but the chaff he would burn with unquenchable fire.

The close of the career of John is introduced by Luke at this point of his narrative to prepare the way for his account of the ministry of Christ. It was actually some time after Jesus had begun his work that Herod the tetrarch arrested John and cast him into prison because he had rebuked the profligate king for his impurity and his sin. John had been a faithful messenger of God, but the world does not reverence its prophets; they are usually imprisoned, beheaded, burned, or crucified.

B. THE BAPTISM OF JESUS Ch. 3:21-22

21 Now it came to pass, when all the people were baptized, that, Jesus also having been baptized, and praying, the heaven was opened, 22 and the Holy Spirit descended in a bodily form, as a dove, upon him, and a voice came out of heaven, Thou art my beloved Son; in thee I am well pleased.

Why did the ideal Man, the Son of God, submit to the baptism of John, a baptism of repentance? Surely not to confess any sin of his own; but first of all to set his seal of approval upon the work of John and to attest the message which declared that repentance and confession of sin are absolutely necessary for all who are to share the salvation of Christ.

Then again by his baptism Jesus identified himself with his people, not as being sinful, but as doing what they were commanded to do and as sympathizing with them in their hatred of sin, in their distress for its burden, and in their hope and expectation of relief. Only those who sympathize can serve and save.

Then again baptism indicated that the penitent had broken with the past to begin a life of new holiness and obedience. So in his baptism Jesus was ending his quiet years of preparation in Nazareth and was about to enter upon the ministry of service and sacrifice which was to be performed in obedience to the will of his Father. It is for this reason that Luke, with the art of a skilled historian, first completed the story of John, the great forerunner, before mentioning that which in reality was the supreme incident in the career of John—his baptism of Jesus. That incident introduced Jesus to his public ministry and that ministry was to form the very substance of the gospel.

That the incident is merely introductory to his narrative is evident also from the way in which Luke records the baptism. He does not describe the event. He merely mentions it to designate the time when Jesus saw the descending Spirit and heard the voice from heaven. The former was a symbolic indication of the power by which the work of Jesus was to be performed; the latter was a declaration that he was the Christ, upon whom rested the approval of God.

We arc not to suppose that Jesus before had lacked the presence of the Holy Spirit, nor that he now assumed any new relation to his Father, but, as in baptism he had yielded himself to his appointed service, so now he was empowered for his task; as in humility he had identified himself with the sons of men, so now he was assured anew that he was the Son of God; as he had shown his sympathy with penitent sinners, he now was declared to be the sinless One in whom God was well pleased.

Thus with the followers of Christ, while all enjoy the abiding presence of his Spirit, yet, as they yield themselves anew to his service, they are filled anew with his power, they are strengthened for their tasks, and are cheered by a new assurance of their sonship and their acceptance with God. Luke alone mentions that this experience came when Jesus was in prayer. He realized that it was a time of crisis. Prayer is usually the condition of those heavenly visions and spiritual experiences which prepare us for our tasks in life.

C. THE GENEALOGY OF JESUS Ch. 3:23-38

23 And Jesus himself, when he began to teach, was about thirty years of age, being the son (as was supposed) of Joseph, the son of Heli, 24 the son of Matthat, the son of Levi, the son of Melchi, the son of Jannai, the son of Joseph, 25 the son of Mattathias, the son of Amos, the son of Nahum, the son of Esli, the son of Naggai, 26 the son of Maath, the son of Mattathias, the son of Semein, the son of Josech, the son of Joda, 27 the son of Joanan, the son of Rhesa, the son of Zerubbabel, the son of Shealtiel, the son of Neri, 28 the son of Melchi, the son of Addi, the son of Cosam, the son of Elmadam, the son of Er, 29 the son of Jesus, the son of Eliezer, the son of Jorim, the son of Matthat, the son of Levi, 30 the son of Symeon, the son of Judas, the son of Joseph, the son of Jonam, the son of Eliakim, 31 the son of Melea, the son of Menna, the son of Mattatha, the son of Nathan, the son of David, 32 the son of Jesse, the son of Obed, the son of Boaz, the son of Salmon, the son of Nahshon, 33 the son of Amminadab, the son of Arni, the son of Hezron, the son of Perez, the son of Judah, 34 the son of Jacob, the son of Isaac, the son of Abraham, the son of Terah, the son of Nahor, 35 the son of Serug, the son of Reu, the son of Peleg, the son of Eber, the son of Shelah, 36 the son of Cainan, the son of Arphaxad, the son of Shem, the son of Noah, the son of Lamech, 37 the son of Methuselah, the son of Enoch, the son of Jared, the son of Mahalaleel, the son of Cainan, 38 the son of Enos, the son of Seth, the son of Adam, the son of God.

The genealogy of Jesus given by Luke contains marked differences from that recorded by Matthew. Possibly some of these differences can be explained and may be found of real significance.

1. First of all, the genealogy is found in a different part of the Gospel. In Matthew it opens the story; in Luke it closes the third chapter. This is of course by no mere chance. The purpose of Matthew is to prove that Jesus is the Christ, the Messiah, who, as the King of Israel, fulfills

all the Old Testament prophecies. It is of the utmost importance that Jesus should be shown to be the Son of David and of Abraham and that the official genealogy containing this record should open the story and even precede the account of the Nativity.

Luke, however, has given the significant account of the birth and infancy and career of the great forerunner, John, because of the light these throw upon the ministry of Christ. Therefore, when the career of John has been related, when the ministry of Jesus is about to be recorded, Luke gives his genealogy to emphasize the fact that the narrative concerning John has closed and the story of the ministry of Jesus is about to begin. The genealogy is thus an artistic interlude, or an important introduction. It suggests the real purpose of the writer and marks the transition from the ministry which called men to repentance to the saving work which secures salvation from sin. The gospel is not good advice but good news. We are not followers of John but of Jesus.

2. Then again, the genealogy in Matthew follows the order of descent; Luke ascends the family line from son to father. The former is the order of an official record; individuals are registered only as they are born; the latter is that of a private document compiled from the public records with a view to fixing the attention upon the particular person whose name stands at the head of the list. This is quite in accord with the literary art of Luke, who desires at this point in the narrative to center the thought upon the supreme importance of Jesus, the Savior, of whose redeeming work he is now to write.

3. In the third place, while the names given by Luke, from Abraham to David, correspond with those given by Matthew, the names from David to Jesus differ. Some have attempted to explain the differences on the ground that Matthew gives the genealogy of Joseph, while Luke gives that of Mary. It is probably wiser to conclude that both give the genealogy of Joseph, but Matthew traces the

line of royal succession showing Jesus to be the heir of David; while Luke gives the line of actual descent. This surely accords with the purpose of Matthew who ever depicts Christ as the King, and also with the purpose of Luke who is painting for us Christ as the true, the ideal Man.

4. Then, too, the genealogy in Matthew begins with Abraham, while Luke traces the line back to Adam. The former proves Jesus to be a Jew, the true son of Abraham, in whom the covenant was fulfilled. The latter reminds us that Jesus belongs to the whole human race. It makes us look beyond all national lines and remember that this ideal Man on whom Luke is fixing our thoughts is the Savior of mankind.

5. When the genealogy closes with the statement that Adam was "the son of God," it does indicate that Jesus was reckoned as one in the great brotherhood of man, and like all his brothers, owed his origin to God; but it does not mean to deny that he also sustained to God a relationship that is absolutely unique. The genealogy opens with the statement that Jesus was the reputed Son of Joseph; he was the legal heir of Joseph and so the promised Son of David because of the marriage of Joseph to Mary: but he was not really the son of Joseph; he was the "only begotten Son" of God.

D. THE TEMPTATION OF JESUS Ch. 4:1-13

1 And Jesus, full of the Holy Spirit, returned from the Jordan, and was led in the Spirit in the wilderness 2 during forty days, being tempted of the devil. And he did eat nothing in those days: and when they were completed, he hungered. 3 And the devil said unto him, If thou art the Son of God, command this stone that it become bread. 4 And Jesus answered unto him, It is written, Man shall not live by bread alone. 5 And he led him up, and showed him all the kingdoms of the world in a moment of time. 6 And the devil said unto him, To thee will I give all this authority, and the glory of them: for it hath been delivered

*unto me; and to whomsoever I will I give it.   7 If thou
therefore wilt worship before me, it shall all be thine.   8
And Jesus answered and said unto him, It is written, Thou
shalt worship the Lord thy God, and him only shalt thou
serve.   9 And he led him to Jerusalem, and set him on the
pinnacle of the temple, and said unto him, If thou art the
Son of God, cast thyself down from hence: 10 for it is
written,*

> *He shall give his angels charge concerning thee, to
> guard thee:*

11 and,

> *On their hands they shall bear thee up,
> Lest haply thou dash thy foot against a stone.*

*12 And Jesus answering said unto him, It is said, Thou
shalt not make trial of the Lord thy God.*

*13 And when the devil had completed every temptation,
he departed from him for a season.*

The temptation of Jesus was the last step in the preparation for his public ministry, and for many of his followers
the final discipline for service consists in such a trial as results in a new determination to live not for self but for
God.

The time of the temptation was significant.   It was just
after Jesus had been filled with the Holy Spirit and had
been assured anew of his divine sonship.   Under the influence of the Spirit he was brought to the place of trial, and
the temptation consisted, in large part, of the suggestion to
use for selfish ends the divine powers of which he was conscious, and to forget his filial relation to his Father.   While
God never tempts us, in the sense of enticing us to sin, it
does seem to be a part of his gracious purpose to allow us
to be tested; these experiences come while we are guided
by his Spirit, and the essence of these temptations usually
consists in some inclination to please self in forgetfulness
of our true relation to God.   The place of temptation was
the wilderness, and there is a sense in which the experience
of moral struggle is always one of intense loneliness.   On
the other hand, to live in a literal desert does not free one

from solicitation to sin. Wherever one may be, he can be certain of the presence and sympathy of Christ; and victory is possible through faith in him. This seems to be the supreme message of the story.

In both Matthew and Luke, three temptations are mentioned. They are probably intended to be symbolic and inclusive; and under one or the other of these enticements to evil can be grouped all the moral trials of mankind. It is to be noted, however, that the order of the temptations given by Luke differs from that of Matthew. In both accounts the first temptation is to make bread of stone; but Luke mentions as the second temptation that which is last in the account of Matthew, the temptation which offered to Jesus all the kingdoms of the world. This was a fitting climax to the testing of the King. Luke, however, mentions last the temptation of Jesus to cast himself from the pinnacle of the Temple and thus to test God. It is the temptation in the sphere of intellectual desire and comes in the subtle form of presumptuous trust. It forms a true climax in the testing of the ideal Man. The order given by Matthew is suggested by the apostle John who mentions "the lust of the flesh and the lust of the eyes and the vainglory of life." The order of Luke takes us back to the story of Eden and to the first human sin, which was due to a love for that which was "good for food" and "a delight to the eyes" and "to be desired to make one wise." As in Eden also, the first temptation is to doubt the goodness of God, the second to doubt his power, and the third to distrust his wisdom. The victory of Jesus, however, was secured by the triumph of his faith, and faith is still the victory which overcomes the world.

The first temptation, then, was in the sphere of bodily appetite; Jesus was urged by Satan to transform a stone into bread. Why not? His appetite was innocent; he possessed the ability to gratify it. The sin, however, would lie in his using divine power to satisfy his human needs. If this should have been his way of life, there would have been for him no hunger, no pain, no sorrow, no cross. He would have defeated the very purpose for which he came into the world; and anyone who makes the gratification of appetite his supreme purpose is wasting his life. The essence of the temptation, however, was to doubt the goodness of God, as Jesus showed by his reply, "Man shall not live by bread alone." He was quoting from the Old Testament; he was declaring that as by a miracle God preserved his people of old, so now he would sustain the life of his Son. Jesus would not be driven into a panic of fear. He believed that God would supply his need and that, however strong the demand of appetite might be, the way and the will of God are certain to secure satisfaction and the truest enjoyment in life.

The second temptation was in the sphere of earthly ambition. It consisted in an offer of unlimited human power. Satan would give to Jesus all the kingdoms of the world on the condition that Jesus should bow down and worship him. The force of the temptation consisted in the fact that Jesus expected someday to rule the world. The Tempter suggested that he himself possessed such power, and that if Jesus would submit to him he would attain the desired goal of universal rule. It was a temptation to doubt the power of God and to be disloyal to him, as is shown by the reply of Jesus, "Thou shalt worship the Lord thy God, and him only shalt thou serve."

This is a familiar form of temptation today. The devil does not ask us to give up our purposes of ultimate helpfulness to others and service to the world; he only asks us to compromise with the evil to attain our goal; he insists that the end will justify the means; he intimates that in the world of commerce, or society, or politics, evil methods are so much in vogue that success can be attained only by complicity with evil. He tells us that this is his world and that we can rule only insofar as we make terms with him. For Christ the issue was clearly drawn. It was submission to Satan or loyalty to God. The latter would involve opposition to the ruler of this world and therefore would mean conflict and toil and tears and a cross; but the ultimate issue would be universal rule. The same choice opens for the followers of Christ. Unswerving loyalty is the way of the cross, but this is the way of the crown.

The last temptation was in the sphere of intellectual curiosity. It suggested to Jesus that he should see for himself what would be the experience of one who should cast himself from a great height and then, by angel hands, be kept from harm. This is the temptation to place oneself needlessly in a situation of moral peril and then to expect to be delivered by God's miraculous power. This is not faith, but presumption. Satan still seeks by this device to destroy human souls. He urges men to see for themselves, to increase their knowledge by experiences which needlessly endanger their credit, their health, and their honor, to place themselves in moral peril, to live beyond their means, to undertake tasks beyond their strength. Jesus replied, "Thou shalt not make trial of the Lord thy God." In the path of actual duty one need not fear the most threatening danger; but one who puts himself in unnecessary peril need not expect divine help. In his own time and way, and in the path of our appointed service, God will open our eyes and give us such knowledge as we need. To seek in presumption for such knowledge while endangering our souls is to doubt the wisdom of God. Real trust preserves us from sinful presumption.

The story closes with the statement that when Jesus had secured his victory the devil "departed from him for a season." The life of faith is a life of repeated moral conflicts, but victory is assured to those who trust in the goodness and power and wisdom of God.

IV
THE MINISTRY
IN GALILEE
Chs. 4:14 to 9:50

A. THE FIRST PERIOD Ch. 4:14-44

1. JESUS PREACHING AT NAZARETH   Ch. 4:14-30

14 And Jesus returned in the power of the Spirit into Galilee: and a fame went out concerning him through all the region round about.   15 And he taught in their synagogues, being glorified of all.

16 And he came to Nazareth, where he had been brought up: and he entered, as his custom was, into the synagogue on the sabbath day, and stood up to read.   17 And there was delivered unto him the book of the prophet Isaiah.   And he opened the book, and found the place where it was written,

18 The Spirit of the Lord is upon me,

> *Because he anointed me to preach good tidings to the poor:*
> *He hath sent me to proclaim release to the captives,*
> *And recovering of sight to the blind,*
> *To set at liberty them that are bruised,*

19 To proclaim the acceptable year of the Lord.

20 And he closed the book, and gave it back to the attendant, and sat down: and the eyes of all in the synagogue were fastened on him.   21 And he began to say unto them, To-day hath this scripture been fulfilled in your ears.   22 And all bare him witness, and wondered at the words of grace which proceeded out of his mouth: and they said, Is not this Joseph's son?   23 And he said unto them, Doubtless ye will say unto me this parable, Physician, heal thyself: whatsoever we have heard done at Capernaum, do also here in thine own country.   24 And he said, Verily

I say unto you, No prophet is acceptable in his own country. 25 But of a truth I say unto you, There were many widows in Israel in the days of Elijah, when the heaven was shut up three years and six months, when there came a great famine over all the land; 26 and unto none of them was Elijah sent, but only to Zarephath, in the land of Sidon, unto a woman that was a widow. 27 And there were many lepers in Israel in the time of Elisha the prophet; and none of them was cleansed, but only Naaman the Syrian. 28 And they were all filled with wrath in the synagogue, as they heard these things; 29 and they rose up, and cast him forth out of the city, and led him unto the brow of the hill whereon their city was built, that they might throw him down headlong. 30 But he passing through the midst of them went his way.

After his baptism and temptation Jesus remained for a time in Jerusalem and in Judea and then returned to Galilee, where he began that ministry to which Luke devotes the next six chapters of his Gospel. Of this ministry he mentions three features: First, it was wrought in the power of the Holy Spirit; secondly, its fame extended through the entire country; and thirdly, its essence consisted in the most arresting and impressive public teaching.

The first recorded sermon of Jesus was preached in the synagogue at Nazareth, the town in which he had spent his youth and early manhood. Luke places this sermon at the very opening of his record of the public ministry of Jesus, probably because he regarded it as containing the program of that ministry, or as forming the proclamation of the saving work of our Lord.

It was a Sabbath Day. The place of worship was crowded with the relatives and friends and townsmen of Jesus. All were eager to hear one whom they knew so well, and who had attained so sudden a renown. Either at his request, or providentially, Jesus was handed the book of Isaiah to lead in the reading of the Scripture. He found the place in the prophecy where, in terms of the joy of jubilee, the writer is describing the gladness of those who are to return from their long captivity in Babylon. When Jesus had finished the lesson he sat down, thereby taking the attitude of a public teacher. As all gazed upon him intently, he undertook to show that the prophecy was to be fulfilled by himself, claiming thereby to be the promised Messiah. The very phrase with which the prophecy begins, "The Spirit of the Lord is upon me," indicates, when applied to himself, that he had been anointed, not with oil as a prophet or a priest or a king, but with the Holy Spirit as the Anointed One, or the Christ of God. As such he was "to preach good tidings to the poor," that is, to those in spiritual as well as in physical poverty. He was to proclaim deliverance for those enslaved by sin and to establish those principles which will result in political freedom for mankind. He was "to set at liberty them that are bruised," that is, to remove the consequences and the cruelties of selfishness and of crime. He was to proclaim the era of universal blessedness which will result from his perfected reign. Thus in these words, which combine the figures of deliverance from captivity with those of the joy of jubilee, Jesus expressed the gracious and beneficent character of his ministry.

His auditors listened in amazement, unable to resist the charm of his address or to deny the fascinating beauty of his words, but unable also to admit his claim; they received his predictions with stubborn unbelief. They expressed their incredulity and at the same time explained it by their question, "Is not this Joseph's son?" They were saying in effect: "Is not this man our neighbor, the carpenter, with whom we have all been acquainted; do we not know him and his family? Surely he cannot be the Messiah."

The reply of Jesus was to the effect that their unwillingness to accept him was due in part to the fact that he had not wrought in their presence the miracles which marked his ministry in other places. This is what he meant by quoting the proverb, "Physician, heal thyself," that is, "Establish your claim here as you have done elsewhere, if you expect to be received as the Christ." Jesus also quoted another proverb to explain more fully their jealous doubts: "No prophet is acceptable in his own country." Those most familiar with great men usually are least able to appreciate their greatness; "Familiarity breeds contempt," because men are so apt to judge one another by false standards and by that which is accidental and external and because so frequently men do not know those whom they think they know the best. This same stupid lack of appreciation shadows human lives today, and makes us fail to realize the worth of our friends and the value of our opportunities, until it is too late. It even has its tragic bearing upon the present ministry of Christ; some reject him for reasons altogether superficial and foolish, thinking that they know him perfectly because they long have been familiar with his name, while in reality they fail to understand the real beauty of his person and the transforming power of his grace.

The unbelief of his auditors was turned to mad hatred as Jesus gave two examples from Old Testament history, both of which indicated that his townsmen, who knew him best, were less worthy of his saving ministry than even men of heathen nations. He even compared himself with Elijah and Elisha and indicated that as the former brought a great blessing to one who lived in Sidon and the latter to a prince in Syria, while the people in Israel were suffering for their unbelief, so the nations of the world would accept the blessed salvation of Christ while those who knew him best would suffer for their unbelief. So maddened were his hearers by this severe rebuke that they drove him from the city and tried to take his life, but he, with majestic calm and divine strength, "passing through the midst of them went his way."

It is still true that those who have enjoyed the best opportunities for knowing Christ often reject him; but, where faith is present, broken hearts are healed as by Elijah of

old and lepers are cleansed as was Naaman by the word of
Elisha.   Thus in this scene in the synagogue of Nazareth,
Jesus indicated not only the grace of his ministry but its
universal power.   He came to relieve all the needs of mankind and in all the world.

2. Jesus Performing Miracles at Capernaum
Ch. 4:31-44

*31 And he came down to Capernaum, a city of Galilee.
And he was teaching them on the sabbath day: 32 and
they were astonished at his teaching; for his word was with
authority.   33 And in the synagogue there was a man, that
had a spirit of an unclean demon; and he cried out with a
loud voice, 34 Ah! what have we to do with thee, Jesus
thou Nazarene? art thou come to destroy us?   I know thee
who thou art, the Holy One of God.   35 And Jesus rebuked him, saying, Hold thy peace, and come out of him.
And when the demon had thrown him down in the midst,
he came out of him, having done him no hurt.   36 And
amazement came upon all, and they spake together, one
with another, saying, What is this word? for with authority
and power he commandeth the unclean spirits, and they
come out.   37 And there went forth a rumor concerning
him into every place of the region round about.*

*38 And he rose up from the synagogue, and entered into
the house of Simon.   And Simon's wife's mother was
holden with a great fever; and they besought him for her.
39 And he stood over her, and rebuked the fever; and it left
her: and immediately she rose up and ministered unto
them.*

*40 And when the sun was setting, all they that had any
sick with divers diseases brought them unto him; and he
laid his hands on every one of them, and healed them.
41 And demons also came out from many, crying out, and
saying, Thou art the Son of God.   And rebuking them, he
suffered them not to speak, because they knew that he was
the Christ.*

*42 And when it was day, he came out and went into a
desert place: and the multitudes sought after him, and came*

unto him, and would have stayed him, that he should not go from them.   43 But he said unto them, I must preach the good tidings of the kingdom of God to the other cities also: for therefore was I sent.

44 And he was preaching in the synagogues of Galilee.

The Sabbath at Nazareth is placed by Luke in sudden contrast with a Sabbath passed at Capernaum. On the former, as the story opens, Jesus was surrounded by his friends and townsmen; as it closes, they had turned into a fierce mob which was seeking his death. In the latter, as the scene opens, Jesus was faced by a demon; but as it closes, he was surrounded by an admiring throng who were eager to have him remain in their midst.

Jesus was again in a synagogue, and was awakening surprise by the character of his message. Unlike the teachers of his day, he spoke with authority instead of quoting reputed "authorities" as he unfolded the Scriptures. Suddenly the service was interrupted by the cries of a man who was possessed by an unclean spirit. Jesus rebuked the demon and compelled him to come out of the man. There can be little doubt that the evil spirit which Jesus thus controlled was an actual malign being who controlled the poor sufferer whom Jesus graciously relieved; yet such an "unclean spirit" is a type of the demoniac power of envy and of lust and of anger, and of the whole host of debasing passions from which Christ alone can give relief.

The second scene of this memorable Sabbath is in the home of Simon Peter; here by a single word Jesus relieved a poor sufferer from a severe fever. The cure was so instantaneous that the woman who had been sick immediately "rose up and ministered unto them." It is probably true that in many homes there are those, not afflicted by the power of evil passions, who nevertheless are suffering from worry and anxiety and fretfulness and unrest and so are unable to render to others the gracious service which they might perform if they could but hear the quieting word of Christ and feel the soothing power of his touch.

The third scene is of peculiar beauty. When the sun had set, a great multitude gathered around the home of Peter, attracted by the report of the miracle wrought in the synagogue. They brought with them great numbers of those who were sick or possessed by demons and Jesus healed them all. This is a picture which in reality is being reproduced today. Amid the shadows and mysteries of suffering and pain the Savior is standing; about him are gathered those whom sin has stricken with its disease, the sad, the loveless, the lonely, the tempted, the hopeless, the lost. His touch "has still its ancient power." In his mercy he is healing them all, and in joy they are going away.

The last scene of this group is at dawn the next morning. Jesus had withdrawn to "a desert place," but the eager multitudes had found him and were beseeching him not to go from them. He reminded them, however, of the other cities which needed to hear "the good tidings of the kingdom of God." Have all of us who have felt the healing touch of Christ something of his sympathy for those who have not yet heard the good news of his grace?

B. THE SECOND PERIOD Chs. 5:1 to 6:11

1. THE CALL OF THE FIRST DISCIPLES   Ch. 5:1-11

1 Now it came to pass, while the multitude pressed upon him and heard the word of God, that he was standing by the lake of Gennesaret; 2 and he saw two boats standing by the lake: but the fishermen had gone out of them, and were washing their nets. 3 And he entered into one of the boats, which was Simon's, and asked him to put out a little from the land. And he sat down and taught the multitudes out of the boat. 4 And when he had left speaking, he said unto Simon, Put out into the deep, and let down your nets for a draught. 5 And Simon answered and said, Master, we toiled all night, and took nothing: but at thy word I will let down the nets. 6 And when they had done this, they inclosed a great multitude of fishes; and their nets were breaking; 7 and they beckoned unto their part-

*ners in the other boat, that they should come and help
them.   And they came, and filled both the boats, so that
they began to sink.   8 But Simon Peter, when he saw it,
fell down at Jesus' knees, saying, Depart from me; for I am
a sinful man, O Lord.   9 For he was amazed, and all that
were with him, at the draught of the fishes which they had
taken;   10 and so were also James and John, sons of Zebe-
dee, who were partners with Simon.   And Jesus said unto
Simon, Fear not; from henceforth thou shalt catch men.
11 And when they had brought their boats to land, they
left all, and followed him.*

The call of his first disciples is regarded by many as
opening a new period in the public ministry of Jesus.   His
work was now to assume a more permanent form.   The
growing popularity of his preaching indicated that the
gospel was designed for the whole world.   For such a
proclamation a definite group of workers must be prepared.   The growth of Christianity ever depends upon securing men who will publicly confess and follow Christ.

The scene of this call is described as being "by the lake
of Gennesaret."   This charming sheet of water brings to
mind so many scenes in the life of our Lord that it has
been termed a "Fifth Gospel."   On its western and northern side were the cities in which most of his work was
done; the eastern shores were not inhabited and thither
Jesus would resort for rest.

Those whom Jesus called were fishermen, sturdy, independent, fearless.   They were not strangers to Jesus, nor
had they been indifferent to spiritual truths.   They had attended the preaching of the Baptist and had come to regard Jesus as the Messiah, but they were now called to
leave their homes and their tasks and to become his constant companions and disciples.

On this occasion Jesus had borrowed the boat belonging
to one of his friends to use as a pulpit and from this he
had addressed the crowds.   When he had finished his discourse, he gave to the four men he was about to call an

impressive object lesson of the character of the work and of the great success which would attend their ministry if they would forsake all and follow him. He wrought a miracle especially impressive because it was in the sphere of their daily calling at a time and place where they were sure it was useless to fish. They were enabled by the guidance of Jesus to take such a draft of fishes that their nets were strained and their boats so loaded as nearly to sink. It was so plainly a manifestation of supernatural power that Peter felt himself to be in the presence of a divine Being and expressed the fear which all have felt when face-to-face with God. Jesus spoke the word which not only removed the terror of Peter but gave to him and his companions courage for all the coming years, "Fear not; from henceforth thou shalt catch men."

So today Jesus is calling men to become his disciples. Obedience may involve sacrifice, but it is certain to result in the saving of human souls.

2. JESUS CLEANSING A LEPER   Ch. 5:12-16

12 And it came to pass, while he was in one of the cities, behold, a man full of leprosy: and when he saw Jesus, he fell on his face, and besought him, saying, Lord, if thou wilt, thou canst make me clean. 13 And he stretched forth his hand, and touched him, saying, I will; be thou made clean. And straightway the leprosy departed from him. 14 And he charged him to tell no man: but go thy way, and show thyself to the priest, and offer for thy cleansing, according as Moses commanded, for a testimony unto them. 15 But so much the more went abroad the report concerning him: and great multitudes came together to hear, and to be healed of their infirmities. 16 But he withdrew himself in the deserts, and prayed.

Leprosy was regarded as the most loathsome and terrible of diseases. It existed in various forms, but its invariable feature was its foul uncleanness. The leper was an outcast; he was compelled to live apart from the dwellings of men. He was required to wear a covering over his mouth and to give warning of his approach by crying, "Unclean! Unclean!" His case was regarded as hopeless; he was reckoned as dead. Loathsome, insidious, corrupting, pervasive, isolating, ceremonially and physically defiling, surely leprosy is a fitting emblem of sin; and this graphic narrative presents a parable of the power of Christ to cleanse and to heal and to restore. It is a vivid picture which Luke draws: the humble trust of the poor sufferer, his pitiful cry, the sympathetic touch of Jesus, the word of command and the instant cure. While Jesus forbade the man to arouse excitement by telling of his healing, he commanded him to report his case to the priest, that the highest religious authorities might have unanswerable testimony to the divine power of Christ, and also that the man might bring the offerings required by the law and thus express his gratitude to God. Our Master does expect all who have felt his healing touch to testify of his grace and to show their gratitude by offering to him the service of their lives.

Such miracles could not be hid. The crowds so pressed upon Jesus that he was forced to withdraw to the desert for rest; and as the scene closed he who had startled the multitude by the manifestation of his divine power was left alone seeking help from God in prayer.

3. Jesus Forgiving Sins   Ch. 5:17-26

17 And it came to pass on one of those days, that he was teaching; and there were Pharisees and doctors of the law sitting by, who were come out of every village of Galilee and Judæa and Jerusalem: and the power of the Lord was with him to heal. 18 And behold, men bring on a bed a man that was palsied: and they sought to bring him in, and to lay him before him. 19 And not finding by what way they might bring him in because of the multitude, they went up to the housetop, and let him down through the

tiles with his couch into the midst before Jesus. 20 And
seeing their faith, he said, Man, thy sins are forgiven thee.
21 And the scribes and the Pharisees began to reason,
saying, Who is this that speaketh blasphemies? Who can
forgive sins, but God alone? 22 But Jesus perceiving their
reasonings, answered and said unto them, Why reason ye
in your hearts? 23 Which is easier, to say, Thy sins are
forgiven thee; or to say, Arise and walk? 24 But that ye
may know that the Son of man hath authority on earth
to forgive sins (he said unto him that was palsied), I say
unto thee, Arise, and take up thy couch, and go unto thy
house. 25 And immediately he rose up before them, and
took up that whereon he lay, and departed to his house,
glorifying God. 26 And amazement took hold on all, and
they glorified God; and they were filled with fear, saying,
We have seen strange things to-day.

Leprosy was the symbol of the uncleanness of sin; par-
alysis of its impotence and pain. On the occasion of healing a paralytic, Jesus, however, did something more startling: he forgave sin. The poor sufferer had been borne
by his four friends who were discouraged by no obstacles.
When they were unable to enter the house where Jesus
was, because of the multitudes which surrounded it, they
went to the roof and let the sick man down through the
tiles into the very presence of Christ. Their earnestness is
a rebuke to us who make so little effort to bring our com-
rades within the healing influence of our Lord.

Jesus recognized the faith both of the man and of his
friends and responded with an utterance which occasioned
his hearers more surprise than had the opening of the roof,
"Man, thy sins are forgiven thee." No request had been
made for such forgiveness, but Jesus read the heart. He
saw the yearning of the sufferer for healing not only of his
body but of his soul. He recognized his sorrow for the sin
which had caused the sickness, and the anguish of remorse, and immediately he spoke the word of pardon and
of peace. Thus Jesus voiced the message which the world

seems reluctant to accept. He declared that physical ills and social evils are less serious than the moral and spiritual maladies of which they are the symptoms and the results; and further, he expressed his claim of divine power to pronounce pardon and to remove guilt.

This claim at once aroused the bitter resentment of the scribes and Pharisees who were present and they began to reason: "Who is this that speaketh blasphemies? Who can forgive sins, but God alone?" Their reasoning was correct. Jesus was a blasphemer worthy of death, or else he was divine.

To prove his deity Jesus proposed an immediate test: "Which is easier, to say, Thy sins are forgiven thee; or to say, Arise and walk?" Of course neither is easier; either requires divine power. Therefore, when at the word of Jesus the man arose and started for his home, "glorifying God," it is not strange that "amazement took hold on all, and they glorified God."

Thus the miracles of Christ were real proofs of his deity as well as expressions of his love; they were moreover parables of his ability and willingness to deliver man from the guilt and power of sin.

4. THE CALL OF LEVI   Ch. 5:27-32

27 And after these things he went forth, and beheld a publican, named Levi, sitting at the place of toll, and said unto him, Follow me. 28 And he forsook all, and rose up and followed him.

29 And Levi made him a great feast in his house: and there was a great multitude of publicans and of others that were sitting at meat with them. 30 And the Pharisees and their scribes murmured against his disciples, saying, Why do ye eat and drink with the publicans and sinners? 31 And Jesus answering said unto them, They that are in health have no need of a physician; but they that are sick. 32 I am not come to call the righteous but sinners to repentance.

Nothing could further emphasize the sympathy of Jesus than his calling a publican to be his close companion and friend. These taxgatherers were everywhere despised for their dishonesty, extortion, and greed; but Jesus chose one of them named Levi, or Matthew, and transformed him into an apostle, an evangelist, and a saint.

There must have been something admirable in the character of the man; at least there was something inspiring in his example, for as soon as he heard the clear call of the Master, "He forsook all, and rose up and followed him."

Probably he had more to leave than any of the twelve men who became apostles of Christ. He must have been possessed of wealth. At least, as soon as he was converted, he made "a great feast in his house" and invited "a great multitude of publicans and of others" to be his guests. He had the courage of his convictions; he was not ashamed of his new Master. He was eager to have his old friends introduced to Christ.

It was on the occasion of this feast that Jesus was criticized by the Pharisees for eating and drinking with publicans and sinners. He made this most significant reply: "They that are in health have no need of a physician; but they that are sick. I am not come to call the righteous but sinners to repentance." By this statement Jesus emphasized and vindicated his conduct and defined his mission. A physician enters a sickroom, not because he delights in disease or rejoices in suffering, but because he desires to cure and to relieve; so Jesus companied with sinners not because he countenanced sin or enjoyed the society of the depraved, but because, as a healer of souls, he was willing to go where he was most needed and to work where the ravages of sin were most severe. He came into the world to save sinners. Their conduct distressed him, their sins pained him; but to accomplish his task he sought them out and showed his sympathy by his presence and by his healing power.

Are there any who do not need the spiritual cure he can effect? Are any "sound"; are some not "sinners"? These questions each must answer for himself. Probably those who like the Pharisees are least conscious of their sickness are in most desperate danger. Then again, are those who know his power willing like the Master to go with his gospel to the places of greatest need?

5. THE QUESTION OF FASTING   Ch. 5:33-39

33 And they said unto him, The disciples of John fast often, and make supplications; likewise also the disciples of the Pharisees; but thine eat and drink. 34 And Jesus said unto them, Can ye make the sons of the bride-chamber fast, while the bridegroom is with them? 35 But the days will come; and when the bridegroom shall be taken away from them, then will they fast in those days. 36 And he spake also a parable unto them: No man rendeth a piece from a new garment and putteth it upon an old garment; else he will rend the new, and also the piece from the new will not agree with the old. 37 And no man putteth new wine into old wine-skins; else the new wine will burst the skins, and itself will be spilled, and the skins will perish. 38 But new wine must be put into fresh wine-skins. 39 And no man having drunk old wine desireth new; for he saith, The old is good.

The Pharisees were disturbed by the attitude of Jesus toward sinners. Much more were they distressed by his attitude toward the forms and ceremonies which to their mind constituted the very essence of religion. This attitude had been expressed by the failure of Jesus to require his disciples to observe the fasts which had become so prominent in the system of legalism taught by the religious leaders of the Jews. The law of Moses prescribed no fasts. The rabbis had so multiplied them that a Pharisee could boast of fasting "twice in the week." The disciples of John the Baptist were taught to fast frequently, not as an empty

form, but to express the solemn character of the ministry
of John who had come preaching "repentance unto remission of sins." It was not strange, therefore, that the enemies of Jesus came to him with a complaint and with the
question, "The disciples of John fast often, and make supplications; likewise also the disciples of the Pharisees; but
thine eat and drink." In his reply Jesus stated distinctly
the view his followers should take, not only of fasting but
of all religious forms: "Can ye make the sons of the bride-
chamber fast, while the bridegroom is with them? But the
days will come; and when the bridegroom shall be taken
away from them, then will they fast in those days." Fasting is an expression of sorrow. How absurd, then, would
it be for Jesus' followers to fast while the heavenly Bridegroom was with them! They might express their distress
thus when he should be taken away. Thus Jesus declared
that fasting, like all religious rites, may be quite fitting if
it is a true expression of religions feeling, but if it is a matter of form, of rule, or requirement, if it is regarded as a
ground of merit, it is an absurdity and an impertinence.

Jesus added a parable which further indicates his attitude toward all the rites and ceremonies in which the
Pharisees took such delight. He declared that he had not
come to regulate the fasts and feasts or to amend the Jewish ritual. That would be like sewing a new patch on an
old garment. This religion of ceremonies had served its
purpose. Jesus had come with something new and better.
The life of freedom and of joy which he was imparting
could not be bound up in the narrow forms and rites of
Judaism. New wine could not be kept in old wineskins.

Christianity cannot be comprehended by any system of
rites and ceremonies. It must not be interpreted as a set
of rules and requirements; it must not be confused with
any ritual. It controls men, not by rules, but by motives.
Its symbol is not a fast but a feast, for its pervasive spirit
is joy.

As reported by Luke, Jesus added a characteristic

phrase indicating his tender sympathy. "And no man having drunk old wine desireth new; for he saith, The old is good." Those who long have been accustomed to a religion of forms find it difficult to be satisfied with the religion of faith. We must be patient with them. It is not easy for them to give up the practices of childhood and it takes time for them to learn the gladness and the freedom of spiritual maturity offered to the followers of Christ.

6. THE SABBATH CONTROVERSY   Ch. 6:1-11

1 Now it came to pass on a sabbath, that he was going through the grainfields; and his disciples plucked the ears, and did eat, rubbing them in their hands. 2 But certain of the Pharisees said, Why do ye that which it is not lawful to do on the sabbath day? 3 And Jesus answering them said, Have ye not read even this, what David did, when he was hungry, he, and they that were with him; 4 how he entered into the house of God and took and ate the showbread, and gave also to them that were with him; which it is not lawful to eat save for the priests alone? 5 And he said unto them, The Son of man is lord of the sabbath.

6 And it came to pass on another sabbath, that he entered into the synagogue and taught: and there was a man there, and his right hand was withered. 7 And the scribes and the Pharisees watched him, whether he would heal on the sabbath; that they might find how to accuse him. 8 But he knew their thoughts; and he said to the man that had his hand withered, Rise up, and stand forth in the midst. And he arose and stood forth. 9 And Jesus said unto them, I ask you, Is it lawful on the sabbath to do good, or to do harm? to save a life, or to destroy it? 10 And he looked round about on them all, and said unto him, Stretch forth thy hand. And he did so: and his hand was restored. 11 But they were filled with madness; and communed one with another what they might do to Jesus.

Jesus had aroused the anger of the Pharisees by his claim to forgive sins. He had further enraged them by his treatment of sinners. But he brought their hatred to a climax of fury by his attitude toward Sabbath observance. Henceforth they sought to destroy him.

The question of the Sabbath has never lost its interest. The followers of Christ need to stand firmly by the principles set forth by their Lord. These principles are few but fundamental: The Sabbath is a day designed for worship and for rest and is to be broken only by works of necessity and of mercy.

The first of these exceptions to the required rest of the Sabbath Day was illustrated by the case of the disciples who were accused by the Pharisees of breaking the Sabbath because as they walked through the fields they picked the ripened ears and thus, according to the interpretation of their enemies, were guilty of working on the Sabbath Day. Our Lord did not deny that the Sabbath law had been broken. He merely referred his enemies to the case of David and his followers who, forced by hunger, broke the Mosaic law in entering the tabernacle and eating the "showbread." Jesus argued that, when necessary to relieve their hunger, his followers were also justified in disregarding the law of rest.

An illustration of the second exception to the law of absolute cessation from labor was given "on another sabbath" when in the synagogue Jesus healed a man whose right hand was "withered." The Pharisees regarded this action of Jesus as another breach of the law of rest. Jesus defended his action on the ground that it was dictated by mercy and that work which secured relief from suffering was allowable on the Sabbath Day. He replied to his enemies by a searching question, assuming the principle that refraining from help is the same as inflicting harm. He asked them whether they regarded the Sabbath Day as of such character as to make it right on that day to do that which on other days was wrong: "I ask you, Is it lawful on the sabbath to do good, or to do harm? to save a life, or to destroy it?"

While Jesus taught that the law of rest might thus be broken to meet the necessities of man and to show mercy to those in need or in distress, he by no means abrogated the Sabbath. He declared, however, that "the Son of man is lord of the sabbath," by which he meant that as the representative of men he had a right to interpret the law for the highest good of man. He was justified in relieving the Sabbath from the narrow and burdensome observances which had been bound upon it by the Pharisees and to restore it to mankind as a glad day of rest and of refreshment and of fellowship with God.

C. THE THIRD PERIOD Chs. 6:12 to 8:56

1. THE CHOICE OF THE TWELVE Ch. 6:12-19

12 And it came to pass in these days, that he went out into the mountain to pray; and he continued all night in prayer to God. 13 And when it was day, he called his disciples; and he chose from them twelve, whom also he named apostles: 14 Simon, whom he also named Peter, and Andrew his brother, and James and John, and Philip and Bartholomew, 15 and Matthew and Thomas, and James the son of Alphæus, and Simon who was called the Zealot, 16 and Judas the son of James, and Judas Iscariot, who became a traitor; 17 and he came down with them, and stood on a level place, and a great multitude of his disciples, and a great number of the people from all Judæa and Jerusalem, and the sea coast of Tyre and Sidon, who came to hear him, and to be healed of their diseases; 18 and they that were troubled with unclean spirits were healed. 19 And all the multitude sought to touch him; for power came forth from him, and healed them all.

The choice of the twelve apostles marks a new and important period in the public ministry of our Lord. The deep significance of the act is indicated by Luke in his statement that Jesus passed the entire preceding night in prayer to God. One reason for his decision may have been the mad hatred of the Pharisees whose anger had now reached a murderous height. To give more assured permanence to his work Jesus saw the necessity of organizing his followers. He had been surrounded by a multitude of disciples, some of whom were his constant companions, but he now determined to appoint officers who would act as trained leaders, who would be his official messengers accredited by miraculous powers.

In all four places in the New Testament where the names of these twelve apostles are found, they are arranged in three invariable groups, possibly in accordance with their intimacy with Jesus and their real service to him. In all ages there have been among his followers such concentric circles, such inner groups, who have been blessed by peculiar intimacy with their Lord, not due to his arbitrary choice, but to their peculiar capacities for love and obedience and faith.

The first six mentioned by Luke were men who under the influence of John the Baptist had become the first followers of Christ. Other things being equal, those who have known Jesus longest are able to serve him best.

The chief place in the first group is always assigned to Simon Peter, bold, impulsive, fickle, but possessing the peculiar powers of leadership which qualified him for the place of primacy among the apostles of our Lord.

With him Luke names his brother Andrew, probably a man of less ability and strength, but one who will ever be remembered as having brought Peter into fellowship with Jesus. None can ever tell what share in the reward of a more famous worker will be enjoyed by one more obscure to whom the greater leader owes his Christian career.

The next to be mentioned are James and John, the "sons of thunder," the courageous, loving, faithful companions who with Peter form the inmost circle of the followers of Christ. James was the first to suffer martyrdom for the sake of his Master, while John lingered longest of all the apostolic band, testifying to the cause of him who had chosen John as his closest friend, and for whose return John continued to watch and to wait.

Of the second four, the first to be mentioned are Philip and Bartholomew; the latter is supposed to be the same as Nathanael, the Israelite without guile whom Philip won as a disciple for Christ.

The next were Matthew and Thomas. The former had been a despised publican, but his training had prepared him to become a careful recorder of facts, so that after his intimate fellowship with Christ he became one of his biographers and wrote that which is numbered as the first of the Gospels. Thomas has won the reputation of being a doubting disciple. He was certainly naturally despondent and incredulous. The fact, however, that such a man became convinced of the resurrection of Christ so soon after the event is one of the most important testimonies to the reality of the fundamental fact of our Christian faith.

As to the last group, we know nothing of James, the son of Alphaeus, commonly called "James the less" in contrast with James the brother of John; but it is surely a mistake to identify him with James the brother of our Lord who became the head of the church in Jerusalem and wrote the Epistle which bears his name. "Simon who was called the Zealot" was by this latter title distinguished from Simon Peter. If this title is correctly interpreted, he had formerly belonged to that fanatical party of Jews who were promoters and supporters of the revolt against Rome, which finally resulted in the destruction of Jerusalem.

Judas, the son of James, is carefully distinguished in the narrative from the traitor whose infamous name always comes last on the list of apostles and is never mentioned in Scripture without some designation of disgrace and shame. Why he should have been chosen as a follower of Christ no one can sufficiently explain, yet there must have been in him original elements of good. There was surely the possibility of development into usefulness and sainthood, but he tried to cherish the passion of greed while companying with Jesus, and the inevitable reaction was so great and rapid that he soon degenerated into a thief and a traitor. His fate serves as a warning to all the followers of Christ and his testimony to the character of Jesus has been repeated through all the years, "I have . . . betrayed innocent blood."

All of the Twelve were men of modest means and humble stations in life; they were men of moderate ability, and most of their names are still obscure; yet they were the first leaders and the real organizers of the most important society the world has known, and their names are yet to be graven on the foundations of the Holy City, the light of which is to fill the earth with glory.

2. THE GREAT SERMON   Ch. 6:20-49

20 And he lifted up his eyes on his disciples, and said, Blessed are ye poor: for yours is the kingdom of God. 21 Blessed are ye that hunger now: for ye shall be filled. Blessed are ye that weep now: for ye shall laugh. 22 Blessed are ye, when men shall hate you, and when they shall separate you from their company, *and reproach you, and cast out your name as evil, for the Son of man's sake. 23 Rejoice in that day, and leap* for joy: *for behold, your reward is great in heaven; for in the same manner did their fathers unto the prophets. 24 But woe unto you that are rich! for ye have received your consolation. 25 Woe unto you, ye that are full now! for ye shall hunger. Woe unto you, ye that laugh now! for ye shall mourn and weep. 26 Woe unto you, when all men shall speak well of you! for in the same manner did their fathers to the false prophets.*

27 But I say unto you that hear, Love your enemies, do good to them that hate you, 28 bless them that curse you, pray for them that despitefully use you. 29 To him that smiteth thee on the one cheek offer also the other; and from him that taketh away thy cloak withhold not thy coat also. 30 Give to every one that asketh thee; and of him that taketh away thy goods ask them not again. 31 And as ye would that men should do to you, do ye also to them

*likewise. 32 And if ye love them that love you, what thank
have ye? for even sinners love those that love them. 33
And if ye do good to them that do good to you, what thank
have ye? for even sinners do the same. 34 And if ye lend
to them of whom ye hope to receive, what thank have ye?
even sinners lend to sinners, to receive again as much. 35
But love your enemies, and do* them *good, and lend, never
despairing; and your reward shall be great, and ye shall be
sons of the Most High: for he is kind toward the unthank-
ful and evil. 36 Be ye merciful, even as your Father is
merciful. 37 And judge not, and ye shall not be judged:
and condemn not, and ye shall not be condemned: release,
and ye shall be released: 38 give, and it shall be given
unto you; good measure, pressed down, shaken together,
running over, shall they give into your bosom. For with
what measure ye mete it shall be measured to you again.*

*39 And he spake also a parable unto them, Can the blind
guide the blind? shall they not both fall into a pit? 40 The
disciple is not above his teacher: but every one when he is
perfected shall be as his teacher. 41 And why beholdest
thou the mote that is in thy brother's eye, but considerest
not the beam that is in thine own eye? 42 Or how canst
thou say to thy brother, Brother, let me cast out the mote
that is in thine eye, when thou thyself beholdest not the
beam that is in thine own eye? Thou hypocrite, cast out
first the beam out of thine own eye, and then shalt thou
see clearly to cast out the mote that is in thy brother's
eye. 43 For there is no good tree that bringeth forth corrupt fruit; nor again a corrupt tree that bringeth forth good
fruit. 44 For each tree is known by its own fruit. For
of thorns men do not gather figs, nor of a bramble bush
gather they grapes. 45 The good man out of the good
treasure of his heart bringeth forth that which is good; and
the evil* man *out of the evil* treasure *bringeth forth that
which is evil: for out of the abundance of the heart his
mouth speaketh.*

*46 And why call ye me, Lord, Lord, and do not the
things which I say? 47 Every one that cometh unto me,
and heareth my words, and doeth them, I will show you to
whom he is like: 48 he is like a man building a house,
who digged and went deep, and laid a foundation upon the*

*rock: and when a flood arose, the stream brake against
that house, and could not shake it: because it had been
well builded.   49 But he that heareth, and doeth not, is
like a man that built a house upon the earth without a
foundation; against which the stream brake, and straightway it fell in; and the ruin of that house was great.*

It might seem difficult to prove that the Sermon on the
Mount is the same as this discourse which has been called
by some the Sermon on the Plain.   The exact relation between the sermon reported by Matthew and this great address recorded by Luke has long been a subject of debate.
It is quite probable, however, that they are identical.
After Jesus had chosen the twelve apostles on the sum-
mit of the mountain where he had spent the night, he descended to a level place on the mountainside and there
met the multitude and delivered the sermon which holds
first place among all the discourses in the world.

If this address is the same as the Sermon on the Mount,
it is to be noted that each account begins with beatitudes
and closes with a warning, while the main body of the discourse differs only in the aspect of truth emphasized by the
two writers.   In Matthew the essence of the Christian life
is described as true righteousness in distinction from the
formalism of the Pharisees.   In Luke the essence of righteousness is found in love.   Matthew was writing with
Jewish Christians in mind.   The Gospel of Luke was for
the world, and many of his readers would not have appreciated the distinction which Matthew was emphasizing.
The word which would describe the sermon as recorded by
Matthew is spirituality, but the substance of the Christian
life as here indicated by Luke is charity.

The Beatitudes here recorded are four in number, while
Matthew mentions eight or nine; but Luke adds four woes,
each one of which is in striking contrast with the parallel
Beatitude, vs. 20-26.   The sermon begins, therefore, by
pronouncing blessings upon the followers of Christ and
contrasted woes upon those who reject him.   Those who

are declared to be blessed are the poor, the hungry, the mourners, and the despised; while woes are pronounced upon the rich, the satisfied, the joyous, and the praised. It is, of course, understood that there are spiritual implications in these different terms. Poverty, hunger, sorrow, reproach, have no merit in themselves and issue in present and eternal blessedness only when accompanied by humility, trust, and patience, and when endured for the sake of Christ. So, too, there is no wrong in riches and satisfaction and laughter and praise unless these are accompanied by the selfishness and greed and frivolity and unworthiness with which they are so often identified. By these blessings and woes the Master indicated the real character as well as the abiding blessedness of those who are his true disciples.

The burden of the discourse, vs. 27-45, sets forth the Christian life as being in essence a life of love. This sermon on love might be accompanied properly by the "hymn of love" composed by Paul, I Cor., ch. 13, and by the "Scripture lesson" on love written by John, I John 4:7-21.

First then, in place of all revenge, vs. 27-30, Jesus established the Golden Rule: "As ye would that men should do to you, do ye also to them likewise." V. 31. Then, in contrast with the self-interest and desire for recompense which so often passes among men as charity, vs. 32-34, he pointed to the perfect example of God and intimated that his mercy should incline us to kindly judgments of our fellows, assuring us of the boundless liberality with which our Father will reward our unselfish love. Vs. 35-38.

The second portion of the main discussion, vs. 39-45, dwells still more definitely upon the fault of unkindly judgments to which Jesus had just referred and which constitutes such a common infraction of the law of love. A man who is unkind in his criticisms and unconscious of his own faults cannot help his fellowman; he is like a blind man trying to lead the blind, like one in whose eye there is a beam trying to help one in whose eye there is a mote. As good fruit is produced only by good trees, only out of hearts full of love can real helpfulness come.

To warn men against calling themselves Christians while they do not observe the law of love, and to encourage his disciples in faithfully keeping his commandments, Jesus concluded this sermon with the familiar figure of the two houses, founded one upon the sand and the other upon the rock. Amid the storms and tempests and floods of the time of judgment, only the latter will stand secure.

3. THE CENTURION OF CAPERNAUM   Ch. 7:1-10

1 After he had ended all his sayings in the ears of the people, he entered into Capernaum.

2 And a certain centurion's servant, who was dear unto him, was sick and at the point of death. 3 And when he heard concerning Jesus, he sent unto him elders of the Jews, asking him that he would come and save his servant. 4 And they, when they came to Jesus, besought him earnestly, saying, He is worthy that thou shouldest do this for him; 5 for he loveth our nation, and himself built us our synagogue. 6 And Jesus went with them. And when he was now not far from the house, the centurion sent friends to him, saying unto him, Lord, trouble not thyself; for I am not worthy that thou shouldest come under my roof: 7 wherefore neither thought I myself worthy to come unto thee: but say the word, and my servant shall be healed. 8 For I also am a man set under authority, having under myself soldiers: and I say to this one, Go, and he goeth; and to another, Come, and he cometh; and to my servant, Do this, and he doeth it. 9 And when Jesus heard these things, he marvelled at him, and turned and said unto the multitude that followed him, I say unto you, I have not found so great faith, no, not in Israel. 10 And they that were sent, returning to the house, found the servant whole.

No more perfect picture of faith has been recorded than that in which Luke sketches the centurion of Capernaum who sent to Jesus the request to heal a favorite servant then lying at the door of death. This military commander, a heathen by birth, was evidently a man of the same high character as is attributed in the New Testament to all soldiers of a similar rank. It may be helpful to notice some features of his faith which was so great that our Lord "marvelled at him." First of all, the centurion was confident that Jesus could cure, because of what he had heard concerning our Lord. This is the very essence of faith, namely belief founded upon evidence. Faith is not credulity or fancy or caprice; it is a purely rational exercise of the mind; it is reasoning from the reports of credible witnesses. The centurion had heard enough of the power and goodness of Jesus to convince him of his ability to heal. Unbelief in the face of evidence is stupidity or sin.

Again, the centurion revealed the sincerity of true faith. He had accepted light as far as this had been revealed. He had been attracted by the pure worship of Judaism and had shown his sympathy with its adherents by building for them a synagogue. When one lives in accordance with the light he has, more light is sure to break.

Then again, he revealed the humility of faith. He regarded himself as unworthy to come into the presence of Jesus to present his request; and when Jesus offered to come to his home, he sent word that he was not worthy to have the Master come under his roof.

Most explicitly of all, he expressed the trust in Christ and the dependence upon his power which characterize true faith. He said that it was unnecessary for Jesus to come to his house; as a soldier and an officer he knew what could be accomplished by a word of command; he knew what it was to obey and to be obeyed, and he had accredited to Jesus such control over the unseen powers of disease that he sent his surprising message, "But say the word, and my servant shall be healed." It was just this aspect of his faith which so impressed our Lord, and it is such humble trust that he still regards with favor and is certain to reward. It is not strange that they "that were sent, returning to the house, found the servant whole," or that Luke rejoiced to tell this story which reveals belief in Christ on the part of one who was found outside of Israel, a belief which was prophetic of the blessings which faith was to bring to men of all the nations in the world.

4. JESUS RAISING THE WIDOW'S SON   Ch. 7:11-17

11 And it came to pass soon afterwards, that he went to a city called Nain; and his disciples went with him, and a great multitude. 12 Now when he drew near to the gate of the city, behold, there was carried out one that was dead, the only son of his mother, and she was a widow: and much people of the city was with her. 13 And when the Lord saw her, he had compassion on her, and said unto her, Weep not. 14 And he came nigh and touched the bier: and the bearers stood still. And he said, Young man, I say unto thee, Arise. 15 And he that was dead sat up, and began to speak. And he gave him to his mother. 16 And fear took hold on all: and they glorified God, saying, A great prophet is arisen among us: and, God hath visited his people. 17 And this report went forth concerning him in the whole of Judæa, and all the region round about.

If it was the purpose of Luke to impress upon his readers the sympathy and tenderness of the Man Christ Jesus, it is easy to understand why he alone of all the Evangelists records this touching story of the raising from the dead of the son of the widow of Nain. No picture could be more full of pity and compassion. Jesus had not been asked to perform the miracle; he was moved wholly by the mute appeal of human sorrow and distress. As he drew near to the gate of the little city, he met the sad procession wending its way out to the place of burial. He was touched by the tears of the lonely mother who had lost her only son; moved with deep compassion, he spoke to her the word of hope, "Weep not." Then he came near and touched the bier on which the lifeless body was being borne. It was a sign more eloquent than a spoken word.

Then came the command: "Young man, I say unto thee, Arise. And he that was dead sat up, and began to speak. And he gave him to his mother." In view of such miracles, possibly we dwell too exclusively upon their purpose as authenticating the mission of Jesus, or as demonstrating his divine message. These purposes are real, but we must never forget that such works were also manifestations of the nature of the ministry of Jesus and revelations of the very heart of God. Such recitals dry the tears of mourners and bind up broken hearts and inspire the despondent with eternal hope. Surely Jesus is the Lord of life and he will yet wipe away all tears from the eyes of those that trust him.

5. JESUS PRAISING JOHN   Ch. 7:18-35

18 And the disciples of John told him of all these things. 19 And John calling unto him two of his disciples sent them to the Lord, saying, Art thou he that cometh, or look we for another? 20 And when the men were come unto him, they said, John the Baptist hath sent us unto thee, saying, Art thou he that cometh, or look we for another? 21 In that hour he cured many of diseases and plagues and evil spirits; and on many that were blind he bestowed sight. 22 And he answered and said unto them, Go and tell John the things which ye have seen and heard; the blind receive their sight, the lame walk, the lepers are cleansed, and the deaf hear, the dead are raised up, the poor have good tidings preached to them. 23 And blessed is he, whosoever shall find no occasion of stumbling in me.

24 And when the messengers of John were departed, he began to say unto the multitudes concerning John, What went ye out into the wilderness to behold? a reed shaken with the wind? 25 But what went ye out to see? a man clothed in soft raiment? Behold, they that are gorgeously apparelled, and live delicately, are in kings' courts. 26 But what went ye out to see? a prophet? Yea, I say unto you, and much more than a prophet. 27 This is he of whom it is written,

Behold, I send my messenger before thy face,
Who shall prepare thy way before thee.

28 *I say unto you, Among them that are born of women there is none greater than John: yet he that is but little in the kingdom of God is greater than he.   29 And all the people when they heard, and the publicans, justified God, being baptized with the baptism of John.   30 But the Pharisees and the lawyers rejected for themselves the counsel of God, being not baptized of him.   31 Whereunto then shall I liken the men of this generation, and to what are they like?   32 They are like unto children that sit in the marketplace, and call one to another; who say, We piped unto you, and ye did not dance; we wailed, and ye did not weep.   33 For John the Baptist is come eating no bread nor drinking wine; and ye say, He hath a demon.   34 The Son of man is come eating and drinking; and ye say, Behold, a gluttonous man, and a winebibber, a friend of publicans and sinners!   35 And wisdom is justified of all her children.*

Because of the darkness of his dungeon or the long delay of Jesus in fulfilling his cherished hopes, the mind of John the Baptist became clouded with doubt and he sent messengers to Jesus to ask whether or not he was really the Messiah whom John had declared him to be: "Art thou he that cometh, or look we for another?"   John had not lost faith in God or in his promises; he believed that if Jesus were not the Messiah, the Messiah was still to come.

The Master lovingly reassured his great herald by sending back the report of the mighty works which he was accomplishing.   John was already familiar with these acts, but the recital must have dispelled his fears.   Jesus sympathizes with us also in our hours of darkness, but his relief usually consists in reminding us of facts we already know concerning his power and love and presence and the truths of his written Word.

Jesus, however, does not praise us for our doubts; he sent to John a gentle and loving rebuke: "And blessed is he, whosoever shall find no occasion of stumbling in me."

This benediction he pronounces upon all who in spite of darkness, imprisonment, delay, and mystery still confidently put their trust in him.

It was upon this occasion when John seems to have failed that Jesus pronounced upon him unparalleled praise, declaring that "among them that are born of women there is none greater than John." He vindicated this deliberate judgment and thereby showed wherein true greatness lies. He spoke first of the character of John and then of his career. He praised the man and then the messenger. He described his moral and then his official greatness.

His expression as to the character of John is voiced by two questions, to each of which a negative answer of course must be given: first, "What went ye out into the wilderness to behold? a reed shaken with the wind?" Surely true greatness does not lie in the moral cowardice which bends before every breeze; quite on the contrary, John was like a rock which no storm could move.

Then there was a second question: "What went ye out to see? a man clothed in soft raiment?" Surely greatness does not lie along the line of self-gratification and indulgence. John endured all hardships and was oblivious to all human delights because he was so devoted to his divine task. Courage and consecration—these constitute prime factors in moral greatness.

The real greatness of John consisted, however, in his mission. Jesus declared that he was the messenger whom Malachi had predicted should prepare the way of the Lord. Other prophets had appeared and had predicted the coming of the Messiah. It was given to John not only to declare that the Christ would come but to point to him and to say: "Behold, the Lamb of God! . . . This is the Son of God." No greater dignity had ever been conferred upon a human soul; and no higher privilege can now be enjoyed than that of turning the thoughts and hearts of men to Jesus Christ, the Savior of the world. The present followers of Christ have a larger knowledge of him than was possessed by John. What their relative positions will be in the glory of the perfected Kingdom will depend upon the comparative faithfulness with which they serve their Master.

The praise of John is sharply contrasted with the condemnation of the Pharisees which Jesus now turned to express. He declared that these professed leaders were like children sitting in the marketplace, complaining one to another that they are willing to play neither at mock funerals nor at mock weddings, for when John came they refused to follow him because his aspect and message were too severe, and when Christ came they criticized him as being too genial, "a friend of publicans and sinners." The trouble with the Pharisees was that they made an excuse of the demeanor of John and the conduct of Jesus for refusing what was essential in their mission and message. They were unwilling to repent at the command of John or to put their trust in Christ in response to his promise of grace and life. Thus some men are still refusing to accept the salvation which is offered because of something in Christianity which is purely external, while they fail to appreciate its true essence; but there were those in the days of Jesus, and there are those today, who are willing to accept both the call to repentance and the offer of life, "And wisdom is justified of all her children."

6. A Sinful Woman Forgiven   Ch. 7:36-50

36 And one of the Pharisees desired him that he would eat with him. And he entered into the Pharisee's house, and sat down to meat. 37 And behold, a woman who was in the city, a sinner; and when she knew that he was sitting at meat in the Pharisee's house, she brought an alabaster cruse of ointment, 38 and standing behind at his feet, weeping, she began to wet his feet with her tears, and wiped them with the hair of her head, and kissed his feet, and anointed them with the ointment. 39 Now when the Pharisee that had bidden him saw it, he spake within him-

self, saying, This man, if he were a prophet, would have perceived who and what manner of woman this is that toucheth him, that she is a sinner. 40 And Jesus answering said unto him, Simon, I have somewhat to say unto thee. And he saith, Teacher, say on. 41 A certain lender had two debtors: the one owed five hundred shillings, and the other fifty. 42 When they had not wherewith to pay, he forgave them both. Which of them therefore will love him most? 43 Simon answered and said, He, I suppose, to whom he forgave the most. And he said unto him, Thou hast rightly judged. 44 And turning to the woman, he said unto Simon, Seest thou this woman? I entered into thy house, thou gavest me no water for my feet: but she hath wetted my feet with her tears, and wiped them with her hair. 45 Thou gavest me no kiss: but she, since the time I came in, hath not ceased to kiss my feet. 46 My head with oil thou didst not anoint: but she hath anointed my feet with ointment. 47 Wherefore I say unto thee, Her sins, which are many, are forgiven; for she loved much: but to whom little is forgiven, the same loveth little. 48 And he said unto her, Thy sins are forgiven. 49 And they that sat at meat with him began to say within themselves, Who is this that even forgiveth sins? 50 And he said unto the woman, Thy faith hath saved thee; go in peace.

The Gospel of Luke appears to place special emphasis upon the grace and forgiveness manifested by Jesus. It alone records his sympathy with the sorrowing widow of Nain, and it is also alone in expressing the sympathy which Jesus felt for the sinful woman who anointed his feet in the house of Simon, the Pharisee. It is a picture, however, not only of the loving mercy of our Lord, but of the unbounded gratitude felt by one who truly appreciated the priceless gift of his pardoning grace.

By an unfortunate error of interpretation, this woman has been confused with Mary of Magdala or with Mary of Bethany. These three persons should be, however, absolutely distinct. It is true that Jesus delivered the first of these from demoniac possession, and that the second, like the woman in this story, anointed his feet with perfume, but there is every reason for believing that of the three only this woman was reputed to be a sinner. She seems to have met Jesus on some previous occasion, to have repented of her sins, and to have received from the Lord his word of forgiveness.

It was her gratitude which gave her courage to enter unbidden into the house of Simon, where Jesus was being entertained as a guest. She had come to anoint his feet but as she beheld him, she thought again of her sins and her hot tears of penitence fell upon the feet of her Lord. She hastily unbound her hair and with it dried his feet and then poured upon them a flask of fragrant ointment. No truer expression could have been given to her gratitude and passionate devotion. The fact that Jesus allowed a woman of such notorious character to express her love for him made Simon conclude that Jesus could not be a prophet, for otherwise he would have been able to discern the nature of so depraved a woman.

By his reply Jesus showed his ability to read even the secret thoughts of his host. The words of Jesus not only answered the silent criticism of Simon but also rebuked him for his own impenitence and lack of faith. Jesus proposed to his host a parable of two forgiven debtors, illustrating the fact that gratitude depends upon the realization of the amount which has been forgiven, and then he applied this principle to Simon and to the woman whom Simon had been regarding with scorn. Jesus showed how keenly he had felt the lack of love shown him by his host, and he contrasted it with the affection shown by the woman. When he had entered the house Simon had neglected the customary service of providing a bath for his feet; the woman had washed his feet with her tears. Simon had withheld the kiss with which a host usually welcomed his guests; the woman had passionately kissed his feet. Simon had not furnished the perfume with which it was usual to anoint an honored guest; the woman had come to the house with the special purpose of pouring fragrant oil upon the feet of her Lord.

In view of the parable, the message of Jesus is plain: "Wherefore I say unto thee, Her sins, which are many, are forgiven; for she loved much: but to whom little is forgiven, the same loveth little." Jesus did not mean to say that until now she had not been pardoned, nor yet that her pardon was conditioned upon her love. He meant that her love resulted from her pardon, and his words have been rightfully interpreted thus: "I say unto thee that her many sins are forgiven, as thou mayest infer from this exhibition of her love." The remainder of the sentence was devoted to Simon: "To whom little is forgiven, the same loveth little." The words do not prove that Simon had been pardoned; rather, they indicate that his lack of love had proved his lack of penitence and so of forgiveness. Jesus then turned to the woman with a word of benediction: "Thy sins are forgiven." He thus assured her of the pardon previously granted, but still more he vindicated her in the eyes of the guests and assured them of the new life upon which the woman already had entered. They marveled as they heard him pronouncing pardon. That is a divine function; but the ideal Man whose sympathy Luke records was likewise the Son of God. Last of all, Jesus turned to the woman with the final word of blessing: "Thy faith hath saved thee; go in peace." This is a clear statement of the fact that faith had secured pardon and pardon had awakened gratitude and gratitude had been expressed by a deed of devoted love. Such a penitent can rightfully go away "into peace," that is, to its present and continual enjoyment.

7. THE MINISTERING WOMEN   Ch. 8:1-3

1 And it came to pass soon afterwards, that he went about through cities and villages, preaching and bringing the good tidings of the kingdom of God, and with him the twelve, 2 and certain women who had been healed of evil spirits and infirmities: Mary that was called Magdalene, from whom seven demons had gone out, 3 and Joanna the wife of Chuzas Herod's steward, and Susanna, and many others, who ministered unto them of their substance.

Luke writes the Gospel of womanhood. He alone records those tender incidents in the lives of Elisabeth, Mary, and Anna which are associated with the infancy of Jesus; he alone tells us of the widow of Nain whose son Jesus restored to life; of the woman bowed down by Satan but relieved by Jesus; of the penitent sinner who anointed his feet; of the domestic scene in the home of Mary and Martha; of the woman who congratulated the mother of Jesus; and of the women who condoled with him on his way to the cross. Perhaps most significant of all is the statement of Luke that as Jesus and his apostles moved about Galilee preaching the gospel, they were attended by a company of women "who ministered unto them of their substance."

Among these women Luke mentions "Mary that was called Magdalene," probably so designated from the town of Magdala where formerly she had lived. By this title she was distinguished from Mary the mother of Jesus, from Mary of Bethany, and from other women of this same name. It is a cruel error to confuse her with the sinful woman of whom Luke has just been writing. Mary had suffered from demon possession, as here stated, but there is nothing in the Gospels to indicate that she had ever been a woman of notoriously evil life.

Luke also mentions Joanna, whose husband, Chuzas, had charge of the household and personal estates of King Herod, evidently then a woman of some social standing; but of her and her companions nothing further is known, excepting this important fact, that their motive in ministering to the Master was that of gratitude; they "had been healed of evil spirits and infirmities."

This statement by Luke is brief but illuminating. It

throws light upon an interesting question to which no other answer is given in the Gospels: How did Jesus and his followers secure financial support during the years of his ministry? Evidently those who had received from him spiritual help gladly supplied his temporal wants and rendered to him all needful service. Thus this passage indicates not only what Jesus did for women, but what women did for him. It suggests a question: Who can estimate how far the gifts and sacrifices of grateful women have been making possible, through the passing ages, the preaching of the gospel in all the world?

8. THE PARABLE OF THE SOWER   Ch. 8:4-18

4 And when a great multitude came together, and they of every city resorted unto him, he spake by a parable: 5 The sower went forth to sow his seed: and as he sowed, some fell by the way side; and it was trodden under foot, and the birds of the heaven devoured it. 6 And other fell on the rock; and as soon as it grew, it withered away, because it had no moisture. 7 And other fell amidst the thorns; and the thorns grew with it, and choked it. 8 And other fell into the good ground, and grew, and brought forth fruit a hundredfold. As he said these things, he cried, He that hath ears to hear, let him hear.

9 And his disciples asked him what this parable might be. 10 And he said, Unto you it is given to know the mysteries of the kingdom of God: but to the rest in parables; that seeing they may not see, and hearing they may not understand. 11 Now the parable is this: The seed is the word of God. 12 And those by the way side are they that have heard; then cometh the devil, and taketh away the word from their heart, that they may not believe and be saved. 13 And those on the rock are they who, when they have heard, receive the word with joy; and these have no root, who for a while believe, and in time of temptation fall away. 14 And that which fell among the thorns, these are they that have heard, and as they go on their way they are choked with cares and riches and pleasures of this life, and bring no fruit to perfection. 15 And that in the good ground, these are such as in an honest and good heart, having heard the word, hold it fast, and bring forth fruit with patience.

*16 And no man, when he hath lighted a lamp, covereth it with a vessel, or putteth it under a bed; but putteth it on a stand, that they that enter in may see the light. 17 For nothing is hid, that shall not be made manifest; nor any-*thing *secret, that shall not be known and come to light. 18 Take heed therefore how ye hear: for whosoever hath, to him shall be given; and whosoever hath not, from him shall be taken away even that which he thinketh he hath.*

Because of its greater length and more elaborate work-manship and greater fullness of detail, this story of the sower is rightly regarded as the first parable of our Lord, even though he had previously used brief illustrations which were designated by the same name. Parables henceforth formed a prominent part of his teaching, and that he was now beginning a somewhat new method of instruction is evident from the fact that the disciples now asked him to explain his meaning, v. 9, and from the fact that he here gave the reason for the use of all his parables. This reason is twofold: these inimitable illustrations would enable those who were attentive and rightly disposed toward him to remember more easily the teachings of the Master; while to inattentive or hostile minds the meaning would be veiled. V. 10. This twofold purpose met the demands of the crisis which had arisen, due on the one hand to the increasing popularity of Jesus' teachings and on the other to the murderous hatred and dark plots of the Pharisees and scribes.

The parable of the sower thus forms a proper introduc-tion to all the parables, for they are vehicles of truth, and our Lord here made it clear that the effect of truth depends upon the spiritual state of the hearers. This is sometimes called the parable of the soils, for it illustrates the various states of heart found among men to whom the Christian message comes.

In some cases "the word of God," whether preached by
Christ or by his followers, falls on hearts which are pictured by the hard-trodden footpath which runs through the
field of grain. No possible impression can be made. The
Word finds no entrance and Satan snatches it away as a
bird picks up the grain which falls by the wayside. Faith
and salvation cannot result.

Other hearers are compared to the thin layer of earth
which covers a ledge of stone. Seed which falls into such
soil springs up most quickly because warmed by the under-
lying rock; but as the roots cannot strike downward, the
grain soon withers beneath the scorching sun. So there
are hearers who receive with joy the message of life, but
when subjected to the persecution and trials which followers of Christ must endure, they quickly desert his
cause.

Other hearers are compared to seed which falls where
thorns are growing. This seed springs into life, but it has
not room for development. It is robbed by the thorns of
its needed nourishment. Thus some Christians are so pre-
occupied by "cares and riches and pleasures" that they can
bear no spiritual fruit.

There are those, however, who are like seed which fell
on "good ground" and "brought forth fruit a hundredfold"; they receive the truth "in an honest and good heart"
and patiently and perseveringly they produce in their lives
a golden harvest of grain.

The great message of the parable is summarized in the
words of our Lord, "Take heed therefore how ye hear."
V. 18. The purpose of his parables, as of all his teachings,
was to give spiritual light. Those who love him and obey
his word will have their understanding quickened and their
knowledge increased; but one who is careless or disobedient to the truth, will lose "even that which he thinketh he
hath." It is a great privilege to hear the gospel of Christ,
but it involves a great responsibility as well.

9. KINSHIP WITH JESUS   Ch. 8:19-21

19 And there came to him his mother and brethren, and they could not come at him for the crowd. 20 And it was told him, Thy mother and thy brethren stand without, desiring to see thee. 21 But he answered and said unto them, My mother and my brethren are these that hear the word of God, and do it.

It is only from the other Gospels that we learn the exact nature and purpose of the visit paid to Jesus by his mother and brethren. Luke does not reveal the fact that it occasioned one of the most delicate and difficult dilemmas by which our Lord was ever confronted. The real purpose of these relatives was to interrupt his work. They feared that his mind was unbalanced and they wished to take him home. Should Jesus repudiate them, or should he allow his work needlessly to be interrupted? This situation Luke does not sketch, but he does state clearly the impressive message which Jesus found occasion to deliver. When Jesus was told that these relatives desired to see him, he pointed to his disciples with the reply, "My mother and my brethren are these that hear the word of God, and do it." Thus Luke connects this incident with the parable of the sower which he has just related. The parable shows the need of careful attention to the gospel truth, and, according to Luke's account of this incident, the same fact is emphasized, namely, the blessed result of heeding the divine Word. According to the statement of Christ, such obedience to him and such true discipleship as was shown by his followers results in a relationship with him more intimate and close than is secured by any human ties. This spiritual kinship is more vital than any relationship of blood or of nature. It results in a fellowship, at once blessed and forever abiding, which is possible for all. The reply of our Lord could not have offended his brethren even though it did contain a delicate rebuke. Only those have a right to claim relationship with him who submit to him as their Lord and are ready to do his will.

10. JESUS STILLING THE STORM   Ch. 8:22-25

22 Now it came to pass on one of those days, that he entered into a boat, himself and his disciples; and he said unto them, Let us go over unto the other side of the lake: and they launched forth. 23 But as they sailed he fell asleep: and there came down a storm of wind on the lake; and they were filling with water, *and were in jeopardy. 24 And they came to him, and awoke him, saying, Master, master, we perish. And he awoke, and rebuked the wind and the raging of the water: and they ceased, and there was a calm. 25 And he said unto them, Where is your faith? And being afraid they marvelled, saying one to another, Who then is this, that he commandeth even the winds and the water, and they obey him?*

Storms were common on the surface of the little lake which Jesus so often crossed with his disciples; and storms are still frequent in the lives of his followers. To accompany the Master does not exempt us from struggles and tempests, from dark skies and angry waves. This, however, was no usual storm. Even the sturdy fishermen of Galilee, who were familiar with all the changeful moods of that inland sea, were filled with terror. Jesus at the time was quietly resting and had fallen asleep in what seemed to his followers to be an hour of greatest peril.

Their fear may have been foolish, but it was wise in them to come to the Master in their moment of pressing need. They awoke him with the cry, "Master, master, we perish." The followers of Christ are not saved from encountering storms, but in the hour of peril they should be comforted by his presence and they can ever turn to him for relief. "He awoke, and rebuked the wind and the raging of the water: and they ceased, and there was a calm." Then when he had rebuked the disordered elements Jesus turned to rebuke his followers, "Where is your faith?" He did not find fault with them for awakening him, or for crying out for help; he rebuked only their lack of trust which should have relieved them from distress of mind while he was so near and so abundantly able to save. Such a miracle must have strengthened their faith, but its first effect was to fill them with wonder and with awe. Every new manifestation of his power came as a surprise to these disciples, and now for the first time they saw his control over the blind forces of nature; thus once again they felt themselves in the presence not only of a perfect Man— but of One who was divine.

11. A DEMONIAC HEALED   Ch. 8:26-39

26 And they arrived at the country of the Gerasenes, which is over against Galilee. 27 And when he was come forth upon the land, there met him a certain man out of the city, who had demons; and for a long time he had worn no clothes, and abode not in any house, but in the tombs. 28 And when he saw Jesus, he cried out, and fell down before him, and with a loud voice said, What have I to do with thee, Jesus, thou Son of the Most High God? I beseech thee, torment me not. 29 For he was commanding the unclean spirit to come out from the man. For oftentimes it had seized him: and he was kept under guard, and bound with chains and fetters; and breaking the bands asunder, he was driven of the demon into the deserts. 30 And Jesus asked him, What is thy name? And he said, Legion; for many demons were entered into him. 31 And they entreated him that he would not command them to depart into the abyss. 32 Now there was there a herd of many swine feeding on the mountain: and they entreated him that he would give them leave to enter into them. And he gave them leave. 33 And the demons came out from the man, and entered into the swine: and the herd rushed down the steep into the lake, and were drowned. 34 And when they that fed them saw what had come to pass, they fled, and told it in the city and in the country.

35 And they went out to see what had come to pass; and they came to Jesus, and found the man, from whom the demons were gone out, sitting, clothed and in his right mind, at the feet of Jesus: and they were afraid. 36 And they that saw it told them how he that was possessed with demons was made whole. 37 And all the people of the country of the Gerasenes round about asked him to depart from them; for they were holden with great fear: and he entered into a boat, and returned. 38 But the man from whom the demons were gone out prayed him that he might be with him: but he sent him away, saying, 39 Return to thy house, and declare how great things God hath done for thee. And he went his way, publishing throughout the whole city how great things Jesus had done for him.

The sufferings of a demoniac were so similar to those of mental disease that by many they are regarded as identical. Those who observe the distinction are faced with a further problem as to whether demon possession exists at the present day. What is most important of all is to note the exact parallel existing between the demoniacs described in the New Testament and those persons who at all times are tormented by envy and lust and anger and greed and other evil passions which dominate the human soul.

On the eastern shore of the Lake of Gennesaret, Jesus was encountered by a man whose suffering and nakedness are types of the anguish and shamelessness of sin. He could not be controlled; he was dwelling among the tombs, and these, too, are pictures of the helplessness and loneliness and hopelessness which evil passions produce. Most of all it is interesting to note that while the demon cried out in dread, the man drew near to Jesus, really hoping for help. The experience was like that of those who suffer from mental disease where a dual consciousness is manifested. Likewise most of us have experienced such a conflict of desires; we have longed for liberty at the very moment when we have felt the controlling power of some passion. Some tell us that we must cease to love the sin before Christ will give us help, but this picture sketched by Luke gives a more hopeful message. It intimates that as we cry out for relief, or even before we speak, Jesus sees the heart and recognizes the longing and assures release.

Jesus asked the sufferer for his name. He wished the real man to be awakened and to be conscious of the distinction between himself and the evil spirit by which he was possessed. The reply of the demoniac was full of pathos. He declared that his name was "Legion," the reason assigned being that "many demons were entered into him." His case was particularly desperate; but the evil spirits realized that they stood before One whose power was absolute. Certain that they were to be expelled from the sufferer, they asked permission to enter into a herd of swine which was feeding on the mountainside. A question has often been raised as to why Jesus granted this request. Probably one reason was that the sight which followed assured the sufferer of his cure; another may have been that the destruction of the herd would give to the men of the region an arresting message both of their own peril and of the power of Christ. However, when "they went out to see what had come to pass," they were full of terror and they requested Jesus to leave their land. They were evidently more concerned for the beasts which had been lost than for the soul that had been saved, when they saw their countryman sitting clothed and in his right mind as a disciple at the feet of Jesus. Their request was granted; our Lord never continues the gracious manifestations of his presence when these are not desired. However, he refused the request of the man whom he had healed. The latter wished to accompany Jesus as he entered the boat to cross to the other side of the lake; but Jesus bade him to remain as a witness for Christ in his own home and among his own people. It is ever the desire of the Master that the testimony of those who have known his power should be given first to those by whom they are best known.

12. THE DAUGHTER OF JAIRUS AND THE WOMAN WITH AN ISSUE OF BLOOD   Ch. 8:40-56

40 And as Jesus returned, the multitude welcomed him; for they were all waiting for him. 41 And behold, there came a man named Jaïrus, and he was a ruler of the synagogue: and he fell down at Jesus' feet, and besought him to come into his house; 42 for he had an only daughter, about twelve years of age, and she was dying. But as he went the multitudes thronged him.

43 And a woman having an issue of blood twelve years, who had spent all her living upon physicians, and could not be healed of any, 44 came behind him, and touched the border of his garment: and immediately the issue of her blood stanched. 45 And Jesus said, Who is it that touched me? And when all denied, Peter said, and they that were with him, Master, the multitudes press thee and crush thee. 46 But Jesus said, Some one did touch me; for I perceived that power had gone forth from me. 47 And when the woman saw that she was not hid, she came trembling, and falling down before him declared in the presence of all the people for what cause she touched him, and how she was healed immediately. 48 And he said unto her, Daughter, thy faith hath made thee whole; go in peace.

49 While he yet spake, there cometh one from the ruler of the synagogue's house, saying, Thy daughter is dead; trouble not the Teacher. 50 But Jesus hearing it, answered him, Fear not: only believe, and she shall be made whole. 51 And when he came to the house, he suffered not any man to enter in with him, save Peter, and John, and James, and the father of the maiden and her mother. 52 And all were weeping, and bewailing her: but he said, Weep not; for she is not dead, but sleepeth. 53 And they laughed him to scorn, knowing that she was dead. 54 But he, taking her by the hand, called, saying, Maiden, arise. 55 And her spirit returned, and she rose up immediately: and he commanded that something be given her to eat. 56 And her parents were amazed: but he charged them to tell no man what had been done.

As Jesus returned to Capernaum after curing the demoniac across the lake, he was welcomed by a great multitude in the midst of which were two sufferers for whom the Savior showed his sympathy as he perfected their faith and relieved their distress. They were strangely contrasted in circumstances, alike only in their desperate need. One was Jairus, a man of prominence in his community, "a ruler of the synagogue," a person of comparative wealth and power and social position, whose home for twelve years had been brightened by the presence of a little daughter, an only child, who was now lying at the point of death.

The other was a woman, poor, weak, ceremonially unclean, friendless, who for twelve years had been suffering from an incurable disease and who knew that by no human power could her life be prolonged.

As Jesus was starting for the home of Jairus, this woman came up behind him, touched the border of his garment, and was instantly healed. Her faith was imperfect, but it was real. She had supposed the power of Christ to be merely magical and mechanical. Jesus showed that it is inseparable from divine knowledge and love. He had felt the touch of her trembling finger. He had distinguished it from the press of the jostling throng; and now for her own sake he required the woman "in the presence of all the people" to acknowledge her cure. Jesus would have us know that faith is a dependence upon his gracious person and purpose, and also that only after public confession of our relation to him can we receive the assurance that we are saved and can hear his blessed word, "Thy faith hath made thee whole; go in peace."

The faith of Jairus was likewise imperfect. It was more intelligent than the faith of the woman, but it fell short of that revealed by the centurion in the same city who felt it unnecessary for Jesus to come to his house but only to speak a word and a cure would be effected. Nevertheless this faith was genuine and so Jesus strengthened it and rewarded it. The very fact that Jesus started toward his home was reassuring to the father, but his faith was tested by the delay caused in curing the woman. However, it was also strengthened by this proof of divine wisdom and power. Most terribly was his faith tested by the message which then reached him, "Thy daughter is dead; trouble not the Teacher." Yet again, it was confirmed by the word of Jesus, "Fear not: only believe, and she shall be made whole." As he entered the house, Jesus spoke another word which rebuked the faithless mourners and cheered the agonized parents, "Weep not; for she is not dead, but sleepeth." He meant that in his presence and in virtue of his power death loses its reality and is robbed of its victory. Nor has the word lost its meaning and its comfort for the followers of Christ during all the subsequent years.

Jesus showed clearly what he meant as he took into the death chamber his three closest friends and the two trembling parents, as he stood before the sleeping child and "taking her by the hand, called, saying, Maiden, arise. And her spirit returned, and she rose up immediately: and he commanded that something be given her to eat." The record indicates the supreme thoughtfulness and tenderness of the Master. He took with him only three disciples, for he would not have the awakened child terrified by the sight of more strangers. When the miracle had been performed he requested that the little girl should be given food; this was for her own comfort but also to break for the parents the spell of awe and terror which had been cast upon them by the presence of death, and also as a proof not only that life had returned but also that complete recovery from disease had been secured. One other command is recorded: "He charged them to tell no man what had been done." The three disciples would be competent witnesses of the miracle, but a widespread report by the parents and their friends might arouse such an outburst of excitement as to interrupt his work and precipitate a crisis before the earthly ministry of our Lord was complete.

D. THE FOURTH PERIOD Ch. 9:1-50

1. THE MISSION OF THE TWELVE   Ch. 9:1-9

1 And he called the twelve together, and gave them power and authority over all demons, and to cure diseases. 2 And he sent them forth to preach the kingdom of God, and to heal the sick. 3 And he said unto them, Take nothing for your journey, neither staff, nor wallet, nor bread, nor money; neither have two coats. 4 And into whatsoever house ye enter, there abide, and thence depart. 5 And as many as receive you not, when ye depart from that city, shake off the dust from your feet for a testimony against them. 6 And they departed, and went throughout the villages, preaching the gospel, and healing everywhere.

7 Now Herod the tetrarch heard of all that was done: and he was much perplexed, because that it was said by some, that John was risen from the dead; 8 and by some, that Elijah had appeared; and by others, that one of the old prophets was risen again. 9 And Herod said, John I beheaded: but who is this, about whom I hear such things? And he sought to see him.

As Jesus sent forth his twelve disciples on their first mission, he was entering the closing period of his ministry in Galilee. Until now the apostles had been his companions; henceforth they were to be more strictly messengers and representatives. Jesus foresaw his approaching rejection and death, but before leaving for Jerusalem and the cross, he wished to offer himself once more to the people of Galilee among whom he had long been laboring; and for this purpose he sent out the Twelve. Their circumstances and the directions given them by Jesus were peculiar to the time and occasion. However, these commands are not without application to the messengers of the Master in all ages of the world. They were given "power and authority over all demons, and to cure diseases." Such miraculous gifts were limited to their own day and were designed as credentials of their mission. It is true, however, that those who represent Christ must ever be concerned for the mental and physical conditions of mankind, even though the great purpose is to bring a message of spiritual import. The latter was, of course, the great purpose of the apostles. They went forth "to preach the kingdom of God," as well as "to heal the sick."

When Christ commanded the disciples to take nothing for their journey, he did not intend to impose needless hardships or even to suggest peculiar denial. Rather, he intimated the principle that his heralds must not be encumbered with worldly cares and burdens and that those who proclaim his gospel may expect to be supported by those to whom the message is preached.

In advising the disciples to remain in the first home where they were properly received, he indicated the wisdom of having a fixed center for their work, of being content with their entertainment and surroundings, and of avoiding social complications which might hinder their work. They were instructed, in case they were not received and welcomed as the messengers of Christ, to show their just displeasure as they departed from the place, by shaking off the dust from their feet, an Oriental custom which in this case indicated the disavowal of any possible relationship with the enemies of their Lord.

"And they departed, and went throughout the villages, preaching the gospel, and healing everywhere." These were the supreme representatives of the great band of heroes who have continued the work and have made known their message in all times and lands. They were prepared by the divine instruction of their Master. It has been said that there is something greater than preaching; it is to prepare preachers. Surely none were ever so trained and none ever accomplished their work so well; but it is possible for every follower of Christ to have some part in making known the gospel of his grace.

The great success of the disciples and the tremendous excitement produced by their mission is indicated by the fact that the reports of their work reached Herod the king and made him tremble on his throne.   It was not that he feared what Jesus might do; it was rather because there was something in the rumor which awakened his sleeping conscience and filled him with a secret alarm and dread. "It was said by some, that John was risen from the dead." Herod had beheaded John, but the memory of his foul deed could not be buried; now he was wondering what might be the real nature of the miracles which were being reported and of the Man in whose name they were wrought.   He "sought to see" Jesus.   That was mere curiosity.   He probably wished to see some miracles performed.   Before long an opportunity was to be given him to stand face-to-face with the divine Man, but it was to be on an unexpected occasion when the latter would stand before him as a prisoner, when Herod might offer him protection or release; but when the occasion came he was disappointed by the silence of the Lord and allowed him to go away to crucifixion and death.   One who beheaded John need not have hoped to understand Jesus.   One who violates his own conscience today and refuses solemn warnings to repent need not expect that Christ will be revealed to him in his beauty and grace and saving power.

2. THE FIVE THOUSAND FED   Ch. 9:10-17

10 And the apostles, when they were returned, declared unto him what things they had done.   And he took them, and withdrew apart to a city called Bethsaida.   11 But the multitudes perceiving it followed him: and he welcomed them, and spake to them of the kingdom of God, and them that had need of healing he cured.   12 And the day began to wear away; and the twelve came, and said unto him, Send the multitude away, that they may go into the villages and country round about, and lodge, and get provisions:

for we are here in a desert place. 13 But he said unto them, Give ye them to eat. And they said, We have no more than five loaves and two fishes; except we should go and buy food for all this people. 14 For they were about five thousand men. And he said unto his disciples, Make them sit down in companies, about fifty each. 15 And they did so, and made them all sit down. 16 And he took the five loaves and the two fishes, and looking up to heaven, he blessed them, and brake; and gave to the disciples to set before the multitude. 17 And they ate, and were all filled: and there was taken up that which remained over to them of broken pieces, twelve baskets.

The feeding of the five thousand is the only miracle recorded by all four Evangelists—in fact, the only incident of the Galilean ministry of our Lord common to them all. Here this ministry attains its climax. This was the hour of the greatest popularity of Jesus; the multitudes would have offered him a crown, but he saw before him the shadow of the cross.

The Twelve had returned weary with labor but elated by success. Jesus desired for them a season of retirement, of rest, and instruction. They withdrew to a secluded place beyond Bethsaida on the east shore of the lake; but there they were discovered by the eager multitudes. Jesus showed his infinite sympathy by cordially welcoming the crowds which had intruded upon his privacy and interrupted his plans; he gladdened their hearts with the gospel message and healed their diseases. And as the day declined he pitied their hunger and met their needs by miraculously multiplying five loaves and two fishes which the disciples had secured.

For the disciples of today there are serious messages in this familiar story; perhaps none is more obvious than that of the measureless compassion of Christ. With something of his sympathy we should look upon the multitudes perishing for lack of physical and spiritual food. Their call for help should not be regarded as an interruption but

as a guide in shaping our personal plans. While of ourselves we are unable to give relief, yet if our all is offered
to the Master, it will be multiplied marvelously by his divine power. The miracle seems to have been wrought
as Jesus looked up in prayer. We must surely look to him
and seek his blessing in our service. We must allow no
broken fragments to be lost; some families could live on
what other families waste; then, too, the followers of
Christ must learn a true economy of time and talents and
wealth if the Bread of life is to be brought to a famishing
world.

3. JESUS PREDICTING HIS DEATH   Ch. 9:18-27

*18 And it came to pass, as he was praying apart, the dis-
ciples were with him: and he asked them, saying, Who do
the multitudes say that I am? 19 And they answering said,
John the Baptist; but others say, Elijah; and others, that
one of the old prophets is risen again. 20 And he said
unto them, But who say ye that I am? And Peter answering said, The Christ of God. 21 But he charged them,
and commanded them to tell this to no man; 22 saying,
The Son of man must suffer many things, and be rejected
of the elders and chief priests and scribes, and be killed,
and the third day be raised up. 23 And he said unto all,
If any man would come after me, let him deny himself, and
take up his cross daily, and follow me. 24 For whosoever
would save his life shall lose it; but whosoever shall lose
his life for my sake, the same shall save it. 25 For what
is a man profited, if he gain the whole world, and lose or
forfeit his own self? 26 For whosoever shall be ashamed
of me and of my words, of him shall the Son of man be
ashamed, when he cometh in his own glory, and the glory
of the Father, and of the holy angels. 27 But I tell you of
a truth, There are some of them that stand here, who shall
in no wise taste of death, till they see the kingdom of God.*

The first clear prediction of his death was made by
Jesus directly after he had heard the famous confession of

Peter. The latter was occasioned by a question Jesus himself had asked: "Who do the multitudes say that I am?" The answer is exactly that given by multitudes in modern days: "And they answering said, John the Baptist; but others say, Elijah; and others, that one of the old prophets is risen again"; that is to say, a reformer, a great preacher, a messenger of God. Such an estimate of himself never satisfied our Lord, and so he asked pointedly: "But who say ye that I am? And Peter answering said, The Christ of God." This is the great affirmation concerning Christ which the world today needs to hear; but at that time Jesus earnestly commanded his disciples to "tell this to no man." The message would then have been misunderstood and the disciples themselves needed first to learn the truth concerning the death and resurrection of Jesus. No man today is qualified to testify for Christ who does not know the meaning of his atoning death and "the power of his resurrection."

Then Jesus told his disciples of the absolute necessity of his approaching sufferings and assured them that on the third day he would be raised up. This prediction of death must have astonished the disciples; quite as surprising was the further statement that every follower of Christ must likewise take up his cross daily, and the cross was not merely a symbol of suffering and shame; it was the instrument of death. Every Christian, therefore, must die daily to self and yield himself wholly to the service of Christ. Such self-denial and sacrifice and obedience will result in the only experience worthy of the name "life"; to refuse is to forfeit "life"; and the loss will be eternal, for those who are ashamed to follow the Master now will be rejected by him when he returns "in his own glory, and the glory of the Father, and of the holy angels." Of this future glory of the coming Christ, three of the disciples were to catch a foregleam only eight days later on the Mount of Transfiguration, and Jesus therefore adds, "There are some of them that stand here, who shall in no wise taste of death, till they see the kingdom of God."

4. THE TRANSFIGURATION   Ch. 9:28-36

28 And it came to pass about eight days after these say-ings, that he took with him Peter and John and James, and went up into the mountain to pray. 29 And as he was praying, the fashion of his countenance was altered, and his raiment became white and dazzling. 30 And behold, there talked with him two men, who were Moses and Elijah; 31 who appeared in glory, and spake of his de-cease which he was about to accomplish at Jerusalem. 32 Now Peter and they that were with him were heavy with sleep: but when they were fully awake, they saw his glory, and the two men that stood with him. 33 And it came to pass, as they were parting from him, Peter said unto Jesus, Master, it is good for us to be here: and let us make three tabernacles; one for thee, and one for Moses, and one for Elijah: not knowing what he said. 34 And while he said these things, there came a cloud, and overshadowed them: and they feared as they entered into the cloud. 35 And a voice came out of the cloud, saying, This is my Son, my chosen: hear ye him. 36 And when the voice came, Jesus was found alone. And they held their peace, and told no man in those days any of the things which they had seen.

The transfiguration of Christ was closely associated with the predictions both of his death and of his return in glory. It prepared him and also his disciples for the former and it was a symbol and a foretaste of the latter. Just what the physical experience may have been, it is difficult to con-jecture. It was not like that of Moses on Mt. Sinai when his face glowed with reflected light. In the case of Jesus the glory was from within. A divine splendor shone forth irradiating the body and even the garments of our Lord.

Luke tells us that this occurred as Jesus was praying; and it is more than a mere figure of speech to say that when in prayer his followers find, in some measure, what it is to be transfigured into his likeness from one degree of glory to another by the power of his indwelling Spirit.

Jesus had been accompanied on the mountaintop by only Peter, James, and John; but suddenly "there talked with him two men, who were Moses and Elijah; who appeared in glory, and spake of his decease which he was about to accomplish at Jerusalem." This, then, was the high purpose of the event; it was to interpret to the mind of Christ more perfectly the meaning of his death, and to encourage him to endure its anguish by this glimpse of the glory that would follow. It is easy to understand why Moses and Elijah should be selected for so august a conference. One had been regarded as the symbol of law and the other of prophecy, and both law and prophecy pointed forward to Calvary; and again both Moses and Elijah had received a special revelation of the grace of God, and he was to manifest his grace supremely in the death of his Son.

It is not strange that Peter longed to linger in such heavenly companionship, and in bewilderment absurdly proposed the erection on the mountain of three booths for the comfort of Jesus, Moses, and Elijah. "While he said these things, there came a cloud, and overshadowed them. . . . And a voice came out of the cloud, saying, This is my Son, my chosen: hear ye him." There was no need of detaining Moses and Elijah; if the Master remained with his disciples, that was enough. Henceforth all that the Law and the Prophets had foreshadowed would be completely revealed and embodied in Jesus Christ. Part of that revelation was made in his death; the full revelation will come when he returns in that glory of which the Mount of Transfiguration gave a foregleam.

5. THE DEMONIAC BOY   Ch. 9:37-45

37 And it came to pass, on the next day, when they were come down from the mountain, a great multitude met him. 38 And behold, a man from the multitude cried, saying, Teacher, I beseech thee to look upon my son; for he is mine only child: 39 and behold, a spirit taketh him, and he suddenly crieth out; and it teareth him that he foameth, and it hardly departeth from him, bruising him sorely.

40 And I besought thy disciples to cast it out; and they could not. 41 And Jesus answered and said, O faithless and perverse generation, how long shall I be with you, and bear with you? bring hither thy son. 42 And as he was yet a coming, the demon dashed him down, and tare him grievously. But Jesus rebuked the unclean spirit, and healed the boy, and gave him back to his father. 43 And they were all astonished at the majesty of God.

But while all were marvelling at all the things which he did, he said unto his disciples, 44 Let these words sink into your ears: for the Son of man shall be delivered up into the hands of men. 45 But they understood not this saying, and it was concealed from them, that they should not perceive it; and they were afraid to ask him about this saying.

It is not strange that artists love to paint the contrast between the picture of Jesus on the mountain encompassed by glory and of the demoniac boy surrounded by the multitudes on the plain; yet it requires no canvas or artificial color to heighten the contrast presented by the historian in his simple story. Jesus long before had learned what it was to exchange the glories of heaven for the shadows and sufferings of earth, and the compassion which drew him from the skies was never withheld, even at times when he naturally might have been absorbed in thoughts concerning his coming suffering and redeeming work. He was instantly moved with tender pity as he heard the agonizing words of the father and saw the distress of the son. However, he was even more moved by the unbelief and sin and anguish and godlessness of the world which he had come to save, and of which this scene was but a symbol and a picture. "O faithless and perverse generation," he cried, "how long shall I be with you, and bear with you?" Can it not be said reverently that the contrasted experiences of the mountain and the plain made Jesus for the moment homesick for heaven? Yet Jesus neither hesitated nor delayed in the path of duty or in the presence of human need. He "rebuked the unclean spirit, and healed the boy, and gave him back to his father."

While all were wondering and astonished at his divine power and marvelous works, he turned to his disciples to impress upon them the dark secret which was resting on his soul. He told them that the time was near when he was to be given up to suffer and to die; "but they understood not this saying." Here was a Man whose sympathy was tender toward all; but who sympathized with him? How often some one of his followers has borne a burden of hidden sorrow, even in the company of friends and when surrounded by admiring throngs!

6. JESUS REBUKING PRIDE AND BIGOTRY   Ch. 9:46-50

46 And there arose a reasoning among them, which of them was the greatest. 47 But when Jesus saw the reasoning of their heart, he took a little child, and set him by his side, 48 and said unto them, Whosoever shall receive this little child in my name receiveth me: and whosoever shall receive me receiveth him that sent me: for he that is least among you all, the same is great.

49 And John answered and said, Master, we saw one casting out demons in thy name; and we forbade him, because he followeth not with us. 50 But Jesus said unto him, Forbid him not: for he that is not against you is for you.

This was no new dispute in which the followers of Jesus were engaged. The question was as to which of them should be the greatest in his Kingdom. There was something admirable in the discussion, for it revealed their faith. To them the Master was yet to be King of Kings and Lord of Lords, and they desired to have places nearest to his throne. Our conception of his Kingdom may be more correct, but if its glories were as real to us as they were to them, if we had faith enough to see this Kingdom in its real importance, we, too, might at times question what our relative places in this Kingdom are or will be.

However, Jesus rebuked them, for there is no place for pride among the followers of Christ. Our nearness to him is not won by selfish effort or granted by arbitrary decree: it is conditioned upon the humble service we may render in his name. "He took a little child, and set him by his side"; not because a child is a picture of humility—most children are self-conscious and absurdly proud—but because the care of a child is a symbol of humble service, and it was this spirit which Jesus praised. To care for a child, or for men and women who like children are in need of our help and sympathy and support, if done for the sake of Christ and in the name of Christ, is a service rendered to the Master himself and not only to him but also to his Father. The willingness to undertake such humble service is the measure of true greatness.

The mention of service in the name of the Master reminded John of a recent incident which he felt to be quite to his credit; so "John answered and said, Master, we saw one casting out demons in thy name; and we forbade him, because he followeth not with us." There was something admirable in the spirit and action of John. He was so devoted to Christ that he wished everyone professing his name to join the company of disciples, to live and to labor and to suffer with them. There is always something admirable in loyalty to a denomination or a sect. If one has found what he believes to be the highest form of Christian life and service, if one feels that he is treading the surest and shortest road to heaven, it is certainly commendable in him to wish others to share his peculiar blessedness.

Jesus, however, rebuked him, and said, "Forbid him not: for he that is not against you is for you." After all, there is no place for bigotry among the followers of Christ. We may love and admire our sect or society, but we are never to stop the work of a fellow Christian however much he may differ from us. There are only two questions to ask: First, Is he casting out demons? That is to say, is he really accomplishing good? Second, Is he doing the work in the name of a divine, crucified, risen Christ? If so, "Forbid him not." We must not expect all Christians to repeat the same creed or to enjoy the same ritual or to accept the same polity or to employ the same methods of work. We should remember the word of the Master, "He that is not against you is for you."

V

THE JOURNEYS
TOWARD JERUSALEM

Chs. 9:51 to 19:28

A. THE FIRST STAGES Ch. 9:51 to 13:21

1. THE INHOSPITABLE SAMARITANS Ch. 9:51-56

51 And it came to pass, when the days were well-nigh come that he should be received up, he stedfastly set his face to go to Jerusalem, 52 and sent messengers before his face: and they went, and entered into a village of the Samaritans, to make ready for him. 53 And they did not receive him, because his face was as though he were going to Jerusalem. 54 And when his disciples James and John saw this, they said, Lord, wilt thou that we bid fire to come down from heaven, and consume them? 55 But he turned, and rebuked them. 56 And they went to another village.

The record of the last journeys of our Lord toward Jerusalem forms a unique feature in the Gospel of Luke. In the other Gospels some of these incidents are included, but they occupy only one or two chapters; here, however, they fill ten chapters with events most of which are no where else related.

The direction of the journeying was first eastward through the borders of Galilee and Samaria, then across the Jordan and then southward through the region of Perea. This region is not so designated in the Bible but is described by the phrase, "beyond the Jordan," and as most of these incidents occurred there, this period of the life of Jesus is commonly called his "Perean ministry." Luke here emphasizes the divine prevision and at the same time the human courage of our Lord. He indicates that

Jesus saw plainly his coming death and also his glorious ascension, but that he unfalteringly moved forward to the intervening agonies of the cross.

The first incident of these journeys was in a village of the Samaritans. Certain messengers had gone before to prepare entertainment for the large company which followed Jesus, but the Samaritans would not receive him; then his disciples, James and John, suggested that they should "bid fire to come down from heaven, and consume them." There was something admirable in the indignation of these disciples. The Samaritans were moved by a narrow and provincial prejudice and they were offering to Jesus a gratuitous insult. It sometimes seems that the genius for indignation has disappeared, and it is refreshing to see men who feel deeply any disrespect to Christ, any injury to his cause.

But Jesus rebuked his disciples, "and they went to another village." There may be place for righteous indignation, but there is no place among the followers of Christ for anger, for intolerance, or for revenge. This is not a time of judgment, but of grace. It is not for us to attempt to administer vengeance, but to preach the gospel of love.

2. JESUS REBUKING RASHNESS, INSINCERITY, AND INDECISION   Ch. 9:57-62

57 And as they went on the way, a certain man said unto him, I will follow thee whithersoever thou goest. 58 And Jesus said unto him, The foxes have holes, and the birds of the heaven have nests; but the Son of man hath not where to lay his head. 59 And he said unto another, Follow me. But he said, Lord, suffer me first to go and bury my father. 60 But he said unto him, Leave the dead to bury their own dead; but go thou and publish abroad the kingdom of God. 61 And another also said, I will follow thee, Lord; but first suffer me to bid farewell to them that are at my house. 62 But Jesus said unto him, No man, having put his hand to the plow, and looking back, is fit for the kingdom of God.

These three incidents show how carefully Jesus was sifting those who wished to become his followers and how deeply he appreciated the fact that he was passing through this region for the last time. The first of the three men with whom Jesus spoke was being swept along by his emotions, by the sight of the crowd which was following the Master, and by the thought that it would be a great privilege to be in such company. He had not for a moment realized that it might involve sacrifice and pain to become a disciple of the Master. It was for this reason that Jesus turned to him with a statement which implies a rebuke and suggests that the Master realized the thoughtlessness and rashness which were prompting this professed follower. "The foxes have holes, and the birds of the heaven have nests; but the Son of man hath not where to lay his head." Of course Jesus is eager to have men vow their allegiance to him and openly acknowledge their discipleship; but among his followers there is no place for rashness. He would have us count the cost.

In the case of the next man, when he was bidden to follow Christ, he offered an excuse, "Lord, suffer me first to go and bury my father." This was a natural request and it seemed that a tender duty made it necessary for him to decline the invitation of the Master. There seems something rather severe in the reply, "Leave the dead to bury their own dead; but go thou and publish abroad the kingdom of God." It is evident that Jesus had looked into the heart of this man and saw that he was making a selfish excuse out of a sacred duty. If his reply was sincere, it nonetheless merited a reproof, for a more sacred duty than caring for the dead was laid upon him by the invitation of the living Christ. No tie, however tender, can be regarded as a sufficient excuse for refusing to become a follower of Christ. Jesus was passing that way for the last time. Prompt obedience was absolutely necessary. Those who were spiritually "dead" and who had not heard the summons of the Master could provide the needed burial; but it was possible for the one who had been called by Christ to perform a more sacred task: he could begin to proclaim the gospel of salvation and of life.

In the case of the third possible disciple, there was no carelessness; he had counted the cost; it was not his intention to make any excuse; he was sincere and definite in his intention, but he wished to delay. He was not quite certain that it was best just then to leave his family and his friends. At least he wished to delay long enough to return to his home and to bid them farewell. But Jesus rebuked him, "No man, having put his hand to the plow, and looking back, is fit for the kingdom of God." Such hesitation indicates that one has not appreciated the glory and privilege involved in the call of Christ or that he still weighs against it the sacrifices it involves. He is self-condemned. There is no place for indecision among those who are to be heirs of the Kingdom of God.

3. THE MISSION OF THE SEVENTY   Ch. 10:1-24

1 Now after these things the Lord appointed seventy others, and sent them two and two before his face into every city and place, whither he himself was about to come. 2 And he said unto them, The harvest indeed is plenteous, but the laborers are few: pray ye therefore the Lord of the harvest, that he send forth laborers into his harvest. 3 Go your ways; behold, I send you forth as lambs in the midst of wolves. 4 Carry no purse, no wallet, no shoes; and salute no man on the way. 5 And into whatsoever house ye shall enter, first say, Peace be to this house. 6 And if a son of peace be there, your peace shall rest upon him: but if not, it shall turn to you again. 7 And in that same house remain, eating and drinking such things as they give: for the laborer is worthy of his hire. Go not from house to house. 8 And into whatsoever city ye enter, and they receive you, eat such things as are set before you: 9 and heal the sick that are therein, and say unto them, The kingdom of God is come nigh unto you. 10 But into whatsoever city ye shall enter, and they receive you not, go

*out into the streets thereof and say, 11 Even the dust from
your city, that cleaveth to our feet, we wipe off against
you: nevertheless know this, that the kingdom of God is
come nigh. 12 I say unto you, It shall be more tolerable
in that day for Sodom, than for that city. 13 Woe unto
thee, Chorazin! woe unto thee, Bethsaida! for if the mighty
works had been done in Tyre and Sidon, which were done
in you, they would have repented long ago, sitting in sack-
cloth and ashes. 14 But it shall be more tolerable for Tyre
and Sidon in the judgment, than for you. 15 And thou,
Capernaum, shalt thou be exalted unto heaven? thou shalt
be brought down unto Hades. 16 He that heareth you
heareth me; and he that rejecteth you rejecteth me; and he
that rejecteth me rejecteth him that sent me.*

*17 And the seventy returned with joy, saying, Lord, even
the demons are subject unto us in thy name. 18 And he
said unto them, I beheld Satan fallen as lightning from
heaven. 19 Behold, I have given you authority to tread
upon serpents and scorpions, and over all the power of the
enemy: and nothing shall in any wise hurt you. 20 Nevertheless in this rejoice not, that the spirits are subject unto
you; but rejoice that your names are written in heaven.*

*21 In that same hour he rejoiced in the Holy Spirit, and
said, I thank thee, O Father, Lord of heaven and earth,
that thou didst hide these things from the wise and understanding, and didst reveal them unto babes: yea, Father; for
so it was well-pleasing in thy sight. 22 All things have
been delivered unto me of my Father: and no one knoweth
who the Son is, save the Father; and who the Father is,
save the Son, and he to whomsoever the Son willeth to
reveal him. 23 And turning to the disciples, he said pri-
vately, Blessed are the eyes which see the things that ye see:
24 for I say unto you, that many prophets and kings desired to see the things which ye see, and saw them not;
and to hear the things which ye hear, and heard them not.*

The sending out of the seventy messengers who were to
prepare the way for the ministry of Jesus is recorded by
Luke alone. This is in harmony with the fact that only
in this Gospel do we read of the extended journeys toward

Jerusalem made by our Lord on the occasion of which the Seventy were sent forth. The work was for only a limited time and their office was temporary; but in his instructions to them Jesus suggested many principles of life which apply to his followers in all the ages. He first intimated the reason for their being chosen. It was because the harvest field in which they were to work was so great and the laborers so few. He intimated that before the world can receive the message which the Seventy were sent to deliver, they and their successors must earnestly pray the Lord of the harvest to send forth more laborers into the field. This is a prayer which all who serve the Master may offer earnestly and at all times. The work seems to be only begun. Our sympathy with the Master will make us yearn to see the work accomplished with more speed, which can only be possible when larger numbers of laborers are secured. V. 2.

Jesus told his messengers that as they went forth they must expect to meet with dangers. "I send you forth as lambs in the midst of wolves." They were, however, to encumber themselves with nothing superfluous and they were to waste no time in idle ceremonies; they must journey as men who are impelled by one supreme motive. Vs. 3-4.

As they entered a home, they were to offer the peace which the gospel can give, but if rejected, they were to believe that their very message would return to them with added force. Thus our Lord signified that no word spoken for his sake is really wasted. Vs. 5-6.

They were to continue in the home which received them, content with what was given, offering relief to those in distress and using every opportunity to proclaim the message of grace. Vs. 7-9.

Where their message was refused, and they were not received by city or town, they were to turn away, shaking off the dust of their feet, thus intimating by an Oriental symbol that they had no connection with the enemies of Christ.

At no time is the reception of the gospel message universal. There are always some who refuse to accept its gracious offer. Vs. 10-12.

The thought of those who would surely reject his messengers reminded Jesus of the cities which had already rejected him, and he paused for a moment to speak solemnly of their guilty unbelief. He referred to Chorazin and Bethsaida, declaring that in the Day of Judgment it would be more tolerable for Tyre and Sidon than for these cities, for even the heathen world would have repented in the face of such evidence of his divine mission as Jesus had given to the cities of Israel. He referred particularly to Capernaum, to its peculiar privileges and to its consequently greater condemnation. Jesus was stating the abiding principle that unusual opportunities involve unusual responsibilities. He emphasized the seriousness of rejecting his messengers by stating that in despising them, men are really despising himself and that those who reject Jesus are rejecting his Father who sent him. Vs. 13-16.

In order to complete the story of the Seventy, Luke proceeds at once to describe their return. They came back elated, with the report that even the demons were subject to them. Our Lord replied by a statement that in the overthrow of these messengers of Satan he saw the ultimate defeat of the Prince of darkness and of all the forces of evil, and he declared that he was giving to his messengers power over all that might oppose or might threaten to destroy them. Yet, he added, their chief joy should not be in their ability to perform these works of wonder, but rather, in their having a part in his triumphant cause and in receiving his salvation. Vs. 17-20.

At this time our Lord himself shared in the exultation of his followers and returned thanks to the Father for what he was accomplishing through the humble messengers whom Jesus had chosen, so that the results were a manifestation of divine power. He added a striking claim which indicates that the ideal Man is likewise the true Son of God who alone can reveal the Father to men. Then lastly, as he turned to his disciples, he congratulated them upon their great privilege, assuring them that "many prophets and kings" desired to see the things which they were seeing as his servants and as the instruments of his power. He intimated something of the exalted joy which through all the coming years his followers would feel as they realized their privilege of serving such a Master, and of revealing him to men. Vs. 21-24.

4. THE GOOD SAMARITAN   Ch. 10:25-37

25 And behold, a certain lawyer stood up and made trial of him, saying, Teacher, what shall I do to inherit eternal life? 26 And he said unto him, What is written in the law? how readest thou? 27 And he answering said, Thou shalt love the Lord thy God with all thy heart, and with all thy soul, and with all thy strength, and with all thy mind; and thy neighbor as thyself. 28 And he said unto him, Thou hast answered right: this do, and thou shalt live. 29 But he, desiring to justify himself, said unto Jesus, And who is my neighbor? 30 Jesus made answer and said, A certain man was going down from Jerusalem to Jericho; and he fell among robbers, who both stripped him and beat him, and departed, leaving him half dead. 31 And by chance a certain priest was going down that way: and when he saw him, he passed by on the other side. 32 And in like manner a Levite also, when he came to the place, and saw him, passed by on the other side. 33 But a certain Samaritan, as he journeyed, came where he was: and when he saw him, he was moved with compassion, 34 and came to him, and bound up his wounds, pouring on them oil and wine; and he set him on his own beast, and brought him to an inn, and took care of him. 35 And on the morrow he took out two shillings, and gave them to the host, and said, Take care of him; and whatsoever thou spendest more, I, when I come back again, will repay thee. 36 Which of these three, thinkest thou, proved neighbor unto him that fell among the robbers? 37 And he said, He that showed mercy on him. And Jesus said unto him, Go, and do thou likewise.

The parable of the good Samaritan was spoken to a certain lawyer who, trusting to his knowledge of the Old Testament, and of its subtle interpretations by the rabbis, came to Jesus hoping to dispute with him and to defeat him in debate. He asked Jesus this question: "Teacher, what shall I do to inherit eternal life?" He evidently thought that Jesus would prescribe some new rites or ceremonies or would in some other way disparage the law. He was startled, then, to have Jesus reply, "What is written in the law?" This answer robbed the enemy of his own weapon. He, however, made a skillful reply, and declared that the law is summarized in the requirement to love God and man. Jesus again replied, "Thou hast answered right: this do, and thou shalt live." There was no shadow of evasion or deception in the statement of Jesus. Perfect love to God and to man is surely the way of life; but who can show such perfect love? Jesus came not to destroy this requirement of the law but to reveal its complete fulfillment, to secure pardon for those who were guilty of its infraction, and to give power to those who felt their need.

The reply of Jesus not only defeated the lawyer; it smote his conscience. He realized that he himself had never fulfilled the requirement of the law he knew so well. He therefore attempted to justify himself by limiting the sphere to which the law of love applies. This is always the experience of those who seek to save themselves while rejecting the salvation of Christ. No one in his own power can fulfill the demands of this perfect law; either we must secure aid outside ourselves and trust in a loving Savior, or else we must in some way lessen the demands which the law makes. The lawyer suggested that it is impossible to love everyone, even though it be required to love our neighbors, and to justify himself he asked the question, "And who is my neighbor?" Jesus replied by the story of the man, evidently a Jew, who went down the steep road from Jerusalem to Jericho and, as he passed through the narrow gorge, was beset by robbers who stripped him of his garments and his possessions and left him half dead.

The first to approach this pitiful sufferer was a priest, a man whose profession and task in life would induce him to perform a deed of mercy, but in fear of thieves or in blind oblivion to the need of the wounded man, he passed by on the other side. Next came a Levite, one whose office was that of a helper to the priests, a man who supposedly would be less burdened by official duties and would have more time to extend relief; but he likewise passed by. At last came a Samaritan, a man of an alien race and of a despised religion, but he showed compassion; he bound up the wounds of the sufferer and placed him on his beast and brought him to an inn and paid for his entertainment. He showed the spirit of love. Thus Jesus indicated that our neighbor is not only one who "lives near" but one who needs our help, as well as one who helps our need. He demonstrated the truth that the law of love is not limited by rank or station or race or creed. Nor is it limited to man. One must likewise love God with all the heart, and thus he will surely love and serve the Son in whom the love of God is made perfect.

5. MARTHA AND MARY   Ch. 10:38-42

38 Now as they went on their way, he entered into a certain village: and a certain woman named Martha received him into her house. 39 And she had a sister called Mary, who also sat at the Lord's feet, and heard his word. 40 But Martha was cumbered about much serving; and she came up to him, and said, Lord, dost thou not care that my sister did leave me to serve alone? bid her therefore that she help me. 41 But the Lord answered and said unto her, Martha, Martha, thou art anxious and troubled about many things: 42 but one thing is needful: for Mary hath chosen the good part, which shall not be taken away from her.

The unfailing human interest of Luke is nowhere more perfectly expressed than by this exquisite scene in the home at Bethany. It is to be regretted that it has become

the occasion for endless debate as to the relative merits of
Martha and Mary.   Some imagine that the former was
unloving but energetic and efficient, and that the latter was
affectionate, but sentimental and indolent.   In reality both
sisters had admirable qualities; both loved the Master and
longed to please him; but on this occasion Martha, in her
very eagerness to serve, had overburdened herself in the
preparation of an elaborate meal, while Mary, with truer
intuition of what Jesus wished, "sat at the Lord's feet,
and heard his word."   She knew that he desired, not for
his own sake, but for theirs, to reveal himself and to deliver
his heavenly message, and thus according to the fine art
of hospitality, she considered first the wish of her guest
and was thus doing more to entertain the Master than was
her sister.

"Martha was cumbered about much serving"; she was
distracted by the many things she was trying to do.   It is
possible for a follower of Christ to attempt too much;
sometimes this is due to a sense of self-importance and of
pride.   It may result in such a mood of irritation and
temper as was shown by Martha when, in criticizing her
sister, she humiliated her by rebuking her in the presence
of their Guest, and by addressing the remark to him rebuked him as well, "Lord, dost thou not care that my sister
did leave me to serve alone? bid her therefore that she
help me."   In his reply Jesus showed his affection by ten-
derly repeating her name, but he rebuked her spirit and
revealed its cause, "Martha, Martha, thou art anxious and
troubled about many things: but one thing is needful: for
Mary hath chosen the good part, which shall not be taken
away from her."   There was no need for an elaborate
meal; but few things or one would have sufficed; yet one
thing was needful, and that Mary had chosen, for while
the Master does appreciate all that we undertake for him,
he knows that our first need is to sit at his feet and learn
his will; then in our tasks we shall be calm and peaceful
and kindly, and at last our service may attain the perfect-

ness of that of Mary when in a later scene she poured upon the feet of Jesus the ointment, the perfume of which still fills the world.

6. JESUS' TEACHING CONCERNING PRAYER
Ch. 11:1-13

1 And it came to pass, as he was praying in a certain place, that when he ceased, one of his disciples said unto him, Lord, teach us to pray, even as John also taught his disciples. 2 And he said unto them, When ye pray, say, Father, Hallowed be thy name. Thy kingdom come. 3 Give us day by day our daily bread. 4 And forgive us our sins; for we ourselves also forgive every one that is indebted to us. And bring us not into temptation.

5 And he said unto them, Which of you shall have a friend, and shall go unto him at midnight, and say to him, Friend, lend me three loaves; 6 for a friend of mine is come to me from a journey, and I have nothing to set before him; 7 and he from within shall answer and say, Trouble me not: the door is now shut, and my children are with me in bed; I cannot rise and give thee? 8 I say unto you, Though he will not rise and give him because he is his friend, yet because of his importunity he will arise and give him as many as he needeth. 9 And I say unto you, Ask, and it shall be given you; seek, and ye shall find; knock, and it shall be opened unto you. 10 For every one that asketh receiveth; and he that seeketh findeth; and to him that knocketh it shall be opened. 11 And of which of you that is a father shall his son ask a loaf, and he give him a stone? or a fish, and he for a fish give him a serpent? 12 Or if he shall ask an egg, will he give him a scorpion? 13 If ye then, being evil, know how to give good gifts unto your children, how much more shall your heavenly Father give the Holy Spirit to them that ask him?

When the disciples came to the Master with the request, "Lord, teach us to pray," they had already, for some time, been with Christ in the school of prayer, and they had been impressed by that most valuable of object lessons, namely, the example of Christ himself. If in our minds doubt ever arises as to the reality and efficacy of prayer, we need only turn to the Gospel of Luke to be reminded that our Lord spent long hours in intercession and that he prayed at every crisis in his life. Surely we shall not be misled if we follow in his steps!

What the disciples wished, however, was some special form or formula for prayer, such as John the Baptist seems to have given his followers. Jesus replied by granting them a matchless model and then by encouraging them in the assurance that prayer will surely be heard. This "Lord's Prayer," more fully recorded by Matthew, was not intended as a form which must be used rigidly on all occasions, but as a type which should mold all prayer, however free and varied and spontaneous it may be.

The first word, "Father," suggests the filial spirit in which all believers should draw near to God, and it intimates much of the encouragement which Jesus gave his disciples in the verses which immediately follow this prayer.

The prayer contains five petitions, two relating to the cause of God in the world, and three to personal needs of the petitioners. The first is a request that the "name" of God, his revelation, or our conception of God, be so reverenced, or so exalted, on earth as it is in heaven. The second is a parallel request, namely, that his Kingdom may come. This Kingdom is to be external, visible, glorious; it depends upon the inward transformation of individuals, but it will yet appear in a perfected social order, and in the universal reign of Christ. The next petition is for "bread sufficient for our needs," and it implies our right to pray for all that concerns our physical welfare. We are then taught to pray for pardon, as we come to God in a spirit of forgiveness toward others; and lastly, to ask for continual protection from the snares of the adversary and from all the powers of evil.

To encourage his disciples in such petitions Jesus gave

them the story of the man whose ceaseless, almost shameless, asking secured for him the answer to his request for needed bread. Jesus implied, however, that there is, on the part of God, no such reluctance to be overcome, so that all who "ask" of him will receive what they need; if they "seek" relief, he will grant it, if they "knock," even at "midnight," he will open the door without delay.

Further still, Jesus encouraged prayer by again reminding his hearers that they were praying to a Father. Human parents reply to the requests of their children, not by mocking them or with injurious gifts, not by giving a stone when bread is asked, or a serpent for a fish, or a scorpion instead of an egg. If then, with all our imperfections and limitations, we know how to give good gifts to our children, much more can we expect our heavenly Father to give his Holy Spirit, and so all other good if lesser gifts, to them that ask him. Thus again we see that the blessed name of "Father" is the key to the lesson. If we approach him as children, it will be with confidence, but also with submission, as we know that, whether he gives or withholds, his reply will be an expression of infinite mercy and of fatherly love.

7. JESUS REBUKING BLASPHEMY AND UNBELIEF
Ch. 11:14-36

14 And he was casting out a demon that was *dumb. And it came to pass, when the demon was gone out, the dumb man spake; and the multitudes marvelled. 15 But some of them said, By Beelzebub the prince of the demons casteth he out demons. 16 And others, trying him, sought of him a sign from heaven. 17 But he, knowing their thoughts, said unto them, Every kingdom divided against itself is brought to desolation; and a house divided against a house falleth. 18 And if Satan also is divided against himself, how shall his kingdom stand? because ye say that I cast out demons by Beelzebub. 19 And if I by Beelzebub cast out demons, by whom do your sons cast them out?*

therefore shall they be your judges. 20 But if I by the finger of God cast out demons, then is the kingdom of God come upon you. 21 When the strong man fully armed guardeth his own court, his goods are in peace: 22 but when a stronger than he shall come upon him, and overcome him, he taketh from him his whole armor wherein he trusted, and divideth his spoils. 23 He that is not with me is against me; and he that gathereth not with me scattereth. 24 The unclean spirit when he is gone out of the man, passeth through waterless places, seeking rest; and finding none, he saith, I will turn back unto my house whence I came out. 25 And when he is come, he findeth it swept and garnished. 26 Then goeth he, and taketh to him seven other spirits more evil than himself; and they enter in and dwell there: and the last state of that man becometh worse than the first.

27 And it came to pass, as he said these things, a certain woman out of the multitude lifted up her voice, and said unto him, Blessed is the womb that bare thee, and the breasts which thou didst suck. 28 But he said, Yea rather, blessed are they that hear the word of God, and keep it.

29 And when the multitudes were gathering together unto him, he began to say, This generation is an evil generation: it seeketh after a sign; and there shall no sign be given to it but the sign of Jonah. 30 For even as Jonah became a sign unto the Ninevites, so shall also the Son of man be to this generation. 31 The queen of the south shall rise up in the judgment with the men of this generation, and shall condemn them: for she came from the ends of the earth to hear the wisdom of Solomon; and behold, a greater than Solomon is here. 32 The men of Nineveh shall stand up in the judgment with this generation, and shall condemn it: for they repented at the preaching of Jonah; and behold, a greater than Jonah is here.

33 No man, when he hath lighted a lamp, putteth it in a cellar, neither under the bushel, but on the stand, that they which enter in may see the light. 34 The lamp of thy body is thine eye: when thine eye is single, thy whole body also is full of light; but when it is evil, thy body also is full of darkness. 35 Look therefore whether the light that is in thee be not darkness. 36 If therefore thy whole body be

*full of light, having no part dark, it shall be wholly full of
light, as when the lamp with its bright shining doth give
thee light.*

The first of these two discourses, vs. 14-26, was given
by Jesus in reply to the charge that he wrought his miracles
by Satanic power, v. 15; the second, vs. 29-36, was an
answer to the demand that he should compel his enemies
to believe in him by giving them "a sign from heaven,"
v. 16.

Jesus had just cast out a demon. His enemies did not
attempt to deny that a miracle had been performed; but,
in order to discredit him with the people, they explained
the miracle on the ground that Jesus must be in league
with the devil. He replied by showing the absurdity of
suggesting that the devil was casting out devils, or "demons," for in that case his power would be like a kingdom
"divided against itself" and so certain to be "brought to
desolation," or like a house thus divided and sure to fall.
Vs. 17-18. He then turned the charge against themselves:
some of their countrymen claimed the power to cast out
demons; Jesus did not discuss the reality of these reputed
cures but pointedly asked by what power they were effected; is it also demonic power? V. 19. Jesus then declared definitely that his miracles were being wrought by
divine power and that their character was a certain proof
that he was representing not the kingdom of the devil but
"the kingdom of God." V. 20. Instead of aiding the
devil, he was despoiling him. He described the devil as
though a strong man, fully armed and guarding his goods,
but Jesus himself was a "stronger than he," and was taking
away his armor and delivering his captives by miracles of
grace. Vs. 21-22. In this conflict there can be no neutrality; one must be on the side either of the devil or of
Christ. V. 23.

Jesus then rebuked his enemies by the parable of the
unclean spirit. The demon of unbelief had once possessed

the Jews, and had been manifested in the form of idolatry; it had been cast out, but it had returned with more terrible manifestations of hypocrisy, covetousness, hatred, fanaticism, and pride. Such had been the fate of the nation; and such is the experience of an individual who turns from sin and rebels against Satan but fails to accept the Lordship of Christ. The empty heart is in peril. Reformation is not regeneration. One must beware of the demon of unbelief. Vs. 24-26.

At this juncture a "woman out of the multitude" interrupted with an expression of congratulation for the mother of Jesus. In reply Jesus intimated that his mother might rightly be called "blessed," but that the woman had missed the real point; it was a privilege to sustain to Christ such a close human and natural relationship, but better far to possess that spiritual kinship which is indicated by faith and by obedience to God. Vs. 27-28.

Jesus continued to rebuke the unbelief of the Jews as he now turned to answer directly the demand for "a sign from heaven." He declared that such a sign would be given, in his resurrection from the dead. This miracle would be wrought without any human intervention; it would be a direct act of God and would fulfill the conditions of "a sign from heaven"; it would be the counterpart of the miraculous deliverance of Jonah from the sea. However, the very demand for such a sign was an impertinence and an insult; it reflected discredit upon the divine character of the miracles which Jesus had already wrought. It failed to recognize the nature of his teachings, which surpassed the wisdom of Solomon and the startling message of Jonah. The eagerness of the heathen queen to hear, the willingness of the Ninevites to repent, rebuked the stubborn unbelief of the Jews who refused to accept "a greater than Solomon," "a greater than Jonah." Vs. 29-32.

Finally Jesus showed that their guilty unbelief was not due to lack of evidence or to the need of a new "sign," but to their indifference and their impenitence. As a lamp is

designed to light a house, and as the eye is intended to il-
lumine the body, so the soul which is right with God possesses the faculty of spiritual sight. This sight is dimmed
and destroyed by sin. The inability of the Jews to believe
was not due to lack of "signs" and proofs, but to lack of
sight. No amount of light will help a blind man. Those
who turn to Christ in repentance and faith and love will
find him to be the Light of the World, and their whole
souls will become radiant with divine splendor. Vs. 33-36.

8. PHARISAISM EXPOSED AND DENOUNCED
Ch. 11:37-54

*37 Now as he spake, a Pharisee asketh him to dine with
him: and he went in, and sat down to meat. 38 And when
the Pharisee saw it, he marvelled that he had not first
bathed himself before dinner. 39 And the Lord said unto
him, Now ye the Pharisees cleanse the outside of the cup
and of the platter; but your inward part is full of extortion
and wickedness. 40 Ye foolish ones, did not he that made
the outside make the inside also? 41 But give for alms
those things which are within; and behold, all things are
clean unto you.*

*42 But woe unto you Pharisees! for ye tithe mint and rue
and every herb, and pass over justice and the love of God:
but these ought ye to have done, and not to leave the other
undone. 43 Woe unto you Pharisees! for ye love the chief
seats in the synagogues, and the salutations in the marketplaces. 44 Woe unto you! for ye are as the tombs which
appear not, and the men that walk over them know it not.*

*45 And one of the lawyers answering saith unto him,
Teacher, in saying this thou reproachest us also. 46 And
he said, Woe unto you lawyers also! for ye load men with
burdens grievous to be borne, and ye yourselves touch not
the burdens with one of your fingers. 47 Woe unto you!
for ye build the tombs of the prophets, and your fathers
killed them. 48 So ye are witnesses and consent unto the
works of your fathers: for they killed them, and ye build
their tombs. 49 Therefore also said the wisdom of God, I*

*will send unto them prophets and apostles; and some of
them they shall kill and persecute;   50 that the blood of all
the prophets, which was shed from the foundation of the
world, may be required of this generation;   51 from the
blood of Abel unto the blood of Zachariah, who perished
between the altar and the sanctuary: yea, I say unto you,
it shall be required of this generation.   52 Woe unto you
lawyers! for ye took away the key of knowledge: ye entered not in yourselves, and them that were entering in ye
hindered.*

*53 And when he was come out from thence, the scribes
and the Pharisees began to press upon him vehemently, and
to provoke him to speak of many things;   54 laying wait
for him, to catch something out of his mouth.*

The conflict between Jesus and his enemies here reached
its climax. He rebuked their hypocrisy, and pronounced
upon them six solemn woes. His words are full of warning for his followers in all ages; religion ever tends to become a matter of form and ritual; hypocrisy is often unconscious; its practice is almost universal.

A Pharisee whose heart was foul with sinful thoughts
wondered that Jesus had sat down to eat without first
washing his hands according to the Jewish ritual. No such
ceremony was required by the law, but only by the traditions upon which the Pharisees laid such stress. Jesus declared that to wash the body while the heart is impure is
as absurd as to cleanse the outside of an unclean cup or
platter. He declared that God who made the body created
the soul also, and that God is more concerned with the
latter than with the former. He insisted that while it may
be well to wash the hands, a better preparation for a meal
would consist in filling the heart with love, which might be
expressed in gifts to the poor. It was much more important that the Pharisee should take the hatred from his
heart, than that Jesus should wash his hands. Vs. 37-41.

Hypocrisy, however, is ever concerned with external
forms while disregarding realities. Therefore Jesus pro-

nounced a woe upon the Pharisees for tithing the small garden herbs while neglecting justice toward men and love toward God, for observing some minute religious rite while breaking all the Ten Commandments. Yet he did not condemn them for caring for these trifles, but for neglecting things essential. "These ought ye to have done, and not to leave the other undone." V. 42. Jesus further rebuked the vanity and the desire for prominence and public recognition which is at once a mark and a cloak of hypocrisy. V. 43. He further compared the evil influence of hypocrites to the defiling contact with a grave, which is level with the ground, upon which one may unconsciously tread and so become ceremonially unclean. Men are not on their guard against those who make loud boasts of religion. V. 44.

At this juncture a lawyer interrupted Jesus with the statement that these severe denunciations seemed to include him and his associates. It was true that most lawyers were Pharisees, but they were the professional teachers of this sect, the recognized leaders of the party; and in denouncing all Pharisees, Jesus seemed to include even these proud expounders of the law. Jesus replied that religious teachers who are insincere, or who allow their religion to become a mere matter of form, are most of all to be rebuked. He pronounced upon them three woes: the first, for extracting from the law minute and burdensome requirements which they were not careful to observe themselves. It is a grievous fault for students and scholars to make religion a matter of weariness and distaste, instead of a delight to the common people. Vs. 45-46.

Secondly, Jesus rebuked their heartless cruelty and fanaticism. Teachers of religion are ever tempted to become bitter partisans, and even to have a share in killing the very prophets and apostles of God. The hatred of Jesus shown by his enemies was like that of their fathers who had killed the divine messengers of old. The blood of these martyrs, from the first to the last mentioned in the Hebrew Bible, was yet to be required of the nation, and those who rejected Jesus would partake in the judgment as they were partakers of the crime. Vs. 47-51.

Lastly, the lawyers were rebuked for keeping back the knowledge of God, by their false interpretations of Scripture and their disregard of the real spiritual needs of the people. Such teachers of religion are like men who hold the key to a sacred temple: they themselves will not enter and they keep back all who would. It is a solemn responsibility to be a professed teacher of divine truth; and to be at once a "lawyer" and a "hypocrite" is to merit these solemn woes which fell from the lips of Christ. So enraged were his hearers that they threatened him with physical violence. Hypocrites hate to be exposed. Wise men are glad to be warned and to repent before it is too late. He who spoke these bitter words of rebuke is ready to pardon and to purify and to lead his followers in the paths of service and of peace. Vs. 52-54.

9. FAITHFUL TESTIMONY ENCOURAGED   Ch. 12:1-12

1 In the mean time, when the many thousands of the multitude were gathered together, insomuch that they trod one upon another, he began to say unto his disciples first of all, Beware ye of the leaven of the Pharisees, which is hypocrisy. 2 But there is nothing covered up, that shall not be revealed; and hid, that shall not be known. 3 Wherefore whatsoever ye have said in the darkness shall be heard in the light; and what ye have spoken in the ear in the inner chambers shall be proclaimed upon the housetops. 4 And I say unto you my friends, Be not afraid of them that kill the body, and after that have no more that they can do. 5 But I will warn you whom ye shall fear: Fear him, who after he hath killed hath power to cast into hell; yea, I say unto you, Fear him. 6 Are not five sparrows sold for two pence? and not one of them is forgotten in the sight of God. 7 But the very hairs of your head are all numbered. Fear not: ye are of more value than many sparrows. 8 And I say unto you, Every one who shall confess me before men, him shall the Son of man also confess before the angels of God: 9 but he that denieth me in the presence of men shall be denied in the presence of the angels of God. 10 And every one who shall speak a word against the Son of man, it shall be forgiven him: but unto him that blasphemeth against the Holy Spirit it shall not be forgiven. 11 And when they bring you before the synagogues, and the rulers, and the authorities, be not anxious how or what ye shall answer, or what ye shall say: 12 for the Holy Spirit shall teach you in that very hour what ye ought to say.

When Jesus had bitterly rebuked the public religious teachers of his day he turned to his disciples and spoke words of cheer which have strengthened his followers in all days. Such encouragement was needed; the bitter hatred of his enemies now threatened the life of Jesus, and made it evident that his disciples could expect no kinder treatment than their Lord. Then, too, Jesus had shown the special guilt of those who professed to be guides in matters of religion; his disciples therefore needed courage to continue their public witness both because of the great responsibility involved and because it would bring upon them the hatred of men. He encouraged them, first, by the assurance that the corrupting influence of the Pharisees would come to an end; their hypocrisy would be mercilessly unmasked; their power would cease; while on the other hand the witness of the disciples would not always be confined to places of obscurity but would be heard in all the world. Vs. 1-3. How truly has this prophecy been fulfilled! Compare the present influence of Hillel or Gamaliel with that of Peter or John. No one can measure the power for good possessed by the humblest witness for Christ.

Jesus further encouraged his disciples by assuring them of the loving care of God. They should look to him in reverent trust; this would give confidence and strength and free them from the fear of man. Their enemies could harm only the body; God controls the eternal destiny of souls, and to him even the body is precious, and he is concerned with the most minute details of our lives. If he notes the fall of a sparrow, he must know the peril and need of every one who is testifying for his Son. Vs. 4-7.

Then again for faithful witnesses there remain great rewards, in spite of what they now may suffer from men. As they now acknowledge Jesus Christ as Savior and Lord, so in the glories of heaven he will acknowledge them as his true and loyal warriors who merit and will share the blessedness of his triumphant reign. Vs. 8-9. On the other hand, those who blaspheme his name by ascribing his power to a Satanic source, ch. 11:15, will be regarded as guilty of an unpardonable sin. This would not apply to such as in ignorance rejected Jesus, but to those who had full opportunity of knowing him, and who then scoffed at his claims and maliciously insulted his divine Person, and made of him an impostor and associated him with the powers of evil. V. 10.

Last of all, in spite of opposition and threats of all the earthly powers, and in the presence of the most imposing tribunals, the witnesses of Jesus never need fear, and must never allow themselves to be silenced. The Holy Spirit, whom their enemies opposed and blasphemed, would speak through them; he would teach them both how and what to say, vs. 11-12. This promise was not designed to encourage indolence or lack of possible preparation, but to assure the Christian witness that a divine Presence would ever give him needed wisdom and strength and grace.

It is a grave responsibility to testify for Christ, but it is the duty of everyone who bears his name; and in this service he can be assured that the influence will be measureless, the protection unfailing, the reward heavenly, the sustaining grace divine.

10. A WARNING AGAINST COVETOUSNESS
Ch. 12:13-21

13 And one out of the multitude said unto him, Teacher, bid my brother divide the inheritance with me. 14 But he said unto him, Man, who made me a judge or a divider over you? 15 And he said unto them, Take heed, and keep yourselves from all covetousness: for a man's life consisteth not in the abundance of the things which he possesseth. 16 And he spake a parable unto them, saying, The ground of a certain rich man brought forth plentifully: 17 and he reasoned within himself, saying, What shall I do, because I have not where to bestow my fruits? 18 And he said, This will I do: I will pull down my barns, and build greater; and there will I bestow all my grain and my goods. 19 And I will say to my soul, Soul, thou hast much goods laid up for many years; take thine ease, eat, drink, be merry. 20 But God said unto him, Thou foolish one, this night is thy soul required of thee; and the things which thou hast prepared, whose shall they be? 21 So is he that layeth up treasure for himself, and is not rich toward God.

The parable of the rich fool was related by our Lord to teach that riches neither form the real content nor assure the continuance of life, so that it is the sheerest folly to seek for gold while forgetting God.

A man had come to Jesus with the request, "Teacher, bid my brother divide the inheritance with me." The reply implied that the Master regarded his work as spiritual, and that he was not willing to invade the sphere of civil law or to usurp the place of regularly appointed authorities, "Man, who made me a judge or a divider over you?"

Possibly this reply contains a message for the modern day and warns us against confusing the functions of the church with those of the state. The sphere of the church is spiritual, and its province is not to determine questions which are commercial and political. The church, however, does provide and inculcate principles which are involved in all moral questions and which determine justice and right in every sphere of human life. Thus Jesus refused to "divide the inheritance," but he pierced to the root of the request and saw that the man was neglecting the civil law and seeking the support of a religious teacher because he was moved by avarice; and it is this same "love of money" which lies at the root of most of the injustice and inequity and cruelty which burden the world today.

Therefore Jesus turned to the multitude with the warning: "Take heed, and keep yourselves from all covetousness: for a man's life consisteth not in the abundance of the things which he possesseth." To enforce his message Jesus told the story of the rich man who was heaping up goods for selfish enjoyment in future years, and who was suddenly confronted by the necessity which death brings of leaving to others all that he had amassed. His foolishness consisted in forgetting that fortune and life itself are dependent upon the will of God, and that a man really owns nothing but owes everything to God, and that the real value of life consists in the unselfish use of wealth and of opportunity according to the will of God. How his vain words, "my fruits," "my barns," "my grain," "my goods," "my soul," are contrasted with the solemn message: "This night is thy soul required of thee."

"So is he," continued Jesus, "that layeth up treasure for himself, and is not rich toward God." It is the sheerest folly to forget that riches neither form the real content nor assure the continuance of life; it is madness to heap up goods while neglecting God.

11. THE CURE OF ANXIETY   Ch. 12:22-34

22 And he said unto his disciples, Therefore I say unto you, Be not anxious for your life, what ye shall eat; nor yet for your body, what ye shall put on. 23 For the life is more than the food, and the body than the raiment. 24 Consider the ravens, that they sow not, neither reap; which have no store-chamber nor barn; and God feedeth them:

*of how much more value are ye than the birds!   25 And
which of you by being anxious can add a cubit unto the
measure of his life?   26 If then ye are not able to do even
that which is least, why are ye anxious concerning the rest?
27 Consider the lilies, how they grow: they toil not, neither
do they spin; yet I say unto you, Even Solomon in all his
glory was not arrayed like one of these.   28 But if God
doth so clothe the grass in the field, which to-day is, and
to-morrow is cast into the oven; how much more shall he
clothe you, O ye of little faith?   29 And seek not ye what
ye shall eat, and what ye shall drink, neither be ye of doubt-
ful mind.   30 For all these things do the nations of the
world seek after: but your Father knoweth that ye have
need of these things.   31 Yet seek ye his kingdom, and
these things shall be added unto you.   32 Fear not, little
flock; for it is your Father's good pleasure to give you the
kingdom.   33 Sell that which ye have, and give alms; make
for yourselves purses which wax not old, a treasure in the
heavens that faileth not, where no thief draweth near,
neither moth destroyeth.   34 For where your treasure is,
there will your heart be also.*

In addressing the crowds, Jesus warned them against
covetousness by speaking to them the parable of the foolish rich man who trusted in his goods and forgot God; he
now turned to his disciples to urge them to forget their
worries by trust in God.   While a Christian must not be
selfishly absorbed in amassing wealth, he need not be anxious about even the necessities of life.   The reason is that
"the life is more than the food, and the body than the raiment," and therefore God who gave life and made the
body will surely provide food and clothing; he who did the
greater will not fail to do the less.

For an example of such providential care Jesus points
to the birds: without the "fruits" and the "barns" and the
"goods," which failed to prolong the life of the rich man,
the ravens continue to live; "God feedeth them: of how
much more value are ye than the birds!"   Of course we are
to be diligent and industrious and to exercise thrift and

foresight; but we are not to be anxious. Worry will not prolong life; on the other hand, it is worry and not work that kills. Therefore, if anxiety shortens life, it surely will not supply the necessities of life; trust God for food. Vs. 24-26.

So, too, as for clothing; if God robes in such beautiful colors the perishable flowers of the field, will he not provide garments for his own children? To be anxious about these necessities is to imitate the heathen who know nothing of God's providential care. We show ourselves to be his children by our trust in him. Vs. 27-30.

However, while we are not to be absorbed in seeking wealth, as the foolish rich man, or to be anxious about food and raiment, as are men of the world, there is something about which we should feel a deep concern, and that is the Kingdom of God. If we seek and labor for its coming, we can be sure that our Father will supply our temporal needs. Even though at times we may be in peril and in want, we can be certain that we are to share at last the blessedness of that Kingdom. Vs. 31-32. Therefore we should not be absorbed in gathering the goods that perish, but by deeds of sacrifice and works of charity, inspired by gratitude to God and love to men, we are to lay up "treasure in the heavens" which will never be stolen or destroyed; and as the heart always follows its treasure, our thoughts will be turned upward toward God; trust in his power and love will banish our anxiety and free us from care. Vs. 33-34.

12. AN EXHORTATION TO WATCHFULNESS
Ch. 12:35-48

35 Let your loins be girded about, and your lamps burning; 36 and be ye yourselves like unto men looking for their lord, when he shall return from the marriage feast; that, when he cometh and knocketh, they may straightway open unto him. 37 Blessed are those servants, whom the lord when he cometh shall find watching: verily I say unto you, that he shall gird himself, and make them sit down to meat, and shall come and serve them.   38 And if he shall come in the second watch, and if in the third, and find them *so, blessed are those* servants.   *39 But know this, that if the master of the house had known in what hour the thief was coming, he would have watched, and not have left his house to be broken through.   40 Be ye also ready: for in an hour that ye think not the Son of man cometh.*

41 And Peter said, Lord, speakest thou this parable unto us, or even unto all?   42 And the Lord said, Who then is the faithful and wise steward, whom his lord shall set over his household, to give them their portion of food in due season?   43 Blessed is that servant, whom his lord when he cometh shall find so doing.   44 Of a truth I say unto you, that he will set him over all that he hath.   45 But if that servant shall say in his heart, My lord delayeth his coming; and shall begin to beat the menservants and the maidservants, and to eat and drink, and to be drunken; 46 the lord of that servant shall come in a day when he ex-pecteth not, and in an hour when he knoweth not, and shall cut him asunder, and appoint his portion with the un-faithful.   47 And that servant, who knew his lord's will, and made not ready, nor did according to his will, shall be beaten with many stripes;   *48 but he that knew not, and did things worthy of stripes, shall be beaten with few* stripes.   *And to whomsoever much is given, of him shall much be required: and to whom they commit much, of him will they ask the more.*

Our Lord had been warning his disciples against allow-ing their minds to be absorbed in the selfish acquisition of wealth, and against being anxious about needed food and clothing; they were to be supremely concerned about his Kingdom which would appear in glory at the time of his return.   As to the events preceding this return, as to its circumstances and results, he taught them more definitely just before his death; here he simply enjoined upon them the attitude of watchfulness, implying that if his coming was occupying their thoughts, they would be kept at once from worldliness and from worry and would be diligent in serving him.

He illustrated this attitude of heart and mind by two parables, the parable of the returning lord and the parable of the thief. In the former, the master has been attending a marriage, his servants are awake and clothed, the house is lighted, and all are ready to receive him. So delighted is he on his arrival to find them faithful that he is ready to give any expression to his joy; he even is willing to cause them to sit down and to partake of the banquet they have prepared for him.

The second parable illustrates the truth that as the time when a thief will come is unknown, therefore the only way to act is to be ready at all times for his approach; therefore, our Savior added, "Be ye also ready: for in an hour that ye think not the Son of man cometh."

The Master here as elsewhere indicated that his return was to be delayed; his absence was to be like a long night; much must transpire, much be done before he would reappear, but his followers must ever be prepared for his return. This did not mean that they were to be nervously expectant nor were they to be saying that the day of his coming was just at hand; rather, they were to be at their places of duty, faithfully performing their tasks, and absorbed in the work which the Master had given them to do.

This attitude of watchfulness, and of interest in the return of Christ, should particularly characterize teachers and leaders. This is the force of the question which Peter now asked. He inquired whether all believers would share equally in the blessings of the Lord's return; would not those, like the apostles, who had been most prominent in his service receive from him a greater reward? Jesus replied that larger privileges imply greater temptations and greater responsibilities. If a Christian minister has been faithful in feeding his people with spiritual food, he will be rewarded with even higher opportunities for service; but if the long delay of his Lord's return shall make him forgetful and unmindful of its reality, if he shall use his high position selfishly or shall use his power unkindly, then when the Master appears he will be punished with the utmost severity.

The chief advantage of a religious leader lies in his opportunity for knowing more fully the teachings of Christ; his superior knowledge, therefore, will be the ground of his more terrible punishment in case of unfaithfulness; the principle is abiding and applies in every sphere. "To whomsoever much is given, of him shall much be required."

Thus Christ taught that in the future there will be degrees and gradations both of punishments and rewards.

13. THE DIVISIVE INFLUENCE OF CHRIST
Ch. 12:49-59

49 I came to cast fire upon the earth; and what do I desire, if it is already kindled? 50 But I have a baptism to be baptized with; and how am I straitened till it be accomplished! 51 Think ye that I am come to give peace in the earth? I tell you, Nay; but rather division: 52 for there shall be from henceforth five in one house divided, three against two, and two against three. 53 They shall be divided, father against son, and son against father; mother against daughter, and daughter against her mother; mother in law against her daughter in law, and daughter in law against her mother in law.

54 And he said to the multitudes also, When ye see a cloud rising in the west, straightway ye say, There cometh a shower; and so it cometh to pass. 55 And when ye see a south wind blowing, ye say, There will be a scorching heat; and it cometh to pass. 56 Ye hypocrites, ye know how to interpret the face of the earth and the heaven; but how is it that ye know not how to interpret this time? 57 And why even of yourselves judge ye not what is right? 58 For as thou art going with thine adversary before the magistrate, on the way give diligence to be quit of him; lest haply he drag thee unto the judge, and the judge shall de-

*liver thee to the officer, and the officer shall cast thee into
prison.   59 I say unto thee, Thou shalt by no means come
out thence, till thou have paid the very last mite.*

Jesus had been warning the crowds against the peril of
selfish enjoyment and urging his followers to watch and to
labor for his return and his Kingdom; but he did not want
them to be deceived and to suppose that this Kingdom
could be established without conflict and delay.   The
present age was to be one of strife and division, and the
Master himself was to be their innocent cause.   Someday
he would return to bring justice and holiness and righteousness to complete victory, and then he would be indeed
the Prince of Peace.

Now, however, his coming into the world had cast upon
the earth the burning brand of division and strife.   This
was so inevitable that Jesus had no regret that the fire was
already kindled; but it would not burst into a conflagration
until Jesus had been crucified, and he felt a pathetic impa-
tience to have that dreadful experience accomplished.   As
Jesus emerged from that baptism of fire he would be the
torch which would set the world ablaze with conflict and
separation.   This division would occur even in a home
circle of five: father and mother would be divided against
son and daughter and daughter-in-law.

Thus Christ, and specifically his cross, is now dividing
the world.   Happy are those who interpret his message
and understand his mission and turn to him in repentance
and faith!

The multitudes, however, were still unbelieving, and
Jesus rebuked their stupid ignorance.   He declared that
they could so interpret the signs of weather as to predict
correctly rain or drought, but they could not see in his
words and works the proofs that he was the Christ, the
Savior of the world.   However, he warned them to repent
before it was too late.   They would have wisdom enough
to agree with an adversary while on the way to a court-

room before sentence had been pronounced, much more should they see that it was the part of wisdom to seek peace with God before the day of mercy and grace had passed.

14. A CALL TO REPENTANCE   Ch. 13:1-9

1 Now there were some present at that very season who told him of the Galilæans, whose blood Pilate had mingled with their sacrifices.   2 And he answered and said unto them, Think ye that these Galilæans were sinners above all the Galilæans, because they have suffered these things?   3 I tell you, Nay: but, except ye repent, ye shall all in like manner perish.   4 Or those eighteen, upon whom the tower in Siloam fell, and killed them, think ye that they were offenders above all the men that dwell in Jerusalem?   5 I tell you, Nay: but, except ye repent, ye shall all likewise perish.

6 And he spake this parable; A certain man had a fig tree planted in his vineyard; and he came seeking fruit thereon, and found none.   7 And he said unto the vinedresser, Behold, these three years I come seeking fruit on this fig tree, and find none: cut it down; why doth it also cumber the ground?   8 And he answering said unto him, Lord, let it alone this year also, till I shall dig about it, and dung it: 9 and if it bear fruit thenceforth, well; but if not, thou shalt cut it down.

At the very time when Jesus was urging upon his hearers their need of repentance, a report was made of a cruel slaughter of Galileans at the hand of Pilate.   It was expected that Jesus would declare the poor sufferers to have merited their fate, and that he would fall into the common fallacy of supposing that exceptional suffering is a proof of exceptional guilt on the part of men.   Jesus, however, replied that temporary exemption from suffering is a mark of special grace on the part of God.   All impenitent men are certain to suffer, and deserve to suffer; if judgment has not fallen, the delay should be regarded as a merciful opportunity to repent.

Jesus enforced the same truth by referring to a recent

calamity in which eighteen men had been crushed by the fall of a tower. Their fate was not to be regarded as a sign of their special sinfulness, but as a warning to others that they would likewise suffer unless they repented of their sins.

The Master had in mind the entire Jewish nation and he further enforced his call to repentance by the parable of the fruitless fig tree. This was a true type of Israel, but also a symbol of every impenitent soul. God mercifully preserves and blesses and spares, but the day of mercy will end. The nation, as the individual, which produces no fruit of penitence and of righteousness is certain to be cut down. While the opportunity is given, repentance must be shown. "Now is the acceptable time; . . . now is a day of salvation."

15. A Cure on the Sabbath   Ch. 13:10-21

10 And he was teaching in one of the synagogues on the sabbath day. 11 And behold, a woman that had a spirit of infirmity eighteen years; and she was bowed together, and could in no wise lift herself up. 12 And when Jesus saw her, he called her, and said to her, Woman, thou art loosed from thine infirmity. 13 And he laid his hands upon her: and immediately she was made straight, and glorified God. 14 And the ruler of the synagogue, being moved with indignation because Jesus had healed on the sabbath, answered and said to the multitude, There are six days in which men ought to work: in them therefore come and be healed, and not on the day of the sabbath. 15 But the Lord answered him, and said, Ye hypocrites, doth not each one of you on the sabbath loose his ox or his ass from the stall, and lead him away to watering? 16 And ought not this woman, being a daughter of Abraham, whom Satan had bound, lo, these eighteen years, to have been loosed from this bond on the day of the sabbath? 17 And as he said these things, all his adversaries were put to shame: and all the multitude rejoiced for all the glorious things that were done by him.

18 He said therefore, Unto what is the kingdom of God

like? and whereunto shall I liken it?   19 It is like unto a grain of mustard seed, which a man took, and cast into his own garden; and it grew, and became a tree; and the birds of the heaven lodged in the branches thereof.

20 And again he said, Where unto shall I liken the kingdom of God?   21 It is like unto leaven, which a woman took and hid in three measures of meal, till it was all leavened.

A true follower of Christ will worship in public on the Sabbath Day, for this was the custom of our Lord.   On one of these days he found occasion to reveal his sympathy and power by releasing a poor woman who for eighteen years had been bound by "a spirit of infirmity," just as on such occasions his word today brings deliverance to souls bound by the power of sin.

It was his sympathy which prompted this act and further led him to relieve the consciences of his hearers from the burden of traditions placed upon them by false interpretations of the law.   When the ruler of the synagogue criticized Jesus, by addressing those whom the woman represented, on the ground that such healing broke the law of Sabbath rest, his hypocrisy and that of his sympathizers was unmasked by the reply that where self-interest prompted, they interpreted the law so liberally as to allow them on the Sabbath to loose their cattle which had been bound but a few hours, while they refused to allow Jesus to relieve a daughter of Abraham whom Satan had bound for years.   They were pretending to be zealous for the law while denying its essential principle of love.   Their real breach of the law was shown both by their lack of sympathy for the woman and their hatred of Christ.   Their interpretation of the law was shown to be absurd, for it prevented an act of mercy which, on the Sabbath, was not only allowable but necessary.   Jesus never intimated that he would abolish the Sabbath; he only designed to restore to it the true spirit of worship and love and liberty and joy.

In view of this gracious work of power the multitude rejoiced; and Jesus spoke the parables of the mustard seed and the leaven, the former to indicate that his power yet was to extend over all the earth and the latter that it was to transform all human life. Some readers interpret the former parable as indicating the unsubstantial forms that Christianity at times assumes, and the latter the false doctrine which at times permeates the church. Whichever interpretation one accepts, it is hardly wise to base upon it any theories as to the order of events related to the coming and Kingdom of Christ. All will agree that small beginnings and invisible forces are not to be despised or distrusted by the followers of the Christ who someday will deliver the whole suffering creation "from the bondage of corruption into the liberty of the glory of the children of God."

B. THE SECOND STAGES Chs. 13:22 to 17:10

1. THE NARROW DOOR   Ch. 13:22-30

22 And he went on his way through cities and villages, teaching, and journeying on unto Jerusalem. 23 And one said unto him, Lord, are they few that are saved? And he said unto them, 24 Strive to enter in by the narrow door: for many, I say unto you, shall seek to enter in, and shall not be able. 25 When once the master of the house is risen up, and hath shut to the door, and ye begin to stand without, and to knock at the door, saying, Lord, open to us; and he shall answer and say to you, I know you not whence ye are; 26 then shall ye begin to say, We did eat and drink in thy presence, and thou didst teach in our streets; 27 and he shall say, I tell you, I know not whence ye are; depart from me, all ye workers of iniquity. 28 There shall be the weeping and the gnashing of teeth, when ye shall see Abraham, and Isaac, and Jacob, and all the prophets, in the kingdom of God, and yourselves cast forth without. 29 And they shall come from the east and west, and from the north and south, and shall sit down in the kingdom

*of God. 30 And behold, there are last who shall be first,
and there are first who shall be last.*

This is the first in a new series of incidents on the last
journeys of Jesus toward Jerusalem. He realized the
seriousness of the situation. He knew that he was offering his salvation to the people for the last time, and therefore he was making an effort to reach every possible city
and village with his message.

Someone among his hearers asked him the question,
"Lord, are they few that are saved?" He did not reply
directly, but his answer implied that many Jews who expected to be saved would be lost and many Gentiles whom
the Jews expected to be lost would be saved. Jesus
likened the blessings of his Kingdom to a banquet served
in a palace. The door into this palace is narrow, and
many who are invited refuse to pass in thereby; after a
time this door is shut, and then those who before have refused to enter, entreat the Master of the house to reopen
it, but in vain; they are forever excluded, and are over-
whelmed with remorse and chagrin. The narrow door is
that of repentance and faith in Christ; the opportunity for
entrance is present but not endless; those who reject Christ
will be excluded from his Kingdom; among these will be
many whose folly will be specially apparent. In the parable they are represented as pleading for entrance, and on
the very ground which condemned them. They are pictured as saying that they had known Christ well; they had
eaten in his presence and he had taught in their streets.
Why, then, had they not accepted him? These privileges
only increase their guilt; and the Lord refused to recognize
them as his own. Thus did Jesus describe the exclusion
from his Kingdom of many Jews; and he added the equally
surprising statement of the reception of Gentiles: "They
shall come from the east and west, and from the north and
south, and shall sit down in the kingdom of God."

Thus Jesus gave a very practical turn to the question

which had been asked in mere curiosity. It is not important to know exactly how many will be saved; it is for each
who hears the gospel to place himself in that number, now
and at any cost. It is not enough that one lives in a Christian land, and in a religious home, and possesses knowledge of saving truth; each must repent and accept Christ
for himself. The sad truth is that many who, like the
Jews, have the largest religious opportunities are the fur-
thest from salvation: "There are last who shall be first, and
there are first who shall be last."

2. The Message to Herod and the Lament Over Jerusalem   Ch. 13:31-35

*31 In that very hour there came certain Pharisees, saying
to him, Get thee out, and go hence: for Herod would fain
kill thee. 32 And he said unto them, Go and say to that
fox, Behold, I cast out demons and perform cures to-day
and to-morrow, and the third* day *I am perfected. 33
Nevertheless I must go on my way to-day and to-morrow
and the* day *following: for it cannot be that a prophet
perish out of Jerusalem. 34 O Jerusalem, Jerusalem, that
killeth the prophets, and stoneth them that are sent unto
her! how often would I have gathered thy children together, even as a hen* gathereth *her own brood under her
wings, and ye would not! 35 Behold, your house is left
unto you* desolate: *and I say unto you, Ye shall not see
me, until ye shall say, Blessed* is *he that cometh in the
name of the Lord.*

A report reached Jesus that Herod was threatening his
life. This report was brought by the Pharisees who hoped
that it would terrify the followers of Jesus and induce him
to flee to Jerusalem where he would fall into the hands of
the Jewish rulers.

Instead, Jesus sent to the king a message of defiance
and irony; it has no note of insolence but reveals the courage and indignation of a true man. "Go and say to that

fox"—Jesus thus addressed Herod because he saw the craftiness of the king. Herod did not wish the disrepute of killing another prophet so soon after the death of John, but he wished his realm to be rid of one whom he regarded as a dangerous leader; so he did not arrest Jesus but tried to put him to flight. The Pharisees were asked to bear this message to the king because Jesus saw that they were one with the king in the malicious cunning of their report.

"Behold, I cast out demons and perform cures to-day and to-morrow and the third day I am perfected." Thus Jesus declared that his time and task were divinely allotted; no king could shorten the time till the task was done. When his work was complete, then in his death and resurrection the glory and grace and power of Jesus would be made perfect. "Nevertheless I must go on my way." Jesus was to leave Galilee and Perea, the realm of Herod, not because he feared the king, but in fulfillment of his task which would take him to Jerusalem. The explicit reference to Jerusalem was made in a tone of solemn irony, "For it cannot be that a prophet perish out of Jerusalem"; that city had a monopoly in murdering prophets; it would be quite improper for Jesus to be killed in any other place.

However, the reference to Jerusalem led Jesus to pronounce a lament of touching pathos over the city he truly loved. He saw that his rejection and death would hasten the destruction of the city. He saw its doom already hovering over it like a bird of prey. He gladly would have given his divine salvation and protection, but his people would not accept him. Now they would be left to their own defense, that is to say, to the ruin which he alone could have averted. Henceforth they would not see him in his saving power until as a suffering and repentant nation they would finally welcome his return as that of their true Savior and Lord. How Jesus always yearns to bless and to deliver, and how often he is spurned and rejected by those who need him the most!

3. JESUS AS A SABBATH GUEST   Ch. 14:1-24

1 And it came to pass, when he went into the house of one of the rulers of the Pharisees on a sabbath to eat bread, that they were watching him. 2 And behold, there was before him a certain man that had the dropsy. 3 And Jesus answering spake unto the lawyers and Pharisees, saying, Is it lawful to heal on the sabbath, or not? 4 But they held their peace. And he took him, and healed him, and let him go. 5 And he said unto them, Which of you shall have an ass or an ox fallen into a well, and will not straightway draw him up on a sabbath day? 6 And they could not answer again unto these things.

7 And he spake a parable unto those that were bidden, when he marked how they chose out the chief seats; saying unto them, 8 When thou art bidden of any man to a marriage feast, sit not down in the chief seat; lest haply a more honorable man than thou be bidden of him, 9 and he that bade thee and him shall come and say to thee, Give this man place; and then thou shalt begin with shame to take the lowest place. 10 But when thou art bidden, go and sit down in the lowest place; that when he that hath bidden thee cometh, he may say to thee, Friend, go up higher: then shalt thou have glory in the presence of all that sit at meat with thee. 11 For every one that exalteth himself shall be humbled; and he that humbleth himself shall be exalted.

12 And he said to him also that had bidden him, When thou makest a dinner or a supper, call not thy friends, nor thy brethren, nor thy kinsmen, nor rich neighbors; lest haply they also bid thee again, and a recompense be made thee. 13 But when thou makest a feast, bid the poor, the maimed, the lame, the blind: 14 and thou shalt be blessed; because they have not wherewith to recompense thee: for thou shalt be recompensed in the resurrection of the just.

15 And when one of them that sat at meat with him heard these things, he said unto him, Blessed is he that shall eat bread in the kingdom of God. 16 But he said unto him, A certain man made a great supper; and he bade many: 17 and he sent forth his servants at supper time to say to them that were bidden, Come; for all things are now ready.   18 And they all with one consent began to make excuse.   The first said unto him, I have bought a field, and I must needs go out and see it; I pray thee have me excused.   19 And another said, I have bought five yoke of oxen, and I go to prove them; I pray thee have me excused.   20 And another said, I have married a wife, and therefore I cannot come.   21 And the servant came, and told his lord these things.   Then the master of the house being angry said to his servant, Go out quickly into the streets and lanes of the city, and bring in hither the poor and maimed and blind and lame.   22 And the servant said, Lord, what thou didst command is done, and yet there is room.   23 And the lord said unto the servant, Go out into the highways and hedges, and constrain them to come in, that my house may be filled.   24 For I say unto you, that none of those men that were bidden shall taste of my supper.

Luke pictures our Lord not as a severe ascetic but as a man of human sympathies and social instincts, mingling freely with his fellowmen, worshiping with them in their synagogues and eating with them in their homes.   No domestic scene in the life of our Lord is sketched with more detail than that of the Sabbath feast in the house of a Pharisee.   Jesus is pictured as entering with the guests, noting the ranks of society to which they belong, and taking a leading part in their conversation.   Yet he never for a moment forgot his mission; he seized every opportunity for delivering some needed message.   Here his tones were unusually severe, for he was among persons who, while formally courteous, were in their hearts hostile to him; but he showed to all his unfailing grace, and his desire for their highest good.

While the guests were assembling, Jesus saw a man suffering from disease.   He knew that the Pharisees were watching him and would object to his effecting a cure on the Sabbath Day and he therefore turned to ask whether a cure would be lawful.   When they hesitated to reply, he healed the sufferer and then rebuked their hypocrisy, and

warned against all insincerity in religion by reminding
these formalists that they would not hesitate on the Sabbath to rescue a beast they owned; should they regard it
as sinful to deliver a human being from distress? Jesus
never encouraged breaking the Sabbath law, but he taught
that this law must be interpreted by love.

When the guests were seated and Jesus saw how they
chose for themselves the most desirable places, he took
occasion to rebuke selfish ambition and to give a lesson in
humility. Evidently, when Jesus advised a guest to "sit
down in the lowest place; that when he that hath bidden
thee cometh, he may say to thee, Friend, go up higher,"
he was not merely teaching good manners or worldly wisdom, nor was he advising the pride that masquerades as
humility. He was stating the great law that among his followers true lowliness and conscious unworthiness in the
sight of God are the real conditions of advancement and
honor; "For every one that exalteth himself shall be humbled; and he that humbleth himself shall be exalted."

Then as Jesus looked around upon the company, he took
occasion to teach a lesson in true charity. He told his
host—and there was something of playfulness in his voice
—that in selecting guests one should invite not only the
rich, lest he might be so unfortunate (?) as to receive an
invitation in return, but also the poor, who could not return the favor. Here again, Jesus was not giving merely
rules of social hospitality; he was illustrating the great
spiritual principle of unselfish motives in all deeds of kindness. We are not to confer benefits with a view to receiving benefits in return.

However, Jesus did not mean literally to forbid inviting
rich guests to our homes or to insist that all feasts must be
confined to paupers, but to teach that no service is to be
rendered with the mere hope of personal gain. It is proper
and pleasant, it may be even profitable, to entertain
"friends" or "brethren" or "kinsmen" or "rich neighbors";
but in none of these cases is such entertainment a ground

of merit for they may "bid thee again"; but if kindness is shown to the poor or rich simply for their good and with no thought of personal gain either present or future, the deed will not be without its reward: "for thou shalt be recompensed in the resurrection of the just."

Possibly this reference or some similar reference called forth from one of the guests the exclamation, "Blessed is he that shall eat bread in the kingdom of God." Jesus took the occasion to give the parable of the great supper, by which he illustrated the sinful folly of refusing to accept his offer of salvation. In this story those who were bidden to the feast at first feigned a willingness to come, but subsequently, by their refusal and their flimsy excuses, they showed their complete absorption in selfish interests and their utter disregard for their host. However, their places were filled with other guests, some of them poor and helpless, from their own city; others were vagrants from the highways and hedges beyond. Thus Jesus plainly pictured the refusal by the rulers and Pharisees of his offered salvation and its acceptance, first by publicans and sinners, and then by despised Gentiles.

There was, however, a message for each one who heard the story, and there is a message today for anyone who is rejecting Christ. The Pharisees, by inviting Jesus to dine, pretended to feel some sympathy for him as a prophet, while in their hearts they hated him; and the very man whose pious and sentimental remark about "the kingdom of God" occasioned the parable, was unwilling to accept the invitation to "eat bread in the kingdom of God" which Jesus was presenting.

So there are those today who show an outward respect for Christian truth and talk sentimentally about the Kingdom of God, who, however, are so absorbed in selfish interests and have so little real love for God that they refuse the offer of salvation, while social outcasts and despised heathen gladly accept the invitation to life and divine fellowship and eternal joy.

4. COUNTING THE COST   Ch. 14:25-35

25 Now there went with him great multitudes: and he turned, and said unto them, 26 If any man cometh unto me, and hateth not his own father, and mother, and wife, and children, and brethren, and sisters, yea, and his own life also, he cannot be my disciple. 27 Whosoever doth not bear his own cross, and come after me, cannot be my disciple. 28 For which of you, desiring to build a tower, doth not first sit down and count the cost, whether he have wherewith to complete it? 29 Lest haply, when he hath laid a foundation, and is not able to finish, all that behold begin to mock him, 30 saying, This man began to build, and was not able to finish. 31 Or what king, as he goeth to encounter another king in war, will not sit down first and take counsel whether he is able with ten thousand to meet him that cometh against him with twenty thousand? 32 Or else, while the other is yet a great way off, he sendeth an ambassage, and asketh conditions of peace. 33 So therefore whosoever he be of you that renounceth not all that he hath, he cannot be my disciple. 34 Salt therefore is good: but if even the salt have lost its savor, wherewith shall it be seasoned? 35 It is fit neither for the land nor for the dunghill: men cast it out. He that hath ears to hear, let him hear.

As Jesus was journeying on toward Jerusalem the attending crowds were increasing in size and in excitement. The people imagined that he was about to establish a kingdom in pomp and splendor and power, and in these glories they expected to share. To remove the misunderstanding, Jesus turned to declare the true conditions of discipleship. His followers must expect sacrifice and suffering and be willing to part with all they possessed, even with life itself. When he declared that they must hate their kindred and their own lives, he of course meant that they must love them less than they loved him, regarding them with aversion only insofar as they were opposed to him or stood in the way of his service. To be his disciple one must be willing to "bear his own cross," which was a symbol of suffering and of death; one must continually yield his will to the will of Christ, no matter what hardship or loss might be involved.

Jesus did not wish to discourage men from following him, but warned them first to count the cost. This he illustrated by referring to the folly of laying the foundation for a building without first estimating the entire expense and one's ability to meet it; he also stated, as a further illustration, the rashness of entering a war without first calculating what sacrifices must be made to win. Jesus did not mean that it is better not to begin the Christian life than to begin and fail, but that it is not wise even to begin unless one first realizes that it involves a readiness to renounce everything which the service of Christ may demand. "So therefore whosoever he be of you that renounceth not all that he hath, he cannot be my disciple."

Nothing could be more useless than a worldly and selfish and willful follower of Christ; he is like salt that has lost its savor; he lacks the very essence of discipleship; he can be of no possible service to his Lord.

5. THE PRODIGAL SON   Ch. 15

1 Now all the publicans and sinners were drawing near unto him to hear him. 2 And both the Pharisees and the scribes murmured, saying, This man receiveth sinners, and eateth with them.

3 And he spake unto them this parable, saying, 4 What man of you, having a hundred sheep, and having lost one of them, doth not leave the ninety and nine in the wilderness, and go after that which is lost, until he find it? 5 And when he hath found it, he layeth it on his shoulders, rejoicing. 6 And when he cometh home, he calleth together his friends and his neighbors, saying unto them, Rejoice with me, for I have found my sheep which was lost. 7 I say unto you, that even so there shall be joy in heaven over one sinner that repenteth, more than over ninety and nine righteous persons, who need no repentance.

8 Or what woman having ten pieces of silver, if she lose one piece, doth not light a lamp, and sweep the house, and seek diligently until she find it?   9 And when she hath found it, she calleth together her friends and neighbors, saying, Rejoice with me, for I have found the piece which I had lost.   10 Even so, I say unto you, there is joy in the presence of the angels of God over one sinner that repenteth.

11 And he said, A certain man had two sons: 12 and the younger of them said to his father, Father, give me the portion of thy substance that falleth to me.   And he divided unto them his living.   13 And not many days after, the younger son gathered all together and took his journey into a far country; and there he wasted his substance with riotous living.   14 And when he had spent all, there arose a mighty famine in that country; and he began to be in want. 15 And he went and joined himself to one of the citizens of that country; and he sent him into his fields to feed swine. 16 And he would fain have filled his belly with the husks that the swine did eat: and no man gave unto him.   17 But when he came to himself he said, How many hired servants of my father's have bread enough and to spare, and I perish here with hunger!   18 I will arise and go to my father, and will say unto him, Father, I have sinned against heaven, and in thy sight: 19 I am no more worthy to be called thy son: make me as one of thy hired servants. 20 And he arose, and came to his father.   But while he was yet afar off, his father saw him, and was moved with compassion, and ran, and fell on his neck, and kissed him. 21 And the son said unto him, Father, I have sinned against heaven, and in thy sight: I am no more worthy to be called thy son.   22 But the father said to his servants, Bring forth quickly the best robe, and put it on him; and put a ring on his hand, and shoes on his feet: 23 and bring the fatted calf, and kill it, and let us eat, and make merry: 24 for this my son was dead, and is alive again; he was lost, and is found.   And they began to be merry.   25 Now his elder son was in the field: and as he came and drew nigh to the house, he heard music and dancing.   26 And he called to him one of the servants, and inquired what these things might be.   27 And he said unto him, Thy brother is come;

and thy father hath killed the fatted calf, because he hath received him safe and sound. 28 But he was angry, and would not go in: and his father came out, and entreated him. 29 But he answered and said to his father, Lo, these many years do I serve thee, and I never transgressed a commandment of thine; and yet *thou never gavest me a kid, that I might make merry with my friends: 30 but when this thy son came, who hath devoured thy living with harlots, thou killedst for him the fatted calf. 31 And he said unto him, Son, thou art ever with me, and all that is mine is thine. 32 But it was meet to make merry and be glad: for this thy brother was dead, and is alive* again; *and* was *lost, and is found.*

The precious and matchless parable of the prodigal son belongs naturally to Luke. Its literary charm, its tender beauty, its deep human interest, its breadth of sympathy, its perfect picture of the grace and love of God, all are in peculiar accord with the purpose and genius of this Gospel.

The parable is linked with two others, the teachings of which it includes and completes: the parables of the lost sheep and of the last coin. The occasion of all three parables was the censure passed by the Pharisees upon Jesus because of his association with social outcasts and his cordial welcome to penitent sinners. Jesus rebuked his enemies by showing that it is natural to rejoice in the recovery of a lost sheep or a lost coin or a lost son: much more, then, must God rejoice in the recovery of a lost soul. Evidently they who fail to share his joy must be out of sympathy and fellowship with him.

The first parable reveals the love of God in depicting his compassion for the distress and helplessness of the sinner. The second shows how precious a lost soul is in the sight of the loving God. Both of them picture his yearning and patient effort for the recovery of the sinner and his abounding joy in the restoration of the lost. The statement that "there shall be joy in heaven over one sinner that repenteth, more than over ninety and nine righteous persons,

who need no repentance," is not to be interpreted too literally. It does not mean that God finds more satisfaction in
a repentant sinner than in a sinless saint. Jesus was here
referring definitely to the penitent publicans and to the
self-righteous Pharisees. God did not take delight in the
sins of the former, nor did he regard the state of the latter
as perfect, even taking the Pharisees at their best and regarding them as faithful to the laws of God. Whatever
its motive, morality is always better than lawlessness and
impurity. However, a repentant sinner who understands
the grace and mercy of God is always more pleasing to him
than the Pharisee, proud, critical, and unloving, however
correct he may be in his moral behavior.

This truth is made more plain in the parable of the prodigal son. Here we have perfectly described the experience
of the repentant sinner and also the unsympathetic attitude of the disdainful Pharisee. The first is represented
in the story by the prodigal and the second by the conduct
of his elder brother.

In describing the waywardness of this younger son, Jesus
gave a complete picture of the character and consequences
of sin. Some have thought that the parable of the lost
sheep indicates that sin is due in part to ignorance and folly
and that the parable of the lost coin shows that it may be
occasioned by misfortune or accident. The parable of the
prodigal son, however, shows that it is usually due to willful choice and to a desire for indulgence. Its results are
sketched in appalling colors. We are shown all its disil-
lusion, suffering, slavery, and despair. As a picture of the
inevitable consequences of sin, no touch could be added
to the scene of the prodigal in the far country when he had
spent all, when the famine had arisen, when he had sold
himself to feed swine and was unable to be satisfied even
with the coarse food he was providing for beasts.

Nor is there any more beautiful picture of repentance
than was drawn when the Master described the prodigal
as "he came to himself." His sin had not been mere folly;

it had been madness. He remembered a former time of joy and plenty in his early home. He realized his present desperate need; he resolved to arise and go to his father. Most of all, he saw that his offense had been not only against a loving, earthly parent but against God, and that he was wholly undeserving of fellowship with his father. Repentance is not only sorrow for sin; it is an acknowledgment that the offense has been committed against a holy God; it is a change of heart toward him, and a resolution for a new life which manifests itself in definite action. "He arose, and came to his father."

Strictly speaking, this is the end of the parable of the prodigal son. In another sense the most beautiful part immediately follows. It is a description of the matchless love shown by God to every repentant soul. The father had never ceased to love the prodigal or to hope and yearn for his return. He had been eagerly looking for his wayward son. The first sight of the prodigal filled his heart with compassion; he "ran, and fell on his neck, and kissed him." The prodigal was ready to confess his fault, but the father scarcely heard his words as he commanded the servants to "bring forth quickly the best robe, and put it on him; and put a ring on his hand, and shoes on his feet: and bring the fatted calf, and kill it, and let us eat, and make merry." It is a picture not only of pardon but of complete restoration. It assures the sinner that as he turns to God he will be received into the closest fellowship of a son and heir and that his return will give joy to the heart of God who will regard him as one that "was dead, and is alive again," as one who "was lost, and is found."

The picture of the elder son is exquisitely sketched. It was unquestionably intended to describe the loveless Pharisees who envied the joy of the repentant publicans and sinners. It furthermore brings a message to all persons in every age to whom religion is merely a matter of unwilling obedience and of loveless faithfulness to the laws of God. It depicts souls out of fellowship with God, feeling no real joy in his service and sharing none of his gladness in the salvation of lost souls.

The elder brother knew nothing of the experience of a true son. He was merely a slave. When the prodigal returned he was not watching with his father, he was "in the field"; when he learned that his brother had been welcomed to the home he was filled with anger. He refused to enter the house and when his father came out to entreat him, he accused him of partiality and unkindness. His words described admirably the self-righteousness of the Pharisees: "I never transgressed a commandment of thine"; they also show how little he appreciated his true privileges: "thou never gavest me a kid." The reply of his father intimates the possibilities which he never had appreciated and the privileges which he never had enjoyed: "Son, thou art ever with me, and all that is mine is thine." It had always been possible for the Pharisees to enjoy the grace and mercy and love of God; but to them, religion had been a mere burdensome round of rites and duties. It had given no satisfaction, no gladness, to their hearts. Something of their experience is paralleled even by Christians of the present day. Failing to appreciate the gracious pardon of God and his willingness to supply every spiritual need, forgetting the possibility of living in daily communion and fellowship with him, knowing nothing of his joys in the salvation and repentance of lost souls, they are seeking in their own strength, wearily and joylessly, to do the things that they believe to be right and to obey the commands of God, but their lives are like those of servants, not like the free, joyous, loving experience of true sons.

Possibly the most artistic touch in the parable is its abrupt close. We do not know whether the elder son yielded to the entreaty of his father or not. It was an appeal to the Pharisees; would they accept the grace of God and further his plans for the salvation of the lost, or would they continue to criticize and envy the repentant sinner? Shall we live as servants or as sons?

6. THE UNRIGHTEOUS STEWARD   Ch. 16:1-13

*1 And he said also unto the disciples, There was a cer-
tain rich man, who had a steward; and the same was accused unto him that he was wasting his goods. 2 And he
called him, and said unto him, What is this that I hear of
thee? render the account of thy stewardship; for thou canst
be no longer steward. 3 And the steward said within himself, What shall I do, seeing that my lord taketh away the
stewardship from me? I have not strength to dig; to beg
I am ashamed. 4 I am resolved what to do, that, when I
am put out of the stewardship, they may receive me into
their houses. 5 And calling to him each one of his lord's
debtors, he said to the first, How much owest thou unto
my lord? 6 And he said, A hundred measures of oil. And
he said unto him, Take thy bond, and sit down quickly and
write fifty. 7 Then said he to another, And how much
owest thou? And he said, A hundred measures of wheat.
He saith unto him, Take thy bond, and write fourscore.
8 And his lord commanded the unrighteous steward because he had done wisely: for the sons of this world are for
their own generation wiser than the sons of the light. 9
And I say unto you, Make to yourselves friends by means
of the mammon of unrighteousness; that, when it shall fail,
they may receive you into the eternal tabernacles. 10 He
that is faithful in a very little is faithful also in much: and
he that is unrighteous in a very little is unrighteous also in
much. 11 If therefore ye have not been faithful in the unrighteous mammon, who will commit to your trust the true
riches? 12 And if ye have not been faithful in that which
is another's, who will give you that which is your own?
13 No servant can serve two masters: for either he will hate
the one, and love the other; or else he will hold to one,
and despise the other. Ye cannot serve God and mammon.*

The parable of the unrighteous steward is often regarded as the most perplexing of all the parables of our
Lord. It seems to picture a man who robbed his master
and received his master's praise and was pointed to by

Jesus as an example for his followers; further, it seems to indicate that a place in heaven can be purchased with money. A more careful reading shows that the praise was bestowed, not for dishonesty, but for prudence and foresight, that our Lord would have his followers imitate these good qualities in a bad man, and further that it is possible to use wealth so generously as to secure endless satisfaction and joy.

The story is that of a steward or a trustee who was in charge of the property of a rich landowner. Report had reached his master of the extravagance and dishonesty of this servant. An account was demanded and he was certain to lose his position. However, he seized on the opportunity which was still his so to use the wealth entrusted to him as to secure friends who would provide a home for him when his stewardship had been lost.

The story is intended to illustrate the stewardship of wealth. No money is really owned by a follower of Christ; it is simply entrusted to him to be wisely used in accordance with the will of the Master. For its use a strict account must someday be made. It will, therefore, be the part of wisdom and of prudence so to use that which is now entrusted that in the eternity to come there will be no regret but only joy for the way in which wealth was employed. In the parable the steward was guilty of fraud, as he reduced the debts of those who owed money to his master. He was really using for his future benefit money which was not his own. Of course the Christian is to act with scrupulous honesty; nevertheless, as he benefits others by his generous gifts, he really is using money which belongs to the Lord, but of course he is using it in accordance with the will of his Master.

In applying the parable, Jesus indicated that the right use of money, which seeks the welfare of others, applies not only to the rich but also to the poor, "He that is faithful in a very little is faithful also in much."

Jesus further indicated that the stewardship which all

Christians now enjoy is a training for larger service in the life to come. "If therefore ye have not been faithful in the unrighteous mammon, who will commit to your trust the true riches?"

The motive which inspires fidelity as stewards is that of love. The difficulty with the dishonest servant was that he was disloyal to his master and was really seeking to serve himself. One who really loves his Lord will be faithful in the use of that which is entrusted to him. The danger of stewards is that of divided allegiance. "No servant can serve two masters: for either he will hate the one, and love the other; or else he will hold to one, and despise the other. Ye cannot serve God and mammon."

7. THE RICH MAN AND LAZARUS   Ch. 16:14-31

14 And the Pharisees, who were lovers of money, heard all these things; and they scoffed at him. 15 And he said unto them, Ye are they that justify yourselves in the sight of men; but God knoweth your hearts: for that which is exalted among men is an abomination in the sight of God. 16 The law and the prophets were until John: from that time the gospel of the kingdom of God is preached, and every man entereth violently into it. 17 But it is easier for heaven and earth to pass away, than for one tittle of the law to fall.

18 Every one that putteth away his wife, and marrieth another, committeth adultery: and he that marrieth one that is put away from a husband committeth adultery.

19 Now there was a certain rich man, and he was clothed in purple and fine linen, faring sumptuously every day: 20 and a certain beggar named Lazarus was laid at his gate, full of sores, 21 and desiring to be fed with the crumbs that fell from the rich man's table; yea, even the dogs came and licked his sores. 22 And it came to pass, that the beggar died, and that he was carried away by the angels into Abraham's bosom: and the rich man also died, and was buried. 23 And in Hades he lifted up his eyes, being in torments, and seeth Abraham afar off, and Lazarus

in his bosom.   24 And he cried and said, Father Abraham,
have mercy on me, and send Lazarus, that he may dip the
tip of his finger in water, and cool my tongue; for I am in
anguish in this flame.   25 But Abraham said, Son, remem-
ber that thou in thy lifetime receivedst thy good things,
and Lazarus in like manner evil things: but now here he
is comforted, and thou art in anguish.   26 And besides
all this, between us and you there is a great gulf fixed, that
they that would pass from hence to you may not be able,
and that none may cross over from thence to us.   27 And
he said, I pray thee therefore, father, that thou wouldst
send him to my father's house;   28 for I have five brethren;
that he may testify unto them, lest they also come into this
place of torment.   29 But Abraham saith, They have
Moses and the prophets; let them hear them.   30 And he
said, Nay, father Abraham: but if one go to them from the
dead, they will repent.   31 And he said unto him, If they
hear not Moses and the prophets, neither will they be per-
suaded, if one rise from the dead.

The parable of the unrighteous steward was intended to
teach the possibility of the right use of wealth.   The parable of the rich man and Lazarus was designed by our
Lord to warn his hearers against its abuse.   Between the
two parables Luke records a number of sayings, the connection of which cannot be determined beyond question
but they seem to have been quoted by him as an introduc-
tion to the second of these parables, vs. 14-18.   They
contain a rebuke of the Pharisees for their besetting sin of
avarice and a statement of the unfailing authority of the
law, the letter of which they observed, but by the spirit
of which they were condemned.

These Pharisees ridiculed our Lord for teaching the absolute necessity of generosity and benevolence and the unselfish use of wealth.   Our Lord replied that while these
enemies of his might receive the approval of men, God
read their hearts and many who received human praise
were but abominable in the sight of God.   Jesus stated that
while the gospel message did differ from the law and while

many were eagerly accepting its blessed privileges, it did not set aside the law, but only showed how its demands could be met. When he stated that "one tittle of the law" could not fall, he referred to the minute projections which distinguish Hebrew letters, and meant that the slightest requirement of the law was sacred and abiding. He illustrated these truths by a reference to the Seventh Commandment, and insisted that adultery did not lose its sinful character because of any interpretation of the law such as was put upon it by those who were teaching lax theories of divorce. It was still sinful, even when justified by civil enactment. Thus Jesus was reminding the Pharisees that the law might abide and be sacred even when legalists who observed its letter were condemned.

In the parable of the rich man and Lazarus, Jesus by no means taught that it is sinful to be rich or that the poor are all saved. He did mean to suggest the solemn peril of the selfish use of wealth. The sin of the rich man did not consist either in the way in which he had acquired his wealth or in the fact that he possessed it, nor yet in any breach of moral law, but in the plain statement that while he was living in selfish luxury, one who was in sore need lay unrelieved at his door. The rich man is commonly called Dives, the Latin name for "a man of wealth." Lazarus is the only person in any parable of our Lord to whom a special name is given. It is just possible that the name was intended to indicate the character of the man as one who trusted in the help of God. The story shows not only the contrast between the two men in the present life but the still greater contrast in the life that is to come. The picture is not to be interpreted with absurd literalness; but it does contain a serious warning, and behind its figures of speech are solemn realities. It does indicate the remorse and the anguish which forever may be experienced by those who upon earth make only a selfish and heartless use of wealth and position and opportunity. The consequences are shown to be as endless as they are distressing.

A time of reversal is to come, a time of judgment and retribution.

It is evident that Jesus was especially warning the Pharisees; the rich man was a representative of this class who were notorious for their scrupulous observance of law and for their lives of selfish luxury and indulgence. The rich man addressed Abraham as his father, and was addressed by Abraham as his son. This is an intimation that the most orthodox Jew might be lost and come at last to a place of torment.

As the rich man requested that a special warning be sent to his brethren, it is possible that he was expressing his sympathy; more probably he was making an excuse and intimating that had he been given more light he would not have so grievously sinned. The reply is, therefore, very significant, "If they hear not Moses and the prophets, neither will they be persuaded, if one rise from the dead." It was an answer to the Pharisees for their continual request that Jesus should give some striking sign by which they would recognize his divine mission. Our Lord indicated that a striking prodigy or miracle will never convince those whose hearts are not right with God. He declared further that the Law and the Prophets plainly set forth the divine requirement of love. One who fails to observe this supreme law in the use of wealth and of all similar opportunities and privileges is under condemnation and is in peril of eternal pain.

8. WARNINGS TO THE DISCIPLES   Ch. 17:1-10

1 And he said unto his disciples, It is impossible but that occasions of stumbling should come; but woe unto him, through whom they come! 2 It were well for him if a millstone were hanged about his neck, and he were thrown into the sea, rather than that he should cause one of these little ones to stumble. 3 Take heed to yourselves: if thy brother sin, rebuke him; and if he repent, forgive him 4 And if he sin against thee seven times in the day, and seven times turn again to thee, saying, I repent; thou shalt forgive him.

5 And the apostles said unto the Lord, Increase our faith. 6 And the Lord said, If ye had faith as a grain of mustard seed, ye would say unto this sycamine tree, Be thou rooted up, and be thou planted in the sea; and it would obey you. 7 But who is there of you, having a servant plowing or keeping sheep, that will say unto him, when he is come in from the field, Come straightway and sit down to meat; 8 and will not rather say unto him, Make ready wherewith I may sup, and gird thyself, and serve me, till I have eaten and drunken; and afterward thou shalt eat and drink? 9 Doth he thank the servant because he did the things that were commanded? 10 Even so ye also, when ye shall have done all the things that are commanded you, say, We are unprofitable servants; we have done that which it was our duty to do.

After the severe rebuke given by our Lord to the Pharisees in view of their selfish abuse of wealth, Luke records four apparently disconnected warnings given to the disciples. The first, vs. 1-2, was against the peril of causing others to sin. In this world of selfishness and of evil desire, our Lord declared, it is inevitable that such offenses will be committed, but he pronounced a solemn woe upon anyone guilty of this grievous fault. He declared that it would be better for such a person to be drowned in the sea rather than to allow himself to become guilty of such a sin. The death of the body is far preferable to the death of the soul. Therefore, Jesus warned his followers lest they might lead anyone astray or cause anyone to stumble, particularly such as might be in years or experience less mature than themselves. No age of the church has been without its tragedies in which power and influence have been selfishly used to mislead innocent souls, and no life is beyond the possibility of placing stumbling blocks in the paths of others or of exerting even unconsciously influences which may cause others to sin.

In the second warning, here recorded by Luke, vs. 3-4,

Jesus guarded his disciples against lack of charity. He intimated that his followers should be ready always to forgive. He did not advise weakness or indifference to sin; he suggested that a brother who offends may deserve and should receive a rebuke. It is proper that he should be made to feel and to appreciate his fault. Nevertheless, he is to be treated with kindness and if he sincerely repents, he is to be forgiven freely. Even if he repeats his sin with frequency, no revenge is to be harbored against him. Jesus suggested that his offense might be committed, "seven times in the day," by which he meant an unlimited repetition of the fault; even then if his repentance is sincere, forgiveness must not be denied.

The twelve apostles, probably in view of the particular responsibilities which rested upon them, turned to their Master with the petition, "Lord, Increase our faith." The reply contains a solemn warning, that there is need of such increase, a far greater need than the petitioners realized. Nevertheless, there is also in the reply a gracious promise. They were lovingly rebuked for their lack of faith, but they were reassured by a revelation of the unlimited power of faith. Our Lord asserted that if they possessed real faith, even so small as to be compared with one of the most minute objects in nature, namely, "a grain of mustard seed," they would be able by a word to accomplish incredible results, speaking figuratively, to cause a mulberry tree to be rooted up and planted in the sea. The followers of Christ today need to be reminded of these same truths, namely, of the narrow limits to which faith is usually confined and the unbounded possibilities which might be theirs if their trust in Christ were more simple, more unquestioning, and more real. Vs. 5-6.

The fourth warning here recorded rebukes the pride, the self-confidence, the desire for praise and for reward, which too often characterize the followers of Christ. Jesus taught that no human works, however perfect, give a claim upon God, but are merely the fulfillment of duty. This truth is set forth in the parable of the unprofitable servant. Vs. 7-10. The word "unprofitable" does not mean worthless, but merely implies one who has not gone beyond his obligation or duty. The picture is that of a slave who has labored faithfully in the field and who when the day is done merely continues in the evening to accomplish his appointed tasks. His master does not show any particular gratitude to one who is doing that which he is expected to do. He does not especially praise his servant for doing the things commanded.

So in the case of every man, a life of the most blameless holiness and love is no more than God requires. It is no ground on which a special reward can be demanded. It is no reason for expecting promotion or praise. To do less would be to neglect an obvious duty, and to do more than duty is impossible. While this parable rebukes all pride and cuts off all merit of works, it is nevertheless true that in other parables our Lord taught the certainty of rewards which he is to grant faithful servants not as a matter of compulsion on his part but in loving grace.

C. THE LAST STAGES Chs. 17:11 to 19:28

1. THE SAMARITAN LEPER   Ch. 17:11-19

11 And it came to pass, as they were on the way to Jerusalem, that he was passing along the borders of Samaria and Galilee. 12 And as he entered into a certain village, there met him ten men that were lepers, who stood afar off: 13 and they lifted up their voices, saying, Jesus, Master, have mercy on us. 14 And when he saw them, he said unto them, Go and show yourselves unto the priests. And it came to pass, as they went, they were cleansed. 15 And one of them, when he saw that he was healed, turned back, with a loud voice glorifying God; 16 and he fell upon his face at his feet, giving him thanks: and he was a Samaritan. 17 And Jesus answering said, Were not the ten cleansed? but where are the nine? 18 Were there none found that returned to give glory to God, save

*this stranger? 19 And he said unto him, Arise, and go thy
way: thy faith hath made thee whole.*

The healing of ten lepers begins the closing cycle of incidents which marked the last journeys of Jesus toward
Jerusalem. It is quite like Luke to record this miracle,
for the chief feature of the story is the gratitude and the
blessing of a Samaritan, and Luke is ever describing Jesus
as the Savior, not only of the Jews, but of the whole human
race.

There is in this miracle, however, another peculiar feature; before the lepers were cured they were bidden to go
to the priests and to declare that the cure had been effected, and "as they went, they were cleansed." It required no little faith to start upon that journey; but they
started, and their faith was rewarded. So today when men
come to Christ with their request to be delivered from sin,
he commands them to act as though the petition already
were granted, and with the act of faith comes the answer
to the prayer. The command of Christ involved a promise and upon his promises we can always rely with absolute safety.

One of the lepers "when he saw that he was healed,
turned back, with a loud voice glorifying God; and he fell
upon his face at his feet, giving him thanks: and he was
a Samaritan." There is something of surprise and sad-
ness in the question of Jesus as he saw this restored leper
lying at his feet: "Were not the ten cleansed? but where
are the nine? Were there none found that returned to
give glory to God, save this stranger?" It is always surprising to find that ingratitude is so common among men.
Nine out of ten probably will forget every favor they may
receive. It is rare that one realizes and acknowledges his
debt. Still more sad it is to see so few among those who
have accepted the salvation of Christ showing real gratitude in lives of joyous service and declaring that they are
constrained to live for him who died for them.

There was, however, for the Samaritan a glad word of blessed assurance and promise: "Arise, and go thy way: thy faith hath made thee whole." Jesus either meant to call attention to the means of the cure, namely faith in himself, and so to nurture that germ of new life into fuller trust in his divine person; or he meant to say that the faith which first had secured the healing of the body and which was manifested in the man's return and his gratitude now secured for him the salvation of his soul. In either case we are reminded that gratitude is often found where least it is expected; that it is always pleasing to our Lord; and that it is the certain condition of further blessedness and joy.

2. THE COMING OF THE KINGDOM   Ch. 17:20-37

20 And being asked by the Pharisees, when the kingdom of God cometh, he answered them and said, The kingdom of God cometh not with observation: 21 neither shall they say, Lo, here! or, There! for lo, the kingdom of God is within you.

22 And he said unto the disciples, The days will come, when ye shall desire to see one of the days of the Son of man, and ye shall not see it. 23 And they shall say to you, Lo, there! Lo, here! go not away, nor follow after them: 24 for as the lightning, when it lighteneth out of the one part under the heaven, shineth unto the other part under heaven; so shall the Son of man be in his day. 25 But first must he suffer many things and be rejected of this generation. 26 And as it came to pass in the days of Noah, even so shall it be also in the days of the Son of man. 27 They ate, they drank, they married, they were given in marriage, until the day that Noah entered into the ark, and the flood came, and destroyed them all. 28 Likewise even as it came to pass in the days of Lot; they ate, they drank, they bought, they sold, they planted, they builded; 29 but in the day that Lot went out from Sodom it rained fire and brimstone from heaven, and destroyed them all: 30 after the same manner shall it be in the day that the

*Son of man is revealed. 31 In that day, he that shall be
on the housetop, and his goods in the house, let him not
go down to take them away: and let him that is in the field
likewise not return back. 32 Remember Lot's wife. 33
Whosoever shall seek to gain his life shall lose it: but whosoever shall lose his life shall preserve it. 34 I say unto
you, In that night there shall be two men on one bed; the
one shall be taken, and the other shall be left. 35 There
shall be two women grinding together; the one shall be
taken, and the other shall be left. 37 And they answering
say unto him, Where, Lord?   And he said unto them,
Where the body is, thither will the eagles also be gathered
together.*

Either in mere curiosity or with a desire for debate the
Pharisees approached Jesus with a question as to when the
Kingdom of God would come. Jesus replied that it would
not come in such manner as they were expecting, nor
would it appear as a visible development of which they
could say, It is "here," or "there," for, in the person of
the King, it was already "in the midst" of them and they
did not recognize it. Thus when Jesus said, "The kingdom of God is within you," he could hardly have meant
that it was in the hearts of the hostile and godless Pharisees; nor is the familiar and beautiful conception of the
Kingdom as "a reign of God in human hearts" thus expressed in the New Testament.   Jesus more probably
meant that in his own person and work the Kingdom was
present. The essence of this Kingdom is always spiritual
and consists in "righteousness and peace and joy." It is
to have, however, a future, visible manifestation at the appearing of the King. The question as to the time and
manner of its coming is not to be asked either to satisfy
mere curiosity or to arouse controversy; for men of the
world, like the Pharisees, the important fact is that Christ,
who is ever a divine and spiritual presence, is to be accepted as Master and Lord; his service always issues in
new and more blessed life.

To the disciples, who trusted him, it was possible for Jesus to answer more in detail the question as to the coming of the Kingdom which is to be inaugurated in splendor on his return. He told them that they must expect first a period of long delay in which their weary hearts would often yearn for a single day of the coming glory and that many deceivers would point to places and times of his appearing. However, when he did appear it would be with suddenness and unmistakable splendor, like the lightning which in an instant flashes across the whole heaven.

First, however, this King who will then come to reign must suffer and die; and the world which has rejected him will not be expecting his return. When he does reappear the race will be in the same carnal security, careless and indifferent and absorbed in the usual occupations of life, as were the men in the time of the Flood or the inhabitants of Sodom in the day of its doom.

On the contrary, those who are to share the glories of the Kingdom must be looking for their returning Lord. Their proper attitude of mind is pictured by a series of acts; one who is on the housetop is not to come down to secure his goods; one in the field will not return to his house; they will not look backward, but will go forth eagerly to meet their Master in whom alone is their safety and their hope.

It will be a time of certain separations even for those most closely related; for example, two men will be sleeping in the same bed: one will be taken and the other left; two women will be sharing a common task: one will be taken and the other left. This word "taken" is the same beautiful expression found in the Gospel of John, where is recorded Jesus' promise, "I . . . will receive you unto myself." It speaks of the peace and joy and blessedness of those who gladly welcome the coming of the King.

At a question from the disciples as to where such judgment would take place, our Lord replied that it will be universal; wherever the carcass is, there the vultures will be gathered together; where there is corruption and sin, there will judgment fall.   Yet this judgment will be followed by the splendor of the Kingdom for which the followers of Christ watch and pray and labor and wait.

3. THE UNRIGHTEOUS JUDGE   Ch. 18:1-8

1 And he spake a parable unto them to the end that they ought always to pray, and not to faint; 2 saying, There was in a city a judge, who feared not God, and regarded not man: 3 and there was a widow in that city; and she came oft unto him, saying, Avenge me of mine adversary. 4 And he would not for a while: but afterward he said within himself, Though I fear not God, nor regard man; 5 yet because this widow troubleth me, I will avenge her, lest she wear me out by her continual coming. 6 And the Lord said, Hear what the unrighteous judge saith. 7 And shall not God avenge his elect, that cry to him day and night, and yet he is longsuffering over them? 8 I say unto you, that he will avenge them speedily. Nevertheless, when the Son of man cometh, shall he find faith on the earth?

The parable of the unrighteous judge was spoken in direct connection with the instructions given to the disciples by their Master in reference to his return.   It is, therefore, not merely a general exhortation to prayer, but to prayer for the coming of Christ, and more specifically to the confident expectation of this event and of the blessedness which will result.

It does, however, contain a very real encouragement to prayer and for all Christians and at all times.   The argument is this: If an unjust judge, who has regard for neither God nor man, would yield to the importunity of an unknown widow because he feared that she would annoy him by her repeated requests, how much more will a just God be ready to reward the persevering petitions of his own loved ones who cry to him continually!

In spite of all the mysteries involved, the followers of
Christ should pray without ceasing, and with all importu-
nity should present their petitions with the assurance that
God does hear and in his own time will answer.

The particular force of the parable relates, however, to
the church in her conscious weakness and loneliness, in
the age between the crucifixion and the Second Coming of
Christ.   Jesus had just given a description of the world at
the time of his return.   He had pictured the prevalent
carelessness and indifference and absorption in earthly
pursuits, and now he wished to encourage his followers to
be patient and to turn their hearts toward him in expectation and prayer.   The widow in the parable is not so much
requesting that an enemy should be punished as that she
should be given her property rights for which she is applying to the judge.   So the church is pictured, not simply as
crying for vengeance upon persecutors, but rather, as longing and praying for all those blessings which have been
promised and which will be received at the coming of the
Lord.

There is a deep mournfulness in the question which
Jesus asked after expounding his parable: "Nevertheless,
when the Son of man cometh, shall he find faith on the
earth?"   Will there still remain those who are true to
Christ, who love him and are looking for his return?   The
very question is a solemn warning against the peril of being overcome by prevalent worldliness and unbelief.
However, the answer is not to be given in a spirit of hopelessness and pessimism and despair.   The church will always have her adversaries, she ever will need to be on her
guard against the worldly influences by which she is surrounded.   However, there will always be those who are
true to him who has chosen them out of the world, and
after long days of weary waiting, their hearts will rejoice
in the sudden appearing of the righteous judge who will
bring with him glories brighter than they have dared to
ask or to expect.

4. THE PHARISEE AND THE PUBLICAN   Ch. 18:9-14

9 And he spake also this parable unto certain who trusted in themselves that they were righteous, and set all others at nought: 10 Two men went up into the temple to pray; the one a Pharisee, and the other a publican. 11 The Pharisee stood and prayed thus with himself, God, I thank thee, that I am not as the rest of men, extortioners, unjust, adulterers, or even as this publican. 12 I fast twice in the week; I give tithes of all that I get. 13 But the publican, standing afar off, would not lift up so much as his eyes unto heaven, but smote his breast, saying, God, be thou merciful to me a sinner. 14 I say unto you, This man went down to his house justified rather than the other: for every one that exalteth himself shall be humbled; but he that humbleth himself shall be exalted.

The parable of the Pharisee and the publican was designed to teach humility not only in prayer but in every estimate of oneself and in every approach to God. It further contrasts the religion of form with the religion of the heart. It shows that the way of penitence is the only path to pardon and to peace.

It was not addressed to Pharisees, although it is a severe exposure of the hypocrisy and self-deception of Pharisaism of every kind. Jesus seems rather to have had in mind some of his own followers; but whatever their class or professon, Pharisees have their representatives in every age and land. They are described as "certain who trusted in themselves that they were righteous, and set all others at nought."

Such, indeed, was the Pharisee here described. He had gone up to the Temple to pray; he stood in some conspicuous place; he addressed God but he uttered no true prayer. He began by saying, "I thank thee," but he really addressed himself. He rejoiced that in comparison with other men he formed a class by himself. He declared all others to be "extortioners, unjust, adulterers," and as an example of such sinners he pointed to the poor publican at whom he was looking instead of looking to God. He boasted that he had refrained from the sins of other men and also that he had performed more good deeds than the law required. Moses instituted no obligatory fast; but the Pharisee fasted twice in the week. Moses exempted certain things from the tithe; the Pharisee had tithed his entire income. In other words, he had been better than God required. He had placed God under obligation to him. How little does such a man understand the real holiness of God, of the requirements of that law the essence of which is love!

In striking contrast the publican was standing at a respectful distance from the supposed saint whose formal piety had impressed his fellowmen. He did not venture even to look toward heaven. He beat upon his breast, as a sign of mourning, and cried out in anguish, "God, be thou merciful to me a sinner." The original words seem to imply that he regarded himself as likewise distinct from all other men. He felt and confessed himself to be "the sinner"; but as he acknowledged his guilt and turned to God in penitence, he was accepted as righteous in the sight of God and received pardon and peace.

There can be no misunderstanding as to the lesson which the Master wished to impress. "This man went down to his house justified rather than the other." A sense of guilt and a yearning for pardon and a cry to God for mercy—this is the very beginning of a new life; and however far one may progress in holiness, there is ever need of similar humility. The nearer one is to God, the more conscious is he of his sinfulness and the less likely to boast of his own moral attainments. The more one acknowledges his unworthiness, the better is he prepared to serve his Master and his fellowmen. The pride of Pharisaism on the part of nations, as well as in the lives of individuals, stands in the way of helpfulness and brotherhood and the favor of God. What is needed today is universal repentance, a manifestation of the humble and the contrite heart: "For every one that exalteth himself shall be humbled; but he that humbleth himself shall be exalted."

5. JESUS RECEIVING LITTLE CHILDREN
Ch. 18:15-17

15 And they were bringing unto him also their babes, that he should touch them: but when the disciples saw it, they rebuked them. 16 But Jesus called them unto him, saying, Suffer the little children to come unto me, and forbid them not: for to such belongeth the kingdom of God. 17 Verily I say unto you, Whosoever shall not receive the kingdom of God as a little child, he shall in no wise enter therein.

This charming picture of Jesus blessing little children is sketched by Matthew and Mark as well as by Luke. Its attractiveness has given it a place on the canvas of many an artist. Its symbolic message is being accepted by the modern church: "They were bringing unto him also their babes." The parents were probably carrying these children in their arms. They realized that not only the lepers and the infirm needed the touch of Christ, but that the power of the Master would bring blessing to the children as well.

This touch may properly picture that personal relation and spiritual contact with Christ which today, with equal eagerness, should be sought for their children by all parents. "When the disciples saw it, they rebuked them." They seemed to have felt that children were too insignificant to be allowed to interfere with the work or to demand the attention of Christ. At this present time there are many things which tend to keep parents from bringing their children to the Master: custom and carelessness and indifference and fear and diffidence; even friends seem to play the part of those "disciples" and to conspire to prevent and rebuke those who really long to see their children brought into a sanctifying relationship to the Lord. No problem of today is more important than the removal of such barriers and obstacles. The Christian nurture of children is the supreme need of the times. "But Jesus called them unto him, saying, Suffer the little children to come unto me, and forbid them not." This reply of the Master has cast an unfading halo about the faces of all children. Their innocence and their need made a special appeal to the Master. Should it not affect us in like manner, and should we not feel that no work is more Christlike and none more blessed than the care of these little ones whom our Lord so truly loves? We are the real servants of our Master only as we feel the appeal of childhood and as we seek to supply to children their physical and mental and spiritual needs.

"For to such belongeth the kingdom of God." It is theirs by right. It belongs not only to those particular children whom Jesus was then blessing, not only to all children in general, but to all of whatever age who are childlike in their trust and dependence and purity. All those who are entrusted to the care of the Master and who accept his saving grace will find a place in his Kingdom.

As the crowds gazed in wonder and sympathy on this tender scene, our Lord added this word of warning, "Whosoever shall not receive the kingdom of God as a little child, he shall in no wise enter therein."

6. THE RICH RULER   Ch. 18:18-30

18 And a certain ruler asked him, saying, Good Teacher, what shall I do to inherit eternal life? 19 And Jesus said unto him, Why callest thou me good? none is good, save one, even God. 20 Thou knowest the commandments, Do not commit adultery, Do not kill, Do not steal, Do not bear false witness, Honor thy father and mother. 21 And he said, All these things have I observed from my youth up. 22 And when Jesus heard it, he said unto him, One thing thou lackest yet: sell all that thou hast, and distribute unto the poor, and thou shalt have treasure in heaven: and come, follow me. 23 But when he heard these things, he became exceeding sorrowful; for he was very rich. 24 And Jesus seeing him said, How hardly shall they that have riches enter into the kingdom of God! 25 For it is easier for a camel to enter in through a needle's eye, than for a rich man to enter into the kingdom of God. 26 And they that heard it said, Then who can be saved? 27 But he said, The things which are impossible with men are possible with God. 28 And Peter said, Lo, we have left our own, and followed thee. 29 And he said unto them, Verily I say unto you, There is no man that hath left house, or wife, or brethren, or parents, or children, for the kingdom of God's sake, 30 who shall not receive manifold more in this time, and in the world to come eternal life.

In contrast with the penitent publican and with the loving trust of little children which Luke has been depicting, there steps upon the scene a young man, rich, upright, morally earnest, but apparently unconscious of the sinful greed which threatened his soul and of that trust in riches which might prevent his entering the Kingdom of God. In spite of his riches, his youth, his position, and his power, his heart was not satisfied. He had come to Jesus with the question, "Good Teacher, what shall I do to inherit eternal life?" Jesus at once rebuked him, "Why callest thou me good? none is good, save one, even God." By this reproof Jesus was neither defending his own divinity nor denying his sinlessness. He wished to convince the young man of his moral need. He intimated that the thoughtless use of the word "good," addressed to one whom he regarded as a human teacher, was a proof that the young man had a superficial view of goodness. Judged by a divine standard, the young inquirer could not claim to be good, nor can any man regard himself as righteous in the light of divine holiness.

In order to awaken the conscience and to disturb the complacent self-righteousness of the young inquirer, Jesus now tested him in the light of the commandments in which God has revealed his holy will. The youth at once replied, "All these things have I observed from my youth up." Jesus now applied the deep probe which showed that the man had never observed the spirit of the law, even though he believed that he had kept the letter. Jesus disclosed the real selfishness of the heart as he proposed a supreme test: "One thing thou lackest yet: sell all that thou hast, and distribute unto the poor, and thou shalt have treasure in heaven: and come, follow me." In this sentence Jesus convicted the man of having broken the law, the essential requirement of which was to love his neighbor as himself.

Jesus promised an eternal recompense for sacrifice, and he offers by his personal companionship the influence and power which will make the keeping of the law more possible and complete. No one can claim to be righteous when judged by the commandments as interpreted by Christ. Our only hope is to come to him for guidance and help. He will lay bare the secret selfishness of our hearts, and will develop the spirit of love and service which forms the essence of eternal life, and in heaven he will ultimately recompense his followers for every loss.

Jesus does not demand that all who obey him must literally leave their worldly possessions. In his command to the rich ruler he was dealing with a specific case. He does demand, however, that each one shall give up anything which prevents open, honest discipleship and fellowship with himself. In the case of this inquirer the obstacle was his wealth. It was impossible for him to retain it and yet to follow Christ. The Master made plain to him that his goodness had been superficial and inadequate. He showed him that love of money was the canker which had been hidden in his soul. He plainly placed before him the necessity of choosing between his wealth and the eternal life which Jesus alone can give. No wonder that when the young ruler heard the stern requirements and realized for the first time that he was controlled by his wealth, "He became exceeding sorrowful; for he was very rich." He kept his wealth and he rejected his Savior. He saw the possibility of eternal life, but he was not willing to pay the price. He retained his riches, but he lost his soul.

As Jesus looked upon him in pity, he startled his disciples by the statement of a truth which the scene had illustrated: "How hardly shall they that have riches enter into the kingdom of God." This was particularly surprising to the Jews. They imagined that wealth was a positive proof of divine favor. What then did Jesus mean? He did not intend to teach that wealth is sinful or that private property is a social wrong. He meant that riches may possibly keep their possessor from Christian discipleship and that one who seeks to satisfy himself with such wealth as keeps him from Christ can never enter the Kingdom of God. Jesus even added a pardonable hyperbole: "It is easier for a camel to enter in through a needle's eye, than for a rich man to enter into the kingdom of God." One who would enter that Kingdom must become as a little child; he must abandon all trust in self, and be willing to sacrifice anything which prevents his becoming an obedient servant of Christ. When the disciples heard this, they were astonished and asked, "Then who can be saved?" Our Lord replied, "The things which are impossible with men are possible with God." It does require resolution and decision and sacrifice, but God is ready to supply all needed grace. His spirit can strengthen those who turn to him in their conscious need and with a real desire for a higher life.

As the rich man moved away sorrowfully in his costly robes, Peter looked upon him with apparent scorn, and turned to Jesus with the self-complacent remark, "Lo, we have left our own, and followed thee." The reply of Jesus was not intended to encourage men to follow him in hope of gain. His salvation is a matter of grace. We are not to think that by any sacrifice of worldly goods we can purchase eternal life. However, the tender words of the Master do remind us that a rich recompence will be received for all that we may surrender in becoming his disciples. Even in this present time one receives a hundredfold reward, not in literal kind but in experiences which now satisfy the soul and "in the world to come eternal life."

7. JESUS AGAIN FORETELLING HIS DEATH
Ch. 18:31-34

31 And he took unto him the twelve, and said unto them, Behold, we go up to Jerusalem, and all the things that are written through the prophets shall be accomplished unto the Son of man. 32 For he shall be delivered up unto the Gentiles, and shall be mocked, and shamefully treated, and spit upon: 33 and they shall scourge and kill him: and the third day he shall rise again. 34 And they understood none of these things; and this saying was hid from them, and they perceived not the things that were said.

As Jesus moved southward through Perea, nearing the end of his last journey to Jerusalem, he was accompanied by admiring multitudes, but his own heart was heavy with the knowledge of the suffering that awaited him and he clearly saw before him the outline of the cross. Many of his followers today share his experience in part; even in surroundings which all observers envy, their hearts are crushed by secret sorrows and by the knowledge of approaching pain.

Those who then were nearest to him were quite unconscious of his thoughts or his need of sympathy. Then for the third time Jesus clearly predicted his approaching death. He declared that his sufferings were to be in accordance with written prophecy and now more clearly than ever he described the details of all the anguish he must endure. He was to be "delivered up unto the Gentiles" and therefore to be crucified, and with all the sickening accompaniments of mockery and spitting and scourging, he was to be killed.

Such a clear vision of what awaited him enhances for us the revelation of his matchless heroism as he moved forward with unfaltering tread, giving an inspiring example to each one who may be asked to take up the cross and come after him.

Such knowledge reveals one who consciously was more than man, such a confidence that he was fulfilling the prophecies of the inspired Scriptures shows that he regarded himself as the Savior of the world. Such a willingness to suffer demonstrates the fact that he believed his atoning death to be an essential part of his redeeming work.

The grave, however, was by no means his goal. With absolute definiteness he declared that on the third day he would rise again. This vision of triumph was in part the explanation of his courage. It was in virtue of such a resurrection victory that he could be the Savior of mankind.

His disciples, however, understood none of these things; with threefold emphasis Luke describes their dullness of apprehension. They did not believe that his death was necessary and for them the resurrection was not even a dream. Their lack of expectation only made them more credible witnesses of that resurrection when it did occur. However, would not a clearer vision, unclouded by false notions of their own, have enabled them to understand their Master and to bring some cheer to his lonely soul; and does he not always desire his followers to accept his predictions with implicit faith and to rest upon his promises with triumphant hope?

8. THE BLIND MAN AT JERICHO   Ch. 18:35-43

35 And it came to pass, as he drew nigh unto Jericho, a certain blind man sat by the way side begging: 36 and

*hearing a multitude going by, he inquired what this meant.
37 And they told him, that Jesus of Nazareth passeth by.
38 And he cried, saying, Jesus, thou son of David, have
mercy on me. 39 And they that went before rebuked him,
that he should hold his peace: but he cried out the more
a great deal, Thou son of David, have mercy on me. 40
And Jesus stood, and commanded him to be brought unto
him: and when he was come near, he asked him, 41 What
wilt thou that I should do unto thee? And he said, Lord,
that I may receive my sight. 42 And Jesus said unto him,
Receive thy sight: thy faith hath made thee whole. 43
And immediately he received his sight, and followed him,
glorifying God: and all the people, when they saw it, gave
praise unto God.*

As for the last time Jesus was journeying through
Jericho, he healed a blind man whom Mark in his record
named Bartimaeus. This miracle was a proof of divine
power and an expression of human sympathy, but it was
also a parable of the ability which Jesus alone has of giving sight to the morally blind and of imparting that spiritual vision which is absolutely necessary if men are to
live in right relations to one another and to God. In
certain minor details Luke's account differs from those of
Matthew and Mark. The former mentions two blind men
and agrees with Mark in stating that the miracle occurred
as Jesus was leaving the city. Possibly Mark and Luke
refer to the best known of the two men and Luke may
designate the older of the two towns which bore the name
of Jericho. All agree, however, in picturing the pitiful
condition of the helpless man who because of his blindness
was reduced to beggary and was a true symbol of the mis-
ery to which one is brought by the lack of spiritual sight.

Then there is the picture of the obstacles to be overcome, of the doubts and difficulties that lie in the way of
those who seek to come under the healing influence of our
Lord. "They that went before rebuked him, that he
should hold his peace." Often do those who yearn for

light and healing hear words which dishearten and sug-
gestions which lead to hopelessness and despair!

Again there is the picture of eager determination and of
unshaken faith. "He cried out the more a great deal,
Thou son of David, have mercy on me." He had been
told that "Jesus of Nazareth" was passing by. He, however, called him "Jesus, thou son of David." He recognized the Prophet of Nazareth as the promised Messiah,
the Savior of the world, and when rebuked for crying to
him for mercy, he continued steadfast in his faith and his
confident trust that Jesus would sympathize and heal.

Lastly, there is the picture of complete relief. The blind
man was not disappointed. Jesus said unto him, "Receive
thy sight: thy faith hath made thee whole." How many
likewise have found Christ able and willing to give them
spiritual vision! Their eyes have been opened to behold
things unseen and eternal, and they have been enabled to
follow the Master with joyful footsteps as they journey
toward the celestial city where they will see the King in
his beauty and will be like him when they "see him even
as he is."

Such miracles of grace rejoice the hearts not only of
those who are healed; they occasion gratitude and joy to
countless others also as they are assured of the sympathy
and grace and divine power of the Savior. As Luke here
states, "All the people, when they saw it, gave praise unto
God."

9. THE CONVERSION OF ZACCHAEUS   Ch. 19:1-10

*1 And he entered and was passing through Jericho.
2 And behold, a man called by name Zacchæus; and he
was a chief publican, and he was rich. 3 And he sought
to see Jesus who he was; and could not for the crowd, because he was little of stature. 4 And he ran on before,
and climbed up into a sycamore tree to see him: for he
was to pass that way. 5 And when Jesus came to the
place, he looked up, and said unto him, Zacchæus, make*

haste, and come down; for to-day I must abide at thy house. 6 And he made haste, and came down, and received him joyfully. 7 And when they saw it, they all murmured, saying, He is gone in to lodge with a man that is a sinner. 8 And Zacchæus stood, and said unto the Lord, Behold, Lord, the half of my goods I give to the poor: and if I have wrongfully exacted aught of any man, I restore fourfold. 9 And Jesus said unto him, To-day is salvation come to this house, forasmuch as he also is a son of Abraham. 10 For the Son of man came to seek and to save that which was lost.

"And he entered and was passing through Jericho," a city famous alike for faith and unbelief. "By faith the walls of Jericho fell down," and in blind unbelief they were rebuilt and the curse which had been pronounced came upon the defiant builder. As Jesus passed through the city, he was to witness faith and unbelief, the latter to be shown by multitudes, the former by a single man named Zacchaeus. This name signifies "holiness," but it was a poor designation of the man. Those who knew him best called him a "sinner," and they were probably right. "He was a chief publican, and he was rich." A man might be a publican and be honest, but he would probably be poor. Zacchaeus' task was that of a taxgatherer, and when it is remembered that these officials made their wealth by extortion and dishonesty, to say the least, it was suspicious when a taxgatherer was rich.

"He sought to see Jesus who he was." It may have been curiosity, but there was a certain eagerness in his desire. He possibly had heard of the great Prophet who was so kind in his treatment of publicans and sinners. However, he could not see Jesus "for the crowd, because he was little of stature." Obstacles often arise in the way of those whose attention is first turned toward Christ. If, however, they are earnest in their desire, they are certain to learn more of him.

The earnestness of Zacchaeus was shown as "he ran on

before, and climbed up into a sycamore tree to see him." There was something undignified in the action of this little man of wealth, but his eagerness received an unexpected reward, for "when Jesus came to the place, he looked up, and said unto him, Zacchæus, make haste, and come down; for to-day I must abide at thy house." This is the only time, so far as we know, that Jesus invited himself to be a guest, but we are certain that he is ever ready to abide with those whose hearts are open to receive him. It has been said that Zacchaeus was converted before he had reached the ground. There can be no doubt that a great change came into his heart as he realized how fully Jesus knew him and anticipated what the Savior could do for him; and his faith and hope were manifest at once. "He made haste, and came down, and received him joyfully."

What did the crowd say? Exactly what the world always says when a man is turning to Christ and seeking to begin a new life. Men always call to mind the dark past from which the rescued man is turning. "They all murmured, saying, He is gone in to lodge with a man that is a sinner."

What did Zacchaeus say? What every man says who has found the grace which Christ bestows and who realizes that a new life can begin only with repentance and resolution. "Behold, Lord, the half of my goods I give to the poor." Thus he determined, as a Christian, to do far more than was required by the Jewish law; that law required a tenth; Zacchaeus promised that half of all his income would be used in the service of the Lord. "And if I have wrongfully exacted aught of any man, I restore fourfold." There can be little doubt that any publican would find large opportunities for such restoration; and nothing more definitely indicates true repentance than the desire to make amends for the past.

What did Jesus say? This is most important of all, "To-day is salvation come to this house, forasmuch as he also is a son of Abraham." By his faith the publican of Jericho showed himself to be a true son of Abraham, the "father of the faithful." His trust in Christ secured for him that salvation which is offered to all, even to the lowest and most hopeless and despised. "For the Son of man came to seek and to save that which was lost."

10. THE PARABLE OF THE POUNDS   Ch. 19:11-28

11 And as they heard these things, he added and spake a parable, because he was nigh to Jerusalem, and because they supposed that the kingdom of God was immediately to appear. 12 He said therefore, A certain nobleman went into a far country, to receive for himself a kingdom, and to return. 13 And he called ten servants of his, and gave them ten pounds, and said unto them, Trade ye herewith till I come. 14 But his citizens hated him, and sent an ambassage after him, saying, We will not that this man reign over us. 15 And it came to pass, when he was come back again, having received the kingdom, that he commanded these servants, unto whom he had given the money, to be called to him, that he might know what they had gained by trading. 16 And the first came before him, saying, Lord, thy pound hath made ten pounds more. 17 And he said unto him, Well done, thou good servant: because thou wast found faithful in a very little, have thou authority over ten cities. 18 And the second came, saying, Thy pound, Lord, hath made five pounds. 19 And he said unto him also, Be thou also over five cities. 20 And another came, saying, Lord, behold, here is thy pound, which I kept laid up in a napkin: 21 for I feared thee, because thou art an austere man: thou takest up that which thou layedst not down, and reapest that which thou didst not sow. 22 He saith unto him, Out of thine own mouth will I judge thee, thou wicked servant. Thou knewest that I am an austere man, taking up that which I laid not down, and reaping that which I did not sow; 23 then wherefore gavest thou not my money into the bank, and I at my coming should have required it with interest? 24 And he said unto them that stood by, Take away from

him the pound, and give it unto him that hath the ten
pounds. 25 And they said unto him, Lord, he hath ten
pounds. 26 I say unto you, that unto every one that hath
shall be given; but from him that hath not, even that which
he hath shall be taken away from him. 27 But these mine
enemies, that would not that I should reign over them,
bring hither, and slay them before me.

28 And when he had thus spoken, he went on before,
going up to Jerusalem.

Jesus felt impelled to deliver the parable of the pounds
because of the mistaken belief among the crowds that on
his arrival in Jerusalem he would establish his Kingdom.
He well knew that he was to be rejected and crucified, and
that a long interval of time would elapse before his return
in triumph. In this parable he definitely predicted this
rejection and warned the unbelieving Jews of their peril.
On the other hand, he encouraged his disciples to wait
with patience for his return, to watch for his coming, and
to be engaged diligently in his service, promising to the
faithful, abundant and gracious rewards.

This parable of the pounds should be studied in connection with the parables of the unprofitable servant,
ch. 17:7-10, the laborers in the vineyard, Matt. 20:1-16,
and the talents, Matt. 25:14-30. The first teaches that
no reward can be claimed as a matter of merit; in view of
all that the Master has given us, even pouring out his life
for our redemption, we never by the most faithful service
could begin to pay the debt we owe; even the most loyal
devotion would be no ground for claiming a reward.

The parable of the laborers in the vineyard likewise
warns us against a mercenary spirit in which we might
serve the Master for the sake of a reward, bargaining for
so much labor for so much pay, jealous of those who may
receive as much as ourselves, though deserving, as we
believe, less.

However, while no reward may be deserved, and while
the hope of reward should not be the motive for service,

the Master has assured us that, in absolute grace and with perfect justice, rewards will be granted to those who are found faithful when he returns. The parable of the talents teaches that while opportunities and abilities for the service of Christ may differ, those who are equally faithful will receive equal rewards. The parable of the pounds tells us that when opportunities are the same, greater faithfulness will receive greater reward.

This latter parable was delivered, as Luke tells us, because Jesus "was nigh to Jerusalem, and because they supposed that the kingdom of God was immediately to appear." Jesus therefore compared himself with a nobleman who went into a far country, "to receive for himself a kingdom, and to return." Jesus was always indicating the fact that there would be a long delay after his ascension before he would return, and that meanwhile his followers should be faithful to the opportunities granted them for serving their Master. In this parable Jesus pictured these opportunities under the figure of pounds, that is, sums of money amounting to something like sixteen dollars each. In comparison with a "talent," this was an insignificant sum. Our Lord wished to suggest that to every one of his followers something is entrusted which may be used for the advancement of his cause.

Jesus knew that the Jews were not only to reject him but were to continue in unbelief after his departure; thus in the parable he stated that "his citizens hated him, and sent an ambassage after him, saying, We will not that this man reign over us." The main portion of the picture, however, is concerned with the return of the nobleman and the reward of his servants. This reward was proportioned to fidelity during the time of his absence. By way of example, one who had so used his pound as to gain ten pounds was made the ruler over ten cities; and one who had gained five, was appointed over five cities. The reward for service is thus shown to be larger service. Faithfulness in that which is very small is a preparation for larger responsibilities and more glorious tasks. This is true in the present, and the principle will be the same in the future.

One man was found, however, who had made no use of his pound. He had kept it "laid up in a napkin." His excuse was that he feared his master and he said, almost boastfully, that he had not lost what had been entrusted to him. He was giving back that which had been given him. The nobleman, however, properly rebuked this unfaithful servant in the very terms which he himself had used. If the master was known to be so strict, the servant should have been prepared to give a better account of his stewardship. It is true that one cause for unfaithfulness is an ignorance of the true nature of our Lord. Some are really afraid to undertake Christian service because they do not know, what the parable could not indicate, namely, that he who entrusts us with opportunities and abilities will give us grace, if we seek to do our best and with a real desire to advance the interests of our Lord, try to use the little which we have. Thus the nobleman rebuked the unfaithful servant for not having done the least which was possible. He could have placed the money in the bank and then if nothing more, the master would have received the interest on the loan. There is always something which every servant of Christ can do for him. There is never any real excuse for idleness and inactivity and failure to achieve something in the cause of Christ.

The pound was taken from the unfaithful servant and given to him who had secured the ten pounds, because our Lord wished to illustrate the truth that with our opportunities and privileges and gifts, the principle, use or lose, always applies. The right employment of even small gifts results in their enlargement, but failure to appreciate and employ that which we possess results in its ultimate loss. "Unto every one that hath shall be given; but from him that hath not, even that which he hath shall be taken away from him."

The parable closes with a solemn warning to those who reject Christ. It is not only perilous to be unfaithful in his service but pitiful to be found in the class of those who refuse to acknowledge him as Lord. Jesus describes in these last words not only the destruction of Jerusalem but the penalty of all who share in rejecting his rule. "But these mine enemies, that would not that I should reign over them, bring hither, and slay them before me."

The time of his departure was at hand. The nation was about to reject him. The nobleman was just to start for the far country, for "when he had thus spoken, he went on before, going up to Jerusalem."

VI
THE CLOSING
MINISTRY

Chs. 19:29 to 21:38

A. THE TRIUMPHAL ENTRY Ch. 19:29-48

29 And it came to pass, when he drew nigh unto Beth-phage and Bethany, at the mount that is called Olivet, he sent two of the disciples, 30 saying, Go your way into the village over against you; in which as ye enter ye shall find a colt tied, whereon no man ever yet sat: loose him, and bring him. 31 And if anyone ask you, Why do ye loose him? thus shall ye say, The Lord hath need of him. 32 And they that were sent went away, and found even as he had said unto them. 33 And as the were loosing the colt, the owners thereof said unto them, Why loose ye the colt? 34 And they said, The Lord hath need of him. 35 And they brought him to Jesus: and they threw their garments upon the colt, and set Jesus thereon. 36 And as he went, they spread their garments in the way. 37 And as he was now drawing nigh, even at the descent of the mount of Olives, the whole multitude of the disciples began to rejoice and praise God with a loud voice for all the mighty works which they had seen; 38 saying, Blessed is the King that cometh in the name of the Lord: peace in heaven, and glory in the highest. 39 And some of the Pharisees from the multitude said unto him, Teacher, rebuke thy disciples. 40 And he answered and said, I tell you that, if these shall hold their peace, the stones will cry out.

41 And when he drew nigh, he saw the city and wept over it, 42 saying, If thou hadst known in this day, even thou, the things which belong unto peace! but now they are hid from thine eyes. 43 For the days shall come upon thee, when thine enemies shall cast up a bank about thee,

and compass thee round, and keep thee in on every side,
44 and shall dash thee to the ground, and thy children
within thee; and they shall not leave in thee one stone upon
another; because thou knewest not the time of thy visita-
tion.

45 And he entered into the temple, and began to cast
out them that sold, 46 saying unto them, It is written, And
my house shall be a house of prayer: but ye have made it
a den of robbers.

47 And he was teaching daily in the temple. But the
chief priests and the scribes and the principal men of the
people sought to destroy him: 48 and they could not find
what they might do; for the people all hung upon him,
listening.

The story of Luke is never lacking in human interest,
but no scene is more suffused with sentiment, none more
vivid with color, than that which pictures Jesus entering
Jerusalem in triumph. We see our Lord mounted as a
king, surrounded by acclaiming multitudes, sweeping over
the brow of Olivet, while his attendant disciples spread
their garments in the way and hail him as the Messiah.
We see him lamenting over the doomed city and hear the
harsh tones of the rulers who are plotting his death. With
all these shouts of joy and sobs of grief and mutterings of
malice, surely no scene is so full of emotion and none can
illustrate more strikingly the relation between religious
feeling and religious faith.

An appeal to the eye and ear and heart may awaken
sentiment and prepare the way for the surrender of the
will. There is today a proper place for music and archi-
tecture and eloquence as aids to devotion. In the case
of the triumphal entry, Jesus planned every detail. He
sent two disciples to secure the colt on which he was to
ride; he allowed the disciples to place on the colt their garments, and as he rode toward the city, he accepted the ac-
clamations of the crowd. When the Pharisees criticized
Jesus for permitting such praise and arousing such excite-

ment, he declared that such homage to himself was not only proper but necessary, and that if the multitudes were silenced the very stones would "cry out" to welcome and to honor him. Jesus was offering himself as King for the last time, and therefore his offer was to be made in the most impressive way. He appealed to the imagination. He stirred the emotions. He did not mean that he was to be such a king as the people supposed; the borrowed colt, the garments of peasants, the banners of leafy branches were not to be the permanent furnishings of a court. He wished to secure the submission of their wills, the complete surrender of their lives, and therefore he made this stirring, dramatic, emotional appeal to the multitudes. He knew that religious feeling is an aid to religious faith.

However, religious feeling is not to be confused with religious faith. Emotion is no substitute for conviction. Jesus was not deceived. As he caught sight of the sacred city and heard the bitter criticism of the Pharisees, he realized the stubborn unbelief he was to encounter; he saw his rejection and death and the consequent destruction of Jerusalem and he pronounced his pathetic lament, "If thou hadst known in this day, even thou, the things which belong unto peace!" He predicted the ghastly horrors of the coming siege and the desolation of Zion and declared that it was due to inability to see that he had come as a Savior and that his ministry had been a gracious visitation which might have resulted in repentance and in continued life for the nation. It is the sad, sad lament for what might have been.

Jesus entered the Temple and rebuked the rulers for allowing the house of God to be desecrated by degrading traffic. As the story closes, we see Jesus standing in the center of the scene, on one hand the rulers plotting against his life, and on his other the multitudes hanging admiringly upon his words. Only too soon the rulers were to persuade the crowds to cry out for his crucifixion, and we are reminded that religious feeling unaccompanied by conviction may soon be chilled into indifference and hate.

There were those, however, like the disciples, who never forgot this scene of triumph. Its fuller meaning was appreciated in later years and as their trust in Christ strengthened, they looked back with ever deeper emotions upon the experiences of that memorable day; for it is true that religious feeling is after all a natural and inevitable consequence of religious faith.

B. THE QUESTION AS TO AUTHORITY
Ch. 20:1-8

1 And it came to pass, on one of the days, as he was teaching the people in the temple, and preaching the gospel, there came upon him the chief priests and the scribes with the elders; 2 and they spake, saying unto him, Tell us: By what authority doest thou these things? or who is he that gave thee this authority? 3 And he answered and said unto them, I also will ask you a question; and tell me: 4 The baptism of John, was it from heaven, or from men? 5 And they reasoned with themselves, saying, If we shall say, From heaven; he will say, Why did ye not believe him? 6 But if we shall say, From men; all the people will stone us: for they are persuaded that John was a prophet. 7 And they answered, that they knew not whence it was. 8 And Jesus said unto them, Neither tell I you by what authority I do these things.

After his triumphal entry into the city, Jesus continued to be the popular idol of the multitudes that thronged Jerusalem at the Passover season. It was this popularity which delayed the designs of the rulers, as they had determined to put Jesus to death. They must first discredit him with the people. With this in view they sent a deputation from their chief court, the Sanhedrin, to entrap Jesus in his talk or to bring him into conflict with the Jewish or Roman rulers. They challenged him to state by

what authority he was receiving such honors as the Messiah, or driving the traders from the Temple, or performing his miracles.   Their question was framed with subtle
skill: "By what authority doest thou these things?   or who
is he that gave thee this authority?"   They placed Jesus
in a dilemma; if he should claim that authority had been
delegated to him, then he might be accused of disloyalty
and of schism, in supplanting the recognized "authorities"
of the Jewish state; if he should claim inherent divine authority, as identified with God, he might be condemned
for blasphemy.

Jesus silenced his enemies with a question which involved them in a counter dilemma: "The baptism of John,
was it from heaven, or from men?"   They could not say
"from heaven," for they had rejected John; they dared
not say "from men," for they feared the people by whom
John was regarded as a prophet.   So they tried to escape
by cowardly replying that they did not know.   Agnosti-
cism is usually cowardly and deserving of little respect.

But Jesus did more than silence them; he answered
them.   His question was no irrelevant riddle by which he
met a difficulty and delayed the necessity of a reply.   He
definitely implied that the authority of John was divine
and that his own authority was the same; but as they were
afraid to deny the divine authority of John they were also
powerless to deny that of Jesus; and further he implied
that if they had accepted the message of John, they would
be prepared to accept Jesus.   It is true that if we are afraid
to accept the logical conclusions of our doubts and denials,
we never can hope to discover truth.

Jesus further rebuked and exposed his enemies.   When
they said that they did not know, Jesus knew, and they
knew, and the crowds knew, that they were not honest;
the Lord had laid bare their hypocrisy; he had made it
perfectly evident that the real question at issue was not
authority but obedience.   The enemies of Jesus pretended
that they wanted to know more of his credentials; they

really wanted to discredit and entrap him. The modern enemies of our Lord declare that they want more proofs, more evidence; what they really lack is love for God and submission to his will. Those who do not repent when John preaches, will not believe when Jesus offers to save. The world needs today, not more proof of divine authority, but more obedience to the divine will.

Jesus absolutely discredited his enemies in the sight of the people. They were the constituted authorities in all matters civil and religious, and yet they were made to confess publicly that they were not competent to judge a clear, familiar, important case relating to religious authority. They really abdicated their position. They, therefore, were disqualified to pass an opinion on the exactly parallel case of the authority of Jesus. Jesus had defeated them with their own weapon. No wonder that subsequently, when on trial before such judges, he refused to answer them a word. He had shown their incompetence, their insincerity, their unbelief. Honest doubters are deserving of sympathy; but professed seekers after truth, who are unwilling to accept the consequences of belief, should expect to receive no further light. An increasing knowledge of divine realities is conditioned upon humble submission of the heart and the will to what already has been revealed.

C. THE PARABLE OF THE HUSBANDMEN
Ch. 20:9-18

9 And he began to speak unto the people this parable: A man planted a vineyard, and let it out to husbandmen, and went into another country for a long time. 10 And at the season he sent unto the husbandmen a servant, that they should give him of the fruit of the vineyard: but the husbandmen beat him, and sent him away empty. 11 And he sent yet another servant: and him also they beat, and handled him shamefully, and sent him away empty. 12 And he sent yet a third: and him also they wounded, and cast him forth. 13 And the lord of the vineyard said,

What shall I do? I will send my beloved son; it may be they will reverence him. 14 But when the husbandmen saw him, they reasoned one with another, saying, This is the heir; let us kill him, that the inheritance may be ours. 15 And they cast him forth out of the vineyard, and killed him. What therefore will the lord of the vineyard do unto them? 16 He will come and destroy these husbandmen, and will give the vineyard unto others. And when they heard it, they said, God forbid. 17 But he looked upon them, and said, What then is this that is written,

The stone which the builders rejected,

The same was made the head of the corner?

18 Every one that falleth on that stone shall be broken to pieces; but on whomsoever it shall fall, it will scatter him as dust.

To the malicious challenge of his enemies Jesus had already replied, claiming for himself divine authority and condemning the rulers for their guilty unbelief. He now added a parable, more clearly stating his claims and more solemnly rebuking these hostile rulers and pronouncing judgment upon the nation they represented. He told the story of a householder who established and equipped a vineyard and let it out to tenants. He lived at a distance and expected as rent a certain portion of the vintage. When he sent for the fruit, however, his messengers were abused and killed; at last his own son was sent and was slain. He determined to come and to exact justice and to deliver his vineyard to tenants who were more worthy.

The parable was so plain that the enemies of Jesus perfectly understood its meaning. The householder was his Father; the vineyard was Israel; the husbandmen were the rulers to whom the nation had been entrusted; the servants were the prophets sent to summon the people to repent and to render to God the fruits of righteousness; the son was Jesus himself, who thus claimed a unique relation to God, distinct from the prophets and from all human messengers; the death of the heir was his own approaching crucifixion; the return of the householder was the coming visitation of divine judgment, the rejection of

Israel, and the call of the Gentiles. It was aside from the present purpose of Jesus to refer to the individual Jews who would accept him and to the future conversion of the nation of which Paul wrote. He wished now to emphasize his own rejection and the guilt and punishment of the nation. He declared, however, that this death would issue in his exaltation and triumph; that he was "the stone which the builders rejected," which "was made the head of the corner." He also warned his enemies that all who, in unbelief, should stumble on that stone, all who should reject him, would be "broken to pieces," and all who should attempt to drag down that stone would be ground and scattered as dust.

D. THE QUESTION AS TO PAYING TRIBUTE
Ch. 20:19-26

19 And the scribes and the chief priests sought to lay hands on him in that very hour; and they feared the people: for they perceived that he spake this parable against them. 20 And they watched him, and sent forth spies, who feigned themselves to be righteous, that they might take hold of his speech, so as to deliver him up to the rule and to the authority of the governor. 21 And they asked him, saying, Teacher, we know that thou sayest and teachest rightly, and acceptest not the person of any, but of a truth teachest the way of God: 22 Is it lawful for us to give tribute unto Cæsar, or not? 23 But he perceived their craftiness, and said unto them, 24 Show me a denarius. Whose image and superscription hath it? And they said, Cæsar's. 25 And he said unto them, Then render unto Cæsar the things that are Cæsar's, and unto God the things that are God's. 26 And they were not able to take hold of the saying before the people: and they marvelled at his answer, and held their peace.

The rulers had been defeated, discredited, and disgraced, but they had not been discouraged. In their first question they failed utterly to bring Jesus into any unlawful opposition to the religious courts. They now attempted by a new question to draw from him an answer which either would make him unpopular with the people or would bring him under the condemnation of the civil ruler. They asked him a question relative to the payment of tribute to the Roman Government. The more conservative Jews held that God was the ruler of Israel and that possibly it was wrong to pay taxes to support a heathen state. The more liberal party sided with the Herods, who owed their power to Rome. Therefore the enemies of Jesus sent to him representatives of both parties, Pharisees and Herodians, so that if he should avoid offending one party he would displease the other. They approached Jesus with the flattering assurance that he was so truthful and courageous that he would not hesitate to express his true convictions; and then they proposed their artful question: "Is it lawful for us to give tribute unto Cæsar, or not?" Should Jesus say, "Yes"? Then he would cease to be a popular idol, for the people loathed the hateful oppression of Rome. Should Jesus say, "No"? Then his enemies would hurry him away to the Roman governor and the cross, as a traitor and a rebel. The dilemma seemed complete; yet Jesus not only escaped the snare, but, in his reply, he enunciated a law for all time. "Render unto Cæsar the things that are Caesar's, and unto God the things that are God's."

To make plain his meaning, Jesus first called for a Roman coin, and asked whose image and superscription it bore. The reply of course was, "Cæsar's." Jesus therefore declared that those who accept the protection of a government and the privileges provided by a government are under obligation to support that government. Christianity never should be identified with any political party or social theory; but Christians ever should take their stand for loyalty, for order, and for law.

It is not the whole of life, however, to "render unto Cæsar the things that are Cæsar's"; one must also render "unto God the things that are God's." The latter higher allegiance includes the former. The enemies of Jesus suggested a conflict of duties; he showed that there was perfect harmony. He intimated, however, that there was danger of forgetting God, and our obligations to him of trust, service, worship, love. The true basis for citizenship is devotion to God, and no political theory or party allegiance can be taken as a substitute for loyalty to him. The enemies of Jesus were answered and rebuked, and his followers were given guidance for all the coming years.

E. THE QUESTION AS TO THE RESURRECTION
Ch. 20:27-40

27 And there came to him certain of the Sadducees, they that say that there is no resurrection; 28 and they asked him, saying, Teacher, Moses wrote unto us, that if a man's brother die, having a wife, and he be childless, his brother should take the wife, and raise up seed unto his brother. 29 There were therefore seven brethren: and the first took a wife, and died childless; 30 and the second: 31 and the third took her; and likewise the seven also left no children, and died. 32 Afterward the woman also died. 33 In the resurrection therefore whose wife of them shall she be? for the seven had her to wife. 34 And Jesus said unto them, The sons of this world marry, and are given in marriage: 35 but they that are accounted worthy to attain to that world, and the resurrection from the dead, neither marry, nor are given in marriage: 36 for neither can they die any more: for they are equal unto the angels; and are sons of God, being sons of the resurrection. 37 But that the dead are raised, even Moses showed, in the place concerning the Bush, when he calleth the Lord the God of Abraham, and the God of Isaac, and the God of Jacob. 38 Now he is not the God of the dead, but of the living: for all live unto him. 39 And certain of the scribes answering said, Teacher, thou hast well said. 40 For they durst not any more ask him any question.

Jesus had foiled the scribes and the chief priests in their plan to entrap him in his public teaching. He was now attacked by the Sadducees, who were the priestly and most powerful party among the Jews. They denied the immortality of the soul and believed neither in angels nor in spirits; they represented the modern materialists. It is to be noted that the question with which they approached Jesus was not one which referred only to immortality but specifically to the resurrection of the body. They proposed the case of a woman married successively to seven brothers from each of whom she was separated by death; and they asked, "In the resurrection therefore whose wife of them shall she be? for the seven had her to wife." They hoped that Jesus would either deny the orthodox belief as to the resurrection or would make some statement which would contradict the law of Moses in accordance with which the successive marriages were made. They implied that this accepted law was inconsistent with the belief in a resurrection.

In his reply Jesus declared that in the resurrection, life will be regulated by larger laws than are known in this present age. Those who will share the glory of that age, and who will experience the blessedness of "the resurrection from the dead" will be immortal in soul and body. Marriage, which is now necessary for a continuance of the race, will no longer exist. The relationships in that life will be higher than even the most sacred relationship of the present life. Those who have a part in this resurrection will be "equal unto the angels," not in all particulars, but in the fact that their state will be deathless. In that larger sense they will be "sons of God" and "sons of the resurrection," for death will have lost its power over them.

Such a reply should be carefully weighed by men of the present day who deny miracles and refuse to believe in resurrection and immortality. Many beliefs which are now ridiculous because they seem to contradict established laws of science will someday be vindicated by the discovery of higher and more inclusive laws than are now known.

In his answer Jesus already had rebuked the Sadducees for denying the existence of angels. He next established the fact of the resurrection by a quotation from the very law on which they had depended to show that resurrection was impossible. He recalled the words recorded by Moses in reference to "the God of Abraham, and the God of Isaac, and the God of Jacob." He then added, "He is not the God of the dead, but of the living." Jesus meant to establish the fact of the continued existence of the dead; yet not merely this, but to prove the resurrection of the dead. The latter was the question at issue. The word "living," as used by our Lord, indicates those who are enjoying a normal life, not that of disembodied spirits, but of immortal spirits clothed with deathless bodies. Therefore Jesus added, "for all live unto him." In the mind and purpose of God all are to be raised from the dead and to enjoy that complete and blessed existence which resurrection implies. The confident expectation of such a future state is based on our relation to God. If he is truly our God and we are his people, the triumph of death is not real and permanent but will be ended by the glorious immortality of the body and of the soul.

F. THE QUESTION OF JESUS Ch. 20:41-44

41 And he said unto them, How say they that the Christ is David's son? 42 For David himself saith in the book of Psalms,

The Lord said unto my Lord,
Sit thou on my right hand,
43 Till I make thine enemies the footstool of thy feet.
44 David therefore calleth him Lord, and how is he his son?

Jesus had defeated his enemies in debate. They had come to him with a series of crafty questions designed to discredit him as a public teacher and to secure some ground for his arrest. To each of these questions he had given a reply by which his foes had been unmasked and condemned. He then asked them a question. It was intended not only to silence his foes forever, though it accomplished this, for henceforth no man ventured to meet him in public discussion; nor yet did Jesus desire further to humiliate his enemies. In the presence of the people he had already shown them to be ridiculous, contemptible, impotent, and insincere. His real motive was to ask a question, the answer to which would embody the chief of all his claims, namely, the claim that he is divine. It was of supreme importance that this claim should be made at exactly this time. He knew that the rulers had been unable to find a charge on which to arraign him before either the ecclesiastical or the civil court. He realized that they would dare to make no other attempt in public, but he clearly foresaw the fact that, through the treachery of Judas, he would be arrested and, before both these courts, would be arraigned on the charge of blasphemy. His enemies would accuse him of claiming to be not only the Messiah but also divine. On this occasion, therefore, in the presence both of the rulers and the people, he made the defense which never can be broken or forgotten as he definitely demonstrated from Scripture that the Messiah was described by the inspired writers as a divine Being. All that Jesus claimed for himself, as recorded in the Gospel of John, was included in the answer which was implied by the question which he now asked. Even for the present day it involves the supreme problem in the sphere of philosophy and religion. This problem concerns the person of Christ. Is he to be regarded as Man or God, or at once God and Man? Where is he to be placed in the scale of being; or, as Jesus voiced the problem, how could David speak of the coming Messiah as both his son

and his Lord? There was but one answer. There can be
but one. The Messiah was to be divine. The son of
David is also the Son of God. The incarnation is the
only solution of our most serious difficulties in the realm
of religious belief. By his question Jesus not only silenced
his enemies; he also showed their insincerity in condemning him to death and their rejection of the inspired Scriptures in their unwillingness to believe the testimony concerning the person of the Messiah. Jesus unquestionably
claimed to be the divine Savior of the world. The ideal
Man is also the incarnate God.

G. THE WARNING AGAINST THE SCRIBES
Ch. 20:45-47

*45 And in the hearing of all the people he said unto his
disciples, 46 Beware of the scribes, who desire to walk in
long robes, and love salutations in the marketplaces, and
chief seats in the synagogues, and chief places at feasts;
47 who devour widows' houses, and for a pretence make
long prayers: these shall receive greater condemnation.*

As the long day of public controversy drew to its close,
it was not strange that Jesus turned to warn the people
against these enemies who had been seeking to defeat him
and who were determined upon his death. These professed guides could not be followed safely. These rulers
had shown themselves to be unworthy of their place and
power. The people must look elsewhere for true teachers.
They must find other men to interpret for them the will of
God.

The scribes were the professional teachers of the day,
the trained expositors of the law. Most of them were
Pharisees. They were of all men the most bitter enemies
of Christ; they were jealous of his power; they were an-
gered at his claims; and finally they had been goaded to
desperation by their humiliating defeat at his hands.

Upon these men Jesus pronounced the most stern condemnation. His words are recorded at length by Matthew. In the brief summary of the discourse made by Mark and by Luke we find only a few short sentences which sketch three principal features in the character of these unworthy leaders of religious thought. The first is their vanity, their ambition for display and for high position, and their love of flattery. The second is their cruel avarice, expressed by our Lord in the suggestive clause, "who devour widows' houses." The third was their shameful hypocrisy; they are described as men who "for a pretence make long prayers." It has always been remarked that the most bitter denunciations of Jesus were addressed to the men whose outward lives were most respectable and whose religious professions were most loud. This does not mean, however, that open vice and flagrant sin are better than selfish and proud morality; but it does remind us that great religious privileges and the possession of revealed truth involve solemn responsibilities and that hypocrisy and pretense are abominations in the sight of God.

H. THE WIDOW'S MITES Ch. 21:1-4

1 And he looked up, and saw the rich men that were casting their gifts into the treasury. 2 And he saw a certain poor widow casting in thither two mites. 3 And he said, Of a truth I say unto you, This poor widow cast in more than they all: 4 for all these did of their superfluity cast in unto the gifts; but she of her want did cast in all the living that she had.

What a contrast this charming sketch supplies to the picture which Jesus drew of the Pharisees! In the eyes of the world the service of the poor widow was meager and worthless, while the gifts of the hypocrites were costly and great; in the eyes of the Lord their offerings were comparatively worthless and she gave more than they all. As a matter of fact, she had brought but two small coins, worth

214   THE CLOSING MINISTRY Luke 21:5-38

less than a half cent, but they were all that she had. With
this scene in mind we should be careful not to call our
offerings "mites" unless they are all that we possess; we
should be encouraged, however, to know that our Lord
looks upon the heart and estimates the gift by the motive
and the love and the sacrifice involved; above all, we
should be reminded that we can best measure our offerings not by what we give but by how much we keep. The
influence of the woman is still moving multitudes toward
the treasury of the Lord.

I. THE DESTRUCTION OF JERUSALEM AND
THE COMING OF CHRIST Ch. 21:5-38

During the days of his ministry Jesus frequently predicted his death and also his return in glory. He saw
clearly before him a cross, but on the distant horizon a
throne. Again and again he had warned the Jews that
their rejection of him and of his call to repentance would
result in the destruction of Jerusalem and in the anguish
of their race, and quite as frequently he had told his disciples that while indeed he was to die and rise again, a
long period of time would pass before he would return
in glory to establish his Kingdom. The great, final discourse relating to the future was delivered at the close
of his last day of public controversy and teaching. As
Jesus sat with his disciples on the slope of the Mount of
Olives, as he looked westward and saw the sun sinking
behind the majestic buildings of the sacred city, he realized
that in truth the night was gathering over the nation, that
his own day of earthly ministry was done, and that the
real dawning would not break for the world until the Sun
of righteousness should arise in true glory, until he himself would return to fill the earth with the peace and joy
and splendor of his universal reign. He, therefore, told
his disciples with much detail the story of the approaching
destruction of Jerusalem and of his own return after the

long years of faithful service and of eager waiting which
were appointed for his followers.

This prophetic discourse of Jesus is difficult to interpret;
first of all, because it is phrased in figurative terms, the
exact meaning of which is not always apparent. Again it
appears that we have only a partial report of the prophecies then spoken by our Lord; it is necessary to compare
the records of Matthew and Mark with the statements
here given by Luke, and then to remember that we have
probably only a fraction of the whole discourse. In the
third place, it is evident that our Lord was describing
not one event, but two. He was prophesying the literal
overthrow of the holy city by the armies of Rome, but he
was using the colors of this tragic scene to paint the picture of his own return in glory. So interwoven are these
two series of predictions that it is not always evident
whether the reference is to the nearer or to the more re-
mote of these events. While we may note with some definiteness the general outline of the prophecy and while
there need be little doubt as to its two outstanding features, namely, the destruction of the city and the return of
our Lord, the study of this chapter should be undertaken
with humility, and our conclusions should be stated with
caution and with reserve. The result need not be bewilderment or despair; it should be encouragement and more
confident expectation of the coming of Christ and the
ultimate triumph of his cause.

1. THE PRESENT AGE   Ch. 21:5-19

*5 And as some spake of the temple, how it was adorned
with goodly stones and offerings, he said, 6 As for these
things which ye behold, the days will come, in which there
shall not be left here one stone upon another, that shall not
be thrown down. 7 And they asked him, saying, Teacher,
when therefore shall these things be? and what shall be the
sign when these things are about to come to pass? 8 And
he said, Take heed that ye be not led astray: for many shall*

come in my name, saying, I am he; *and, The time is at hand: go ye not after them. 9 And when ye shall hear of wars and tumults, be not terrified: for these things must needs come to pass first; but the end is not immediately.*

10 Then said he unto them, Nation shall rise against nation, and kingdom against kingdom; 11 and there shall be great earthquakes, and in divers places famines and pestilences; and there shall be terrors and great signs from heaven. 12 But before all these things, they shall lay their hands on you, and shall persecute you, delivering you up to the synagogues and prisons, bringing you before kings and governors for my name's sake. 13 It shall turn out unto you for a testimony. 14 Settle it therefore in your hearts, not to meditate beforehand how to answer: 15 for I will give you a mouth and wisdom, which all your adversaries shall not be able to withstand or to gainsay. 16 But ye shall be delivered up even by parents, and brethren, and kinsfolk, and friends; and some *of you shall they cause to be put to death. 17 And ye shall be hated of all men for my name's sake. 18 And not a hair of your head shall perish. 19 In your patience ye shall win your souls.*

The occasion of this prophetic message was the question asked by the disciples, as they gazed on the splendor of the Temple, concerning the destruction of which Jesus had spoken as he declared that the days would come "in which there shall not be left here one stone upon another, that shall not be thrown down. And they asked him, saying, Teacher, when therefore shall these things be? and what shall be the sign when these things are about to come to pass?" In the words of Matthew, they also asked, "What shall be the sign of thy coming, and of the end of the world?"

First of all, then, Jesus sketched for his disciples the character of this present age down to its very end, and described the experiences of his followers, urging them to be faithful to him amid all the commotions and trials of the coming years until he should return. According to his description the age will be characterized by the appearance of many deceivers who will claim the allegiance of his followers and assume to take the place of Christ. Furthermore, there will be wars and tumults but believers are not to be terrified by these. It is always a temptation of shallow minds to interpret every unusual event as a sign of the approaching end of the world. Our Lord assured his disciples that all through the passing years such events would happen without warranting the conclusion that the great event is near; as he declared, "The end is not immediately"; there would be a long period of delay; there would be a political commotion: "Nation shall rise against nation, and kingdom against kingdom." There would also be earthquakes, famines, pestilences, and "great signs from heaven," but these again must be regarded as characteristics of the present age and not as signs of its approaching end.

Furthermore, the followers of Christ must suffer bitter persecution and be brought before kings and governors for his name's sake. They must continue steadfast in their testimony. They need not be troubled as to the exact form of their witness but must trust the unseen Master to give them all needed wisdom as they speak boldly in his name.

Most distressing of all, they must suffer from the treachery of "parents, and brethren, and kinsfolk, and friends" and some of them must taste the bitter cup of martyrdom; they will be hated of all men, yet their souls will not perish. By their steadfast endurance they will win eternal salvation. It is true, the picture is one of great hardship and distress, but its message has encouraged sufferers who in all ages have been faithful in their testimony and have found the comfort and inspiration which is possible for all as they look for the coming and Kingdom of Christ.

2. THE DESTRUCTION OF JERUSALEM   Ch. 21:20-24

20 But when ye see Jerusalem compassed with armies, then know that her desolation is at hand. 21 Then let them that are in Judæa flee unto the mountains; and

let them that are in the midst of her depart out; and let
not them that are in the country enter therein. 22 For
these are days of vengeance, that all things which are writ-
ten may be fulfilled. 23 Woe unto them that are with child
and to them that give suck in those days! for there shall be
great distress upon the land, and wrath unto this people.
24 And they shall fall by the edge of the sword, and shall
be led captive into all the nations: and Jerusalem shall be
trodden down of the Gentiles, until the times of the Gen-
tiles be fulfilled.

As our Lord scanned the future he now fixed his eyes
first of all upon that dreadful event which in some of its
features foreshadowed the end of that age which he had
been describing. On more than one occasion he had predicted the destruction of Jerusalem. He now declared
that the definite sign of the descending doom would be
the siege of the city: "When ye see Jerusalem compassed
with armies, then know that her desolation is at hand."
He warned those within the city to flee to the mountains
and declared that those who were in the country should
not turn to the city for safety, because the days of vengeance will have come and the prophecies of punishment
upon the guilty nation will be about to be fulfilled. It
would be a time of unparalleled distress and horror; as
Jesus declared, "They shall fall by the edge of the sword,
and shall be led captive into all the nations." How literally his words were fulfilled is a familiar fact of history.
It would be difficult to recall another scene of equally hide-
ous carnage. It is estimated that a million Jews fell vic-
tims to the slaughter and outrage of the soldiers under
Titus, and that unnumbered thousands were led as captives to Egypt and other lands.

Last of all Jesus predicted that Jerusalem would be
"trodden down of the Gentiles, until the times of the Gentiles be fulfilled." The first phrase denotes something
more than mere domination and Gentile control; it indicates something of indignity and disgrace and humiliation,

and this state of the holy city is to continue until "the times of the Gentiles" are fulfilled, which probably means during all the ages of Gentile control, and further, during all the seasons of grace in which the gospel is being preached to the Gentile world, indeed, until the return of our Lord. "Gentiles" are plainly contrasted with Jews, and not with Christians. The mere fact that the sacred city has passed into control of Christian powers is no proof that the age is near its end; for this end there will be definite signs as Jesus himself proceeded to declare. However, as one turns from this lurid picture of the destruction of the historic city, and remembers how exactly these prophecies came to pass, it should be with a new confidence in the further predictions made by Christ and with a new belief that the more significant events of which he next proceeded to speak will be fulfilled likewise with exactness and in all their promised glory.

3. THE COMING OF CHRIST Ch. 21:25-28

25 And there shall be signs in sun and moon and stars; and upon the earth distress of nations, in perplexity for the roaring of the sea and the billows; 26 men fainting for fear, and for expectation of the things which are coming on the world: for the powers of the heavens shall be shaken. 27 And then shall they see the Son of man coming in a cloud with power and great glory. 28 But when these things begin to come to pass, look up, and lift up your heads; because your redemption draweth nigh.

Immediately before the return of our Lord, as the age draws to its close, there are to be certain signs so definite, so startling, and so terrifying, that they will leave no doubt that the predicted event is immediately to follow. They are described, however, in terms which may be largely figurative: "signs in sun and moon and stars; and upon the earth distress of nations, in perplexity for the roaring of the sea and the billows; men fainting for fear . . . :

for the powers of the heavens shall be shaken"; then will occur the event toward which all the ages are moving, for which the weary world has waited and by which the work of the church will be crowned and her hopes fulfilled, namely, the personal, glorious appearing of the crucified, risen, ascended Lord. It may be a time of distress for the impenitent but for believers it will be a time of hope and expectation. When the signs of which Jesus spoke "begin to come to pass," then, according to the words of Jesus, his followers may hopefully lift up their heads to greet their Deliverer, for their redemption will be at hand. The coming of Christ will be an event unexpected by the world, but Christians will be so definitely warned that they can be looking for the promised deliverance and for the predicted glory.

4. THE ENCOURAGEMENT TO HOPE AND VIGILANCE
Ch. 21:29-36

29 And he spake to them a parable: Behold the fig tree, and all the trees: 30 when they now shoot forth, ye see it and know of your own selves that the summer is now nigh. 31 Even so ye also, when ye see these things coming to pass, know ye that the kingdom of God is nigh. 32 Verily I say unto you, This generation shall not pass away, till all things be accomplished. 33 Heaven and earth shall pass away: but my words shall not pass away.

34 But take heed to yourselves, lest haply your hearts be overcharged with surfeiting, and drunkenness, and cares of this life, and that day come on you suddenly as a snare: 35 for so shall it come upon all them that dwell on the face of all the earth. 36 But watch ye at every season, making supplication, that ye may prevail to escape all these things that shall come to pass, and to stand before the Son of man.

In speaking of his return in glory, Jesus mentioned certain definite signs by which his followers will know that his coming is near. To explain more clearly the purpose of

these "signs," Jesus spoke a brief parable in which he compared their appearance to the foliage put forth in the
springtime which becomes a certain harbinger of the summer.   Many have supposed that Jesus indicated Israel by
his reference to "the fig tree" and have concluded that a
revival of Judaism and a return of the Jews to Palestine
will be a certain indication that the present age is drawing
to its close.   Whatever may be predicted elsewhere concerning the Jews, there is no such reference here, for Jesus
not only said, "Behold the fig tree," but also, "all the
trees."   His meaning is perfectly plain.   He did not refer
to nations under the figure of trees, but he declared that as
the foliage is a sure precursor of summer, so the signs of
which he spoke are a certain indication of his imminent return.   "Even so ye also, when ye see these things coming
to pass, know ye that the kingdom of God is nigh," the
Kingdom which is to be established in glory at the appearing of our Lord.

Jesus further awakened the expectation of his hearers
by the statement, "This generation shall not pass away, till
all things be accomplished."   It is improbable, as again
many have supposed, that Jesus referred to the Hebrew
race by the term "this generation."   The words are almost
certainly to be interpreted in their usual significance and
"all things" to be "accomplished" refers to the destruction
of Jerusalem regarded as the type and symbol of the return
of Christ.   These two events are thus closely related in this
prophetic discourse, and the literal fulfillment of the first
gives to believers a more confident assurance of the certain
occurrence of the latter: "Heaven and earth shall pass
away: but my words shall not pass away."   The hope that
our Lord will come is not based on human conjectures
but on his own unfailing predictions.   All that is material
and temporal may cease to exist, but his promises are
eternal.

In view of such glorious prophecies the heart of the
Christian is ever to be set upon the gracious realities re-

lating to the coming of the Master. The followers of
Christ must be on their guard lest they be overcome by the
influences which Jesus described as characterizing the days
immediately preceding his return. There will be temptation to self-indulgence and indifference and absorption in
worldly cares. Believers are warned to be on their watch
lest the coming of Christ overtake them unexpectedly, as
indeed it will come upon others. They are urged to watch
and to pray that they may be able to escape from those
judgments which will break upon a guilty world, and may
be counted worthy to take their places in the glorious
Kingdom of their Lord.

5. THE HISTORIC STATEMENT   Ch. 21:37-38

*37 And every day he was teaching in the temple; and
every night he went out, and lodged in the mount that was
called Olivet. 38 And all the people came early in the
morning to him in the temple, to hear him.*

Luke closes his account of the discourse delivered by
Jesus in reference to his return by a statement which sum-
marizes the general conditions which marked the final
events of Jesus' earthly ministry. He states that Jesus
passed his days teaching in the Temple and spent the
nights under the open skies on the slopes of the Mount of
Olives, and that the people were so eager to hear him that
they resorted to the Temple early each morning. This
statement is rather in the nature of a review. It marks a
transition in the narrative. In reality, Jesus seems to have
returned to the city only once more, when he was arrested
and led forth to die. Luke prepares us for these last
events. The story has reached its climax.

VII
THE DEATH AND
RESURRECTION
Chs. 22 to 24

A. THE TREACHERY OF JUDAS
Ch. 22:1-6

1 Now the feast of unleavened bread drew nigh, which is called the Passover. 2 And the chief priests and the scribes sought how they might put him to death; for they feared the people.

3 And Satan entered into Judas who was called Iscariot, being of the number of the twelve. 4 And he went away, and communed with the chief priests and captains, how he might deliver him unto them. 5 And they were glad, and covenanted to give him money. 6 And he consented, and sought opportunity to deliver him unto them in the absence of the multitude.

The statement that "the feast of unleavened bread drew nigh, which is called the Passover," forms a fitting preface to the story of the passion, for the Hebrew feast commemorated the deliverance of Israel when the angel of death passed over the homes which were marked with blood, and now a greater redemption was to be purchased by the blood of Christ, and those who would accept his salvation were to put away sin from their lives, even as leaven was excluded from Hebrew homes during all the days of the feast.

The rulers of the Jews had already determined upon the death of Jesus. Their problem lay in his immense popularity. They were determining to delay until after the feast, when the great crowds would have left the city, when suddenly help came to them from a most unexpected quarter. Judas Iscariot, one of the twelve immediate followers of Jesus, offered to betray his Master into the hands of the rulers at such a time and place as they desired, namely, "in the absence of the multitude." Of course the chief priests and the officers of the Temple guard "were glad" and contracted to pay the money demanded by the traitor for his treachery. Luke states that Judas acted under the direction of Satan. We are not to conclude, however, that he was a demoniac or that he lacked control of his faculties. His act was deliberate, unsolicited, and without excuse. The explanation is that he long had been cherishing his lust for gold. He had listened to the suggestion of Satan and now he yielded himself to his foul service. The alarming truth is that the treachery of Judas was not the act of a unique monster, but only an example of what, finally, may be done by any man who, in daily fellowship with Jesus, does not renounce his one besetting sin. To resist continually the gracious influence of the Savior is to fall the more rapidly under the complete power of Satan.

B. THE LAST SUPPER Ch. 22:7-38

7 And the day of unleavened bread came, on which the passover must be sacrificed. 8 And he sent Peter and John, saying, Go and make ready for us the passover, that we may eat. 9 And they said unto him, Where wilt thou that we make ready? 10 And he said unto them, Behold, when ye are entered into the city, there shall meet you a man bearing a pitcher of water; follow him into the house whereinto he goeth. 11 And ye shall say unto the master of the house, The Teacher saith unto thee, Where is the guest-chamber, where I shall eat the passover with my disciples? 12 And he will show you a large upper room furnished: there make ready. 13 And they went, and found as he had said unto them: and they made ready the passover.

14 And when the hour was come, he sat down, and the

apostles with him.   15 And he said unto them, With desire I have desired to eat this passover with you before I suffer: 16 for I say unto you, I shall not eat it, until it be fulfilled in the kingdom of God.   17 And he received a cup, and when he had given thanks, he said, Take this, and divide it among yourselves: 18 for I say unto you, I shall not drink from henceforth of the fruit of the vine, until the kingdom of God shall come.   19 And he took bread, and when he had given thanks, he brake it, and gave to them, saying, This is my body which is given for you: this do in remembrance of me.   20 And the cup in like manner after supper, saying, This cup is the new covenant in my blood, even that which is poured out for you.   21 But behold, the hand of him that betrayeth me is with me on the table.   22 For the Son of man indeed goeth, as it hath been determined: but woe unto that man through whom he is betrayed!   23 And they began to question among themselves, which of them it was that should do this thing.

24 And there rose also a contention among them, which of them was accounted to be greatest.   25 And he said unto them, The kings of the Gentiles have lordship over them; and they that have authority over them are called Benefactors.   26 But ye shall not be so: but he that is the greater among you, let him become as the younger; and he that is chief, as he that doth serve.   27 For which is greater, he that sitteth at meat, or he that serveth? is not he that sitteth at meat? but I am in the midst of you as he that serveth.   28 But ye are they that have continued with me in my temptations; 29 and I appoint unto you a kingdom, even as my Father appointed unto me, 30 that ye may eat and drink at my table in my kingdom; and ye shall sit on thrones judging the twelve tribes of Israel.   31 Simon, Simon, behold, Satan asked to have you, that he might sift you as wheat: 32 but I made supplication for thee, that thy faith fail not; and do thou, when once thou hast turned again, establish thy brethren.   33 And he said unto him, Lord, with thee I am ready to go both to prison and to death.   34 And he said, I tell thee, Peter, the cock shall not crow this day, until thou shalt thrice deny that thou knowest me.

35 And he said unto them, When I sent you forth without purse, and wallet, and shoes, lacked ye anything? And they said, Nothing. 36 And he said unto them, But now, he that hath a purse, let him take it, and likewise a wallet; and he that hath none, let him sell his cloak, and buy a sword. 37 For I say unto you, that this which is written must be fulfilled in me, And he was reckoned with transgressors: for that which concerneth me hath fulfilment. 38 And they said, Lord, behold, here are two swords. And he said unto them, It is enough.

The last meal of which Jesus partook with his disciples was a Passover feast, and it was the occasion of the establishment of that Sacrament which is known as the Lord's Supper. The Passover called to mind a national deliverance in the past and pointed forward to a greater deliverance to come, which was effected by the death of Christ. The Lord's Supper points us backward to the great redemption he achieved by his atoning death, and forward to the fuller redemption he will accomplish in his return. The "Last Supper" may rightly be reviewed in connection with the Christian Sacrament, and the story here recorded may intimate to us how this Sacrament may be most helpfully observed.

1. It must be for us a time of retirement. So far as possible we must exclude all distracting thoughts and fix our minds upon Christ and his redeeming love. Jesus made such provision for his disciples. He sent Peter and John to the city to prepare a room in which he might partake of the Passover with his disciples, but he was careful to provide against any possible interruption. He did not mention to the disciples the place of meeting. Had he done so, Judas would have disclosed the place to the enemies who would have arrested Jesus in the midst of the supper. Our Lord was careful to say to the two disciples that as they entered the city there would meet them "a man bearing a pitcher of water"; they were to follow him into the house and were there to prepare the Passover.

According to the account of the other Evangelists, it seems that after the Passover feast had been eaten and before Jesus established his memorial supper, he dismissed Judas from the circle. Surely it must be our endeavor to shut out from our hearts all traitorous and intrusive thoughts, that during the sacred service we may be consciously alone with our Lord.

2. It is to be a time of communion. Our Lord had eagerly looked forward to those hours to be spent with his disciples in unbroken fellowship. He had much to tell them. He knew it was to be a season of tender farewell, and he wished to strengthen them by messages of cheer and of hope. Probably in the whole Bible there are no chapters more familiar, more tender, more helpful, than those written by John containing the words spoken by our Lord in the upper room on the occasion of this Last Supper. To those whose hearts are prepared, the unseen Lord is surely present and ready to speak, through the appointed symbols and by his Spirit, truths which will inspire strength and joy.

3. It is to be a season of gratitude. The Sacrament has often been called the "Eucharist," the service of "thanksgiving," for we then call to mind the infinite benefits secured for us by the atoning death of our Lord. This is the supreme purpose of the feast. Jesus stated this clearly when establishing it; the bread was to call to mind his body broken for us, and the wine was to be a symbol of his blood, which as he said to his disciples, was to be poured out for them. This supper is therefore to be a memorial of redeeming grace; it is to show forth the Lord's death, as he himself said, "This do in remembrance of me."

4. It is to be a time of hope. Even under the shadow of the cross our Lord pointed his disciples to the glory of his throne; while their hearts were torn by the thought of separation, he reminded them of a reunion when they would eat and drink together "in the kingdom of God." He declared that they were to have a time of temptation,

but if they suffered with him, they would also reign with him. "I appoint unto you a kingdom, even as my Father appointed unto me, that ye may eat and drink at my table in my kingdom." Thus Communion is a time when we especially look forward to glad reunions with those who have passed on before. We cheer our hearts with visions of coming glory. Under the darkest shadows we look for the opening skies and for the return of Christ; we "proclaim the Lord's death till he come."

5. It is a time of consecration. While the disciples were seated at the table, they were disputing as to which of them was greatest. Our Savior gave them a memorable example when he stooped down and washed their feet, and then most impressively he explained to them the character of true greatness and showed that its essence lay in service; to quote his own words, "He that is the greater among you, let him become as the younger; and he that is chief, as he that doth serve." As we turn from the table of our Lord, it should ever be with a desire to go forth in his name and to do anything in our power to serve our fellowmen, and to follow in his footsteps who came "not to be ministered unto, but to minister, and to give his life a ransom for many."

6. It should be a time of humility, when we realize anew our weakness and our dependence upon Christ and his sustaining grace. Jesus found it necessary to warn his disciples concerning their coming temptations and trials, and particularly to foretell the fall of Peter. Turning to the impulsive, affectionate, fickle disciple, who seems to have been the leader of the apostolic band, he told him that Satan had desired to have the disciples, to sift them as wheat, but that Jesus himself had made special prayer for Peter that his faith should not fail, even though Jesus foresaw that for a time his courage would give way and that he would deny his Master. He urged Peter, however, to repent after his fall and to encourage his fellow disciples. Such a statement of the weakness and unfaithfulness which

Peter was to manifest seemed incredible to him and he protested, "Lord, with thee I am ready to go both to prison and to death." But Jesus sadly replied, "I tell thee, Peter, the cock shall not crow this day, until thou shalt thrice deny that thou knowest me."

It is impossible to observe the Lord's Supper without memories of past failure, and it is only too true that similar experiences of weakness will be shown in days to come. Every such disloyalty gives pain to our Lord, but if our hearts are really yielded to him, our faults will be followed by true repentance. If we really trust in him, he is ready to pardon; as he prayed for Peter, so he is praying for us; though we at times stumble, he will not allow us utterly to fall. He is able to save "to the uttermost . . . , seeing he ever liveth to make intercession" for us.

7. This should be a time of new resolution. We should be humble and trustful in view of past and of possible future failures, but we should determine to stand firmly in the strength which the Master supplies. He told his followers in the upper room of the changed conditions which they were to meet when he had been taken from them. The enemies who would take his life would surely not treat his disciples with kindness. He assured them that they were now to be left more to their own resources and that they were to meet with the most bitter hostility. He even suggested that it would be necessary for each one to buy a sword. They took his words with absurd literalness and they said, "Lord, behold, here are two swords." It was with sad irony that Jesus replied, "It is enough." Of course, he did not mean that his followers are to use violence or are to extend the gospel by means of force. He only wished us to be warned and to resolve anew that in the spiritual conflict which awaits us, we shall be true to him as loyal soldiers of the cross. We go forth to battle, but on some brighter morrow we shall be seated with him at a heavenly feast with banquet and song.

C. THE AGONY IN GETHSEMANE Ch. 22:39-46

39 And he came out, and went, as his custom was, unto the mount of Olives; and the disciples also followed him. 40 And when he was at the place, he said unto them, Pray that ye enter not into temptation. 41 And he was parted from them about a stone's cast; and he kneeled down and prayed, 42 saying, Father, if thou be willing, remove this cup from me: nevertheless not my will, but thine, be done. 43 And there appeared unto him an angel from heaven, strengthening him. 44 And being in an agony he prayed more earnestly; and his sweat became as it were great drops of blood falling down upon the ground. 45 And when he rose up from his prayer, he came unto the disciples, and found them sleeping for sorrow, 46 and said unto them, Why sleep ye? rise and pray, that ye enter not into temptation.

From the quiet fellowship in the upper room Jesus with his disciples, under the shadow of the night, went forth to the Garden of Gethsemane, a favorite resort on the slope of the Mount of Olives, and he there experienced that unequaled anguish of soul which is commonly known as his "agony." To enter the sacred privacy of that scene even in imagination seems to be an intrusion, and yet some glimpses have been revealed for our instruction and encouragement as his disciples.

There can be no doubt that this distress which seized him was due to his clear vision of the death he was to endure on the following day; and this very agony adds beyond measure to the meaning and the mystery of that death. For any sensitive soul to shrink from pain and anguish is but natural and pardonable; yet if Jesus suffered such incomparable agony simply in view of physical torture, he was less heroic than many of his followers have been. If, however, in the hour of death, he was to be so identified with sin as to become the Redeemer of the world; if he was "to give his life a ransom for many"; if his experience as the Lamb of God was to be absolutely unique; if he was to endure the hiding of his Father's face, then we can understand why it was that in the dark hour of anticipation his soul was sorrowful "even unto death." The agony of our Lord must never be supposed to reflect upon his human heroism; it is rather a proof of his divine atonement. The "cup" which Jesus was asked to drink consisted of death as "the Bearer of sin."

In this hour of most bitter trial Jesus found relief in prayer. He had come to Gethsemane that he might be alone with God. He had exhorted his disciples to follow his example. When the agony most fiercely gripped his lonely heart he still prayed and he was heard. The cup was not removed, but "there appeared unto him an angel from heaven, strengthening him." He was given grace to drain the cup to its very dregs and death lost its sting and the grave its terror. He was fitted for perfect sympathy with those who are called upon to face the mystery of "unanswered prayer." "He became unto all them that obey him the author of eternal salvation."

Jesus prayed in faith; and the very essence of such believing prayer is the willingness to obey. This was the petition which comes to us as an example, "Nevertheless not my will, but thine, be done." He won his victory by complete submission to the will of his Father. Henceforth there was no more struggle. He turned with unfaltering step to meet betrayal and agony and death. The hour struck and he was ready. "He was well content."

D. THE ARREST OF JESUS Ch. 22:47-53

47 While he yet spake, behold, a multitude, and he that was called Judas, one of the twelve, went before them; and he drew near unto Jesus to kiss him. 48 But Jesus said unto him, Judas, betrayest thou the Son of man with a kiss? 49 And when they that were about him saw what would follow, they said, Lord, shall we smite with the sword? 50 And a certain one of them smote the servant of the high

*priest, and struck off his right ear. 51 But Jesus answered
and said, Suffer ye them thus far. And he touched his ear,
and healed him. 52 And Jesus said unto the chief
priests, and captains of the temple, and elders, that were
come against him, Are ye come out, as against a robber,
with swords and staves? 53 When I was daily with you in
the temple, ye stretched not forth your hands against me:
but this is your hour, and the power of darkness.*

The manner in which Judas concluded his foul crime
was in perfect keeping with its essential baseness. He led
a multitude armed with swords and clubs into the Garden
where his Master was wont to retire for prayer, and there
betrayed him with a kiss, a sign which had been agreed
upon in order that, in the deep shadows, one of the disciples might not be mistaken for the Master and arrested
in his place. A kiss was a usual sign of friendship, but
the manner of Judas and the rebuke of Jesus indicate that
it was given with a false semblance of deep affection and
was thus the more repulsive to the Lord. Acts of disloyalty to Christ are even more distressing to him in surroundings which are sacred and when committed by those
who have made loud protestations of love.

The fearless composure of the Master is now contrasted
with the conduct of his followers. They asked whether they
should defend him with the sword, and before he could
reply, Peter rashly smote the servant of the high priest and
cut off his right ear. To this act Jesus made reply: "Suffer
ye them thus far"; the exact meaning is not certain, but
probably he was addressing his disciples to prevent further
violence. He then touched the ear of the servant and
healed him. Only Luke, "the beloved physician," mentions this "unique miracle of surgery." The incident has
its message for disciples in all ages. Violence and cruelty
in the defense of the cause of Christ misrepresent him to
the world. The act of Peter gave countenance to charges
which would be preferred against Jesus, and further re-
sistance would have compromised the position of his Lord.

However well intended, such rash defenses weaken the cause they are designed to promote.

Jesus turned to rebuke his enemies and resented the fact that they had come against him as against a robber with swords and clubs. He reminded them that daily he had taught in public. Their coming with violence, in secrecy, and under the cover of night, was a proof that the arrest was false and that it could not be justified. There had been abundant opportunities during many days to seize him in public when he was unprotected. Their present course bore its own condemnation; but he added mournfully, "This is your hour, and the power of darkness." In the mystery of his providence God was allowing this iniquity. He was giving this temporary authority to the forces of evil. It was to be a brief hour, but those who willingly put it to such a use would incur eternal condemnation. Nothing is more solemn than the possibility of using for evil ends the liberty allotted us of God.

E. PETER'S DENIAL Ch. 22:54-62

54 And they seized him, and led him away, and brought him into the high priest's house. But Peter followed afar off. 55 And when they had kindled a fire in the midst of the court, and had sat down together, Peter sat in the midst of them. 56 And a certain maid seeing him as he sat in the light of the fire, and looking stedfastly upon him, said, This man also was with him. 57 But he denied, saying, Woman, I know him not. 58 And after a little while another saw him, and said, Thou also art one of them. But Peter said, Man, I am not. 59 And after the space of about one hour another confidently affirmed, saying, Of a truth this man also was with him; for he is a Galilæan. 60 But Peter said, Man, I know not what thou sayest. And immediately, while he yet spake, the cock crew. 61 And the Lord turned, and looked upon Peter. And Peter remembered the word of the Lord, how that he said unto him, Before the cock crow this day thou shalt deny me thrice. 62 And he went out, and wept bitterly.

Peter really loved Jesus, and his faith in him never failed; but in the hour of trial, which Jesus had predicted, Peter lost courage and denied his Lord. His sin, however, was unlike that of Judas. The latter was the final step in a downward course. The former was an act of cowardice in a career of moral development which resulted in blessing and service to all the followers of Christ.

The fall of Peter may be traced to his self-confidence. When he protested that he would be true to Christ, even though all should forsake him, he was sincere and expressed the true feeling of his heart, but he betrayed his pride. The immediate result was his failure to obey the Master and to watch and pray as he had been bidden; and consequently he was surprised and stunned by the arrest of Jesus, and like the other disciples, after a rash stroke in his defense, he forsook Jesus and fled. He followed Jesus to the palace of the high priest but hoped to conceal his discipleship and to be regarded as one of the excited crowd.

Every follower of Christ is in mortal danger when confident of his moral strength and especially when at the same time he is ashamed to be publicly known as a disciple, and most of all when he feels, as Peter probably felt, that confessed loyalty to Christ can under the circumstances be of no special help to his Lord. At such a time when the cause of Jesus seemed hopeless, when the courage of Peter was gone, when he was wearied by the long night of sleeplessness, when cold and lonely, the unexpected attack was made and Peter suffered his tragic defeat.

It may be easy to point the finger of scorn at the great apostle, but there are few followers of Christ who at times of less severe testing have not as truly denied their Lord, by word or deed, with cowardice and deceit and passion. Three times Peter repeated his denial and then he heard the crowing of a cock. The incident was insignificant in itself, but it recalled the word of his Master; it made Peter conscious of his disgrace but it called him to himself, and then as he turned toward the palace, for a moment he caught sight of his Lord. We may be unable to conjecture what was expressed in the face of Jesus as at that moment he "looked upon Peter." There may have been something of rebuke, but probably there was more of unutterable sorrow and of tender sympathy. We read that as "Peter remembered the word of the Lord, . . . he went out, and wept bitterly." Surely these were tears of repentance and they prepared the way for pardon and for peace. To many a fallen follower of Christ, there has come some minute providence recalling hours of glad fellowship and messages of solemn warning, and the heart has been turned toward the Master, and true repentance has been felt in realizing the pain which the disloyalty has brought to the loving Lord. The consciousness has brought bitter tears and hours of regret and of anguish, but they have been followed by a brighter morning, by a meeting with the risen Christ, by a new confession of love, by words of peace, and by a truer life of deeper devotion to his cause.

F. JESUS BEFORE THE JEWISH RULERS
Ch. 22:63-71

63 And the men that held Jesus mocked him, and beat him. 64 And they blindfolded him, and asked him, saying, Prophesy: who is he that struck thee? 65 And many other things spake they against him, reviling him.

66 And as soon as it was day, the assembly of the elders of the people was gathered together, both chief priests and scribes; and they led him away into their council, saying, 67 If thou art the Christ, tell us. But he said unto them, If I tell you, ye will not believe: 68 and if I ask you, ye will not answer. 69 But from henceforth shall the Son of man be seated at the right hand of the power of God. 70 And they all said, Art thou then the Son of God? And he said unto them, Ye say that I am. 71 And they said, What further need have we of witness? for we ourselves have heard from his own mouth.

After Jesus had been denied by Peter, he was grossly insulted and abused by his captors. He was mocked and beaten and reviled. Those responsible for these indignities were the Jewish rulers, the most cultured and refined and professedly religious men of their day; but the beast within man is more powerful than we commonly suppose. When Christ is rejected, when his teachings are despised, when his Spirit is opposed, then it is only a question of time and of occasion when hatred or malice or lust or anger awaken in man the passions and ferocity of the brute.

When the morning dawned, Jesus was led away to be arraigned formally before the Sanhedrin, the supreme ecclesiastical court of the Jews. He was supposed to be on trial for his life; in reality the council was being judged, and in its guilt the entire nation was involved. The rulers convicted themselves of prejudice, dishonesty, and malice. They did not seek to learn the truth that justice might be done; they sought to find some evidence on which Jesus might be condemned.

When every attempt to convict Jesus had failed, they finally charged him in the words: "If thou art the Christ, tell us." Jesus' reply shows how fully he appreciated their blind hatred and their unwillingness to be just; he told them that no statement he might make would be believed, and that no explanation or defense he might offer would be accepted; nevertheless, he would answer their question, with the statement that his exaltation to the place of divine power was about to take place. Then they asked him directly, "Art thou then the Son of God?" He answered with all distinctness, "Ye say that I am." Then they at once decreed that he was worthy of death. They had prejudged the case. They were unwilling to consider whether his claim to be the Son of God was true; they only wished to be sure that he made the claim. When they had made sure of this, they agreed that he must die as a blasphemer. Their logic was so far true. There is no other alternative. In the presence of Christ there can be no neutrality. Either he was an impostor who deserves our contempt, or else he is the divine Son of God whom we must worship and obey. Every soul must choose between the Sanhedrin and the church.

G. JESUS BEFORE PILATE Ch. 23:1-25

1 And the whole company of them rose up, and brought him before Pilate. 2 And they began to accuse him, saying, We found this man perverting our nation, and forbidding to give tribute to Cæsar, and saying that he himself is Christ a king. 3 And Pilate asked him, saying, Art thou the King of the Jews? And he answered him and said, Thou sayest. 4 And Pilate said unto the chief priests and the multitudes, I find no fault in this man. 5 But they were the more urgent, saying, He stirreth up the people, teaching throughout all Judæa, and beginning from Galilee even unto this place. 6 But when Pilate heard it, he asked whether the man were a Galilæan. 7 And when he knew that he was of Herod's jurisdiction, he sent him unto Herod, who himself also was at Jerusalem in these days.

8 Now when Herod saw Jesus, he was exceeding glad: for he was of a long time desirous to see him, because he had heard concerning him; and he hoped to see some miracle done by him. 9 And he questioned him in many words; but he answered him nothing. 10 And the chief priests and the scribes stood, vehemently accusing him. 11 And Herod with his soldiers set him at nought, and mocked him, and arraying him in gorgeous apparel sent him back to Pilate. 12 And Herod and Pilate became friends with each other that very day: for before they were at enmity between themselves.

13 And Pilate called together the chief priests and the rulers and the people, 14 and said unto them, Ye brought unto me this man, as one that perverteth the people: and behold, I, having examined him before you, found no fault in this man touching those things whereof ye accuse him: 15 no, nor yet Herod: for he sent him back unto us; and behold, nothing worthy of death hath been done by him.

16 I will therefore chastise him, and release him. 18 But they cried out all together, saying, Away with this man, and release unto us Barabbas:—19 one who for a certain insurrection made in the city, and for murder, was cast into prison. 20 And Pilate spake unto them again, desiring to release Jesus; 21 but they shouted, saying, Crucify, crucify him. 22 And he said unto them the third time, Why, what evil hath this man done? I have found no cause of death in him: I will therefore chastise him and release him. 23 But they were urgent with loud voices, asking that he might be crucified. And their voices prevailed. 24 And Pilate gave sentence that what they asked for should be done. 25 And he released him that for insurrection and murder had been cast into prison, whom they asked for; but Jesus he delivered up to their will.

The Jews had been deprived by their Roman conquerors of the right to inflict capital punishment. When, therefore, their chief council had decided that Jesus was worthy of death, the rulers brought him to Pilate, the Roman governor, that he might confirm their sentence and execute the cruel penalty of crucifixion. The trial before Pilate developed into a disgraceful contest between the murderous and determined Jewish rulers and the weak and vacillating Roman governor, who was at last compelled to act contrary to his conscience and his desire and to submit his will to that of the subjects whom he detested.

Luke gives only a bare outline of the story, which is sketched best by the apostle John. Enough, however, is given to show the infamous baseness of the Jews and the futile endeavors of Pilate to avoid the judicial murder which he finally committed. The Jewish rulers had asked Pilate to pronounce sentence without hearing the charge; this Pilate properly refused to do. When the accusation was made, Luke shows most clearly how craftily the decision of the Jewish court was perverted, and how forcibly the false charge was presented. Jesus had been convicted of claiming to be the divine Messiah. It was the claim of deity, and thus of blasphemy, on which he was condemned.

The Jews knew that this would make no impression on Pilate. However, the office of Messiah did imply rule and authority, and therefore the claim of Jesus was distorted into a political offense and he was charged with sedition, with forbidding tribute to Caesar, and with claiming to be a king.

How absurd all these accusations were, Pilate soon learned; he probably was not a little suspicious of the sudden zeal for their Roman tyrants shown by these rebellious Jews. However, he lacked the courage of his convictions; he declared Jesus to be innocent, but fearing to offend the rulers and the crowds whom they had won to their will, he hesitated to release Jesus. That was a fatal step; the only thing to do is to act with decision and promptness as soon as one sees what is right. It is surely true in matters of conscience that "he who hesitates is lost."

Then Pilate did what all weak men are apt to do: he attempted to avoid making a decision; he tried to shift the responsibility; he learned that Jesus was from Galilee, and so Pilate sent Jesus to be judged by King Herod, within whose realm Galilee lay. Herod was then in Jerusalem, and he was eager to see Jesus, of whom he had heard so much, and he hoped that his curiosity might be gratified by seeing Jesus perform some miracle. However, when appearing before Herod, Jesus refused even to answer him by a single word. Jesus has a message for every penitent, and a miracle for every believer; but for the murderer of John and for the shallow, sinful profligate there is only silence and contempt.

To wreak upon Jesus a petty revenge, Herod mocked Jesus by clothing him with royal apparel, and sent him back thus arrayed to Pilate. It was a cruel jest, but it was an acquittal of Jesus as guilty of no political offense. Thus Pilate was forced to act as judge; others cannot decide for us questions of conscience. When compelled to act, Pilate attempted a second maneuver familiar to all weak souls; he proposed to compromise. He would do what was wrong but he would avoid the crime of murder. He offered to scourge Jesus, whom he declared to be absolutely innocent, or to release him as a notable criminal, as one such was usually released at this feast.   On the one hand, he would be subjecting Jesus to the most agonizing bodily torture; on the other, he would brand Jesus as a malefactor who had deserved death.   Compromise in a case of conscience is always a sign of weakness, and the enemy is sure to press his advantage.   As the rulers saw Pilate yielding thus far, they asked for the release of a notorious murderer by the name of Barabbas; and as they saw Jesus coming forth from the scourging, torn and bleeding, they cried out for his life, "Crucify, crucify him."   As Pilate hesitated, the rulers used their most deadly weapon; they suggested that they would report Pilate to the emperor as shielding a political revolutionist; they would imperil the position and life of the governor.   This attack Pilate could not withstand; when some personal loss was involved conscience was no longer to be considered.   He decided to do what he knew to be wrong; he "gave sentence that what they asked for should be done"; and so doing he placed himself near the head of that long list of moral cowards who share his eternal infamy for fearing to do the right.

The degradation of the Jewish rulers was even greater. With all their knowledge of the moral law, they who professed to be special representatives of God put to death his Son, and chose a murderer instead of the Savior.   To the tragedy of such a choice Luke refers with horror in the only personal comment he makes upon the scene.   V. 25. Are not thousands, however, making that same choice today?   There can be no neutral ground; indecision is impossible: one must choose either Barabbas or Christ.

H. THE CRUCIFIXION Ch. 23:26-38

26 And when they led him away, they laid hold upon one Simon of Cyrene, coming from the country, and laid on him the cross, to bear it after Jesus.

27 And there followed him a great multitude of the people, and of women who bewailed and lamented him. 28 But Jesus turning unto them said, Daughters of Jerusalem, weep not for me, but weep for yourselves, and for your children. 29 For behold, the days are coming, in which they shall say, Blessed are the barren, and the wombs that never bare, and the breasts that never gave suck. 30 Then shall they begin to say to the mountains, Fall on us; and to the hills, Cover us. 31 For if they do these things in the green tree, what shall be done in the dry?

32 And there were also two others, malefactors, led with him to be put to death.

33 And when they came unto the place which is called The skull, there they crucified him, and the malefactors, one on the right hand and the other on the left. 34 And Jesus said, Father, forgive them; for they know not what they do. And parting his garments among them, they cast lots. 35 And the people stood beholding. And the rulers also scoffed at him, saying, He saved others; let him save himself, if this is the Christ of God, his chosen. 36 And the soldiers also mocked him, coming to him, offering him vinegar, 37 and saying, If thou art the King of the Jews, save thyself. 38 And there was also a superscription over him, THIS IS THE KING OF THE JEWS.

The Gospel narratives spare us the distressing details of the crucifixion; this was the most cruel and agonizing form of death; but the facts are written with surprising delicacy and reserve. As Jesus was being led from the city, a certain Simon of Cyrene was pressed into the service of bearing his cross. The cause of this action is purely a matter of conjecture. Its result was to give Simon immortal fame and apparently to secure for him eternal salvation; for it seems that this experience, and the knowledge of Christ gained at Calvary, resulted in the conversion of Simon and his household. Mark 15:21; Rom. 16:13. In a figure, he was the first of that long line of men and women who have taken up the cross and followed Christ. Of course this is a mere symbol, and the actual contrasts are vital. In reality no one can share the burden of the cross which our Savior bore. His sufferings, and his alone, made atonement for sin. Then again no one can be compelled to take up the cross. There are burdens in life which cannot be evaded but one can refuse the cross. It is a type of the voluntary suffering endured for the sake of Christ; it is a symbol of the complete sacrifice of self and the complete submission to his will which is necessary for all who share in the redeeming benefits of his death.

Luke alone records the incident of the women who, wailing and lamenting, followed Jesus out of the city. It is quite fitting that in this Gospel, in which womanhood is so exalted, a place should be found for this picture. It is not to be supposed that these were the loyal friends who had followed Jesus on his journeys and helped to supply his needs; these were rather residents of Jerusalem whose hearts were bleeding with sorrow for the loving Prophet who was being led forth to an agonizing death. Our Lord turned to these women with a message of sympathy and told them that they were not to weep for him but for themselves and their children. He was not rebuking them for their compassion; he rather meant to indicate that while his sufferings were pitiful, their own were more worthy of tears, for they were to be even more intense. He had in mind the destruction of the city due to its impenitence and made certain by its rejection of the Redeemer. Jesus declared that the days would come when childlessness would be a ground for congratulation because of the universal distress. He predicted that the horror would be so great that men would call upon the mountains to fall on them and the hills to cover them, preferring such forms of death to the torments which threatened from the armies of Rome. Jesus added a proverb, the force of which is evident even though its exact application may not be clear: "For if they do these things in the green tree, what shall be done in the dry?" In other words, if the sufferings of Christ were so great, what would be the sufferings of the Jews! If the

Romans were putting to death him whom they regarded as innocent, what would they do to the inhabitants of the rebellious and hated city? It is quite in accordance with the character of Luke to note how Jesus, in this very hour of his anguish, thought rather of others than of himself and pronounced this prophecy, not in resentment, but in infinite tenderness and pity.

While the actual sufferings of the crucifixion are not described, Luke tells us of the cruel mockery to which Jesus was subjected. He states that two malefactors were crucified with Jesus, "one on the right hand and the other on the left." This was evidently designed to add to the disgrace and humiliation of his cruel death. The place of the crucifixion was called "The skull," probably because it was a bare, rounded hill located outside the city gates.

Of the seven words spoken by Jesus on the cross, Luke records three, all of them characterized by love and trust. The first is found in no other Gospel. As Jesus tasted the first bitterness of his anguish he was heard to pray, "Father forgive them; for they know not what they do." He did not have in mind simply the soldiers who were involuntary instruments of his death, but rather, the Jews who had not fully recognized the enormity of their crime. For them Jesus felt no hatred in his heart. He yearned for their repentance and their salvation. This prayer was a revelation of the matchless grace and mercy of this ideal Man. Luke adds the details of the mockery to which the other Evangelists likewise refer. The crowds stood gazing upon the Sufferer, but the rulers and the soldiers cruelly mocked him; the former scoffed at him saying, "He saved others; let him save himself." In reality, had he saved himself, he never could have saved others. He died for the very men who were deriding him, to make possible their salvation. The soldiers made sport of him by casting lots for his garments and by offering him drink and hailing him as "King of the Jews." This last title had been placed on the cross above the head of Jesus. It was put there by Pilate in bitter irony. It was his way of taking revenge upon the rulers who, contrary to his conscience, had compelled him to put to death an innocent Man. In place of this superscription the eye of faith sees another: "Behold, the Lamb of God, that taketh away the sin of the world!"

I. THE PENITENT THIEF Ch. 23:39-43

39 And one of the malefactors that were hanged railed on him, saying, Art not thou the Christ? save thyself and us. 40 But the other answered, and rebuking him said, Dost thou not even fear God, seeing thou art in the same condemnation? 41 And we indeed justly; for we receive the due reward of our deeds: but this man hath done nothing amiss. 42 And he said, Jesus, remember me when thou comest in thy kingdom. 43 And he said unto him, Verily I say unto thee, To-day shalt thou be with me in Paradise.

This story which enshrines for us the second saying of our Lord upon the cross has often been regarded as one of the most significant narratives in the Gospels: first, because it gives us such a picture of the unique person of Christ; here was a dying man who at the same time was a forgiving God. Then, here is a picture of the transforming power of Christ who in an instant of time changed a robber into a saint. Most of all, we have here a message of the conditions of salvation which are ever the same, namely, repentance and faith. The first of these conditions is strikingly illustrated from the fact that the repentant thief was thinking of God and remembering that it was against a divine Being that he had sinned. Of this fact he reminded his companion, intimating that they might properly fear him into whose august presence they were so soon to be ushered. It is the very essence of repentance to regard sin, not as a mistake or a weakness, or as an injury to men, but as rebellion and insult against God. His penitence was further shown in his recognition that the penalty which he was suffering was just, and in his recognition of the innocent sufferings of Christ.

His faith was as remarkable as his repentance. He saw in the bleeding, dying Sufferer, One who is yet to return as universal King, and to him he addressed his prayer: "Jesus, remember me when thou comest in thy kingdom." We do not know the source of such faith. The robber may have heard part of the trial of Jesus; he did hear him praying for his enemies; but whatever gave rise to his belief and trust, he regarded Jesus as a Savior and Lord who was yet to reign and who could bring him to eternal glory. This story thus reveals to us the truth that salvation is conditioned upon repentance and faith. However, it contains other important messages also. It declares that salvation is independent of Sacraments. The thief had never been baptized, nor had he partaken of the Lord's Supper. It is obvious that had he lived he would have carried out the requirements of his Lord by accepting these Sacraments. He did, in fact, boldly confess his faith in the presence of a hostile crowd and amid the taunts and jeers of rulers and soldiers, yet he was saved without any formal rites.

It is further evident that salvation is independent of good works. The thief was pardoned before he had lived a single, righteous, innocent day. Of course, good works follow faith; they evidence its reality; but faith precedes and results in holiness. A life of goodness is an expression of gratitude for salvation already begun.

It is further evident that there is no "sleep of the soul." The body may sleep, but consciousness persists after death. The word of the Master was, "To-day shalt thou be . . . in Paradise." Again it is evident that there is no "purgatory." If any man ever needed discipline and "purifying fires," it was this penitent robber. Out of a life of sin and shame he passed immediately into a state of blessedness. This was the promise: "To-day shalt thou be with me in Paradise."

Again it may be remarked that salvation is not universal.

There were two robbers; only one was saved. Jesus had heard them both speaking of him. He did not say "ye," but "Verily I say unto thee, To-day shalt thou be with me in Paradise."

Last of all, it may be noted that the very essence of the joy which lies beyond death consists in personal communion with Christ. The heart of the promise to the dying thief was this: "Thou shalt be with me." This is our blessed assurance, that to depart is to "be with Christ," which is "very far better."

J. THE DEATH AND BURIAL Ch. 23:44-56

44 And it was now about the sixth hour, and a darkness came over the whole land until the ninth hour, 45 the sun's light failing: and the veil of the temple was rent in the midst. 46 And Jesus, crying with a loud voice, said, Father, into thy hands I commend my spirit: and having said this, he gave up the ghost. 47 And when the centurion saw what was done, he glorified God, saying, Certainly this was a righteous man. 48 And all the multitudes that came together to this sight, when they beheld the things that were done, returned smiting their breasts. 49 And all his acquaintance, and the women that followed with him from Galilee, stood afar off, seeing these things.

50 And behold, a man named Joseph, who was a councillor, a good and righteous man 51 (he had not consented to their counsel and deed), a man of Arimathæa, a city of the Jews, who was looking for the kingdom of God: 52 this man went to Pilate, and asked for the body of Jesus. 53 And he took it down, and wrapped it in a linen cloth, and laid him in a tomb that was hewn in stone, where never man had yet lain. 54 And it was the day of the Preparation, and the sabbath drew on. 55 And the women who had come with him out of Galilee, followed after, and beheld the tomb, and how his body was laid. 56 And they returned and prepared spices and ointments.

And on the sabbath they rested according to the commandment.

The death of Christ was an event of such supreme importance that it properly was accompanied by supernatural
signs of deep significance. Of these, Luke mentions two.
The first was the darkened skies, a fit symbol of the black-
est crime in all the history of man. The second was the
rending of the Temple veil, a type of the "new and living
way" opened into the presence of God for all believers.
Thus these two signs correspond to the human and the
divine aspects of this atoning death, and indicate the hei-
nousness of sin and the purpose of redeeming grace.

The last word spoken by Jesus on the cross was an expression of perfect trust and peace. He had shown his
sympathy for others by his prayer, by his promise to the
penitent thief, and by his provision for his mother; by three
other words he had revealed his sufferings of mind and body
and their result in a completed redemption: "My God, my
God . . ."; "I thirst"; "It is finished." He now breathed
out his soul in a sentence of absolute confidence taken from
the psalmist and recorded by Luke alone: "Father, into
they hands I commend my spirit." It was the supreme
utterance of faith. The earthly ministry of the Son of God
had ended.

Luke notes the effects produced by the manner of Jesus'
death, and by the accompanying signs upon the Roman
centurion, the Jewish multitudes, and the Christian disciples. The soldier was so impressed that he "glorified
God," giving his testimony to the fact that the One whom
he had crucified as a criminal was a "righteous man."
Possibly he may be regarded as a type of that host of believing Gentiles, of whom Luke liked to write, who were yet
to enlist under the banner of the cross.

The crowds of Jews had little real desire for the crucifixion of Jesus; they had been hounded by their rulers to cry
out for his death, but they now returned to the city "smiting their breasts" in an agony of remorse, a prophecy of
Israel's future repentance and mourning as they "look on
him whom they pierced."

Most pathetic of all was that group of saddened disciples who "stood afar off" gazing in bewilderment upon the scene; but for them the meaning of that cross would begin to dawn as they should meet their risen Lord. For none of his followers has the cross lost its mystery; yet to them all it has become a symbol of triumph and of hope.

The body of Jesus was given burial by Joseph of Arimathea, a man whom Matthew designates as rich, Mark as a "councillor of honorable estate," and Luke as "good and righteous." Thus together they describe an ideal man from the Jewish and Roman and Greek point of view. Perhaps he is to be criticized for not having identified himself before this more publicly with the cause of Christ; but Luke makes not the slightest unfavorable reflection upon his character. He declares definitely that this powerful and influential member of the Sanhedrin "had not consented" to the "counsel and deed" of the rulers who had compassed the death of Jesus; and now in the hour when his Master was most deeply dishonored, he risked the scorn of the people and the hatred of the rulers and begged from Pilate the body of Jesus, which he wrapped in linen cloth and lay reverently in his own new, rock-hewn tomb. It was a deed of loving devotion, and adds a gratifying contrast and a touch of tenderness to the story of the cross.

Other loving hearts longed to have a part in this expression of affection. The women who had followed Jesus out of Galilee, noted the place of his burial and purchased perfumes to embalm the body of their Lord. However, as the declining sun marked the beginning, at eventide, of the Sabbath, they rested until the first day of the week, and then they found that their task was needless. It was well to show affection for the crucified Master, it is a greater privilege to serve a risen Lord.

K. THE EMPTY TOMB Ch. 24:1-12

1 But on the first day of the week, at early dawn, they came unto the tomb, bringing the spices which they had

*prepared. 2 And they found the stone rolled away from
the tomb. 3 And they entered in, and found not the body
of the Lord Jesus. 4 And it came to pass, while they were
perplexed thereabout, behold, two men stood by them in
dazzling apparel: 5 and as they were affrighted and bowed
down their faces to the earth, they said unto them, Why
seek ye the living among the dead? 6 He is not here, but
is risen: remember how he spake unto you when he was
yet in Galilee, 7 saying that the Son of man must be delivered up into the hands of sinful men, and be crucified, and
the third day rise again. 8 And they remembered his words,
9 and returned from the tomb, and told all these things
to the eleven, and to all the rest. 10 Now they were Mary
Magdalene, and Joanna, and Mary the mother of James:
and the other women with them told these things unto the
apostles. 11 And these words appeared in their sight as
idle talk; and they disbelieved them. 12 But Peter arose,
and ran unto the tomb; and stooping and looking in, he
seeth the linen cloths by themselves; and he departed to his
home, wondering at that which was come to pass.*

After seeing where Jesus was buried, the women who
had followed him from Galilee and had ministered to him
began preparing spices and ointments with which to embalm his body. However, as the day drew to its close, because this Friday evening was the beginning of a Jewish
Sabbath, they rested from their labor of love until Sunday,
"the first day of the week," and then "at early dawn" they
came to the tomb, but were astonished to find that the body
of Jesus was gone.

There are several explanations of this empty tomb, but
only one which is credible and which accords with the facts.
Some persons profess to believe that Jesus did not die, that
he only swooned upon the cross, that he regained consciousness after being laid in the tomb, that he escaped and
then appeared to his disciples; but Jesus had declared that
he was to die and was to rise again on the third day, and
he afterward made his disciples believe that such an experience had been his; this theory, therefore, cannot be held
without denying the honesty and morality of our Lord.

A second theory maintains that "his disciples came by night, and stole" away his body; but these disciples continually declared that he rose from the dead on the third day; according to this theory, then, these disciples were impostors; but this can be believed by no one familiar with their subsequent lives and influence.

It is as impossible to believe the third theory, namely, that the enemies of Jesus stole his body, for had that body been in their possession, how gladly they would have produced it and thus forever have silenced the disciples who declared that Jesus was alive and that his resurrection proved these enemies had put to death an innocent Man, their divine Messiah.

The only true explanation of this empty tomb is that given to the wondering women by two angels: "Why seek ye the living among the dead? He is not here, but is risen: remember how he spake unto you when he was yet in Galilee." This startling statement of the angels embodies the substance of the message delivered by the apostles. The truth it declares forms the cornerstone of Christian faith. The resurrection of our Lord is vitally connected with all the realities which relate to his person and work and to the life of his followers.

When, however, the fact of the resurrection had been reported to the apostles, they regarded the words of the women "as idle talk, and they disbelieved them." This incredulity on the part of the apostles shows the absolute absurdity of another theory advanced by those who deny the resurrection of our Lord, namely, the theory that his followers so eagerly expected him to rise from the dead that their fevered brains finally imagined that he had so risen and they testified to what was only a product of their own fancy. In reality the disciples did not expect Jesus to rise, and, as here recorded, when the truth was reported to them, they refused to accept it until proof upon proof had been given them and doubt and unbelief became absolutely impossible. They were prepared, however, for further proofs by the fact that the tomb in which the body was laid had been found empty. There is even more weighty evidence of the resurrection; but those who deny this supremely important event must give first some rational account of this empty tomb.

L. THE WALK TO EMMAUS Ch. 24:13-35

13 And behold, two of them were going that very day to a village named Emmaus, which was threescore furlongs from Jerusalem. 14 And they communed with each other of all these things which had happened. 15 And it came to pass, while they communed and questioned together, that Jesus himself drew near, and went with them. 16 But their eyes were holden that they should not know him. 17 And he said unto them, What communications are these that ye have one with another, as ye walk? And they stood still, looking sad. 18 And one of them, named Cleopas, answering said unto him, Dost thou alone sojourn in Jerusalem and not know the things which are come to pass there in these days? 19 And he said unto them, What things? And they said unto him, The things concerning Jesus the Nazarene, who was a prophet mighty in deed and word before God and all the people: 20 and how the chief priests and our rulers delivered him up to be condemned to death, and crucified him. 21 But we hoped that it was he who should redeem Israel. Yea and besides all this, it is now the third day since these things came to pass. 22 Moreover certain women of our company amazed us, having been early at the tomb; 23 and when they found not his body, they came, saying, that they had also seen a vision of angels, who said that he was alive. 24 And certain of them that were with us went to the tomb, and found it even so as the women had said: but him they saw not. 25 And he said unto them, O foolish men, and slow of heart to believe in all that the prophets have spoken! 26 Behooved it not the Christ to suffer these things, and to enter into his glory? 27 And beginning from Moses and from all the prophets, he interpreted to them in all the scriptures the things concerning himself. 28 And they drew nigh unto the village, whither they were going: and he made as though he would go further. 29 And they constrained him, saying, Abide with us; for it is toward evening, and the day is now far spent. And he went in to abide with them. 30 And it came to pass, when he had sat down with them to meat, he took the bread and blessed; and breaking it he gave to them. 31 And their eyes were opened, and they knew him; and he vanished out of their sight. 32 And they said one to another, Was not our heart burning within us, while he spake to us in the way, while he opened to us the scriptures? 33 And they rose up that very hour, and returned to Jerusalem, and found the eleven gathered together, and them that were with them, 34 saying, The Lord is risen indeed, and hath appeared to Simon. 35 And they rehearsed the things that happened in the way, and how he was known of them in the breaking of the bread.

No man saw Christ rise; but many saw the risen Christ. He appeared to Mary and to Peter and to James and to "the eleven" and to more than five hundred disciples at one time; but of the appearances on the day of his resurrection none is recorded with more dramatic vividness and more definiteness of detail than that related by Luke when Jesus walked with two disciples toward Emmaus.

This village was probably situated some seven miles northwest of Jerusalem. Thither these two men were moving with sad and discouraged hearts when Jesus joined them and drew from them expressions of their disappointment and despair. The One on whom they had set their hopes of redemption for Israel had been put to death, and although he had spoken mysteriously of a resurrection on the third day, the day was passing, and he had not been seen, although it was true that reports had reached them of a vision of angels who said that he was alive. Such in substance seem to have been their words, in no small measure a confession of obstinate unbelief. They had little expectation that the Lord would fulfill his own promises; the third day of which he had spoken was not ended, and yet they were hopelessly turning their backs upon Jerusalem;

heavenly messengers had sent them an announcement of cheer which they refused to receive.

It was not strange, therefore, that Jesus rebuked them: "O foolish men, and slow of heart to believe in all that the prophets have spoken! Behooved it not the Christ to suffer these things, and to enter into his glory?" It is noticeable that Jesus did not chide them for refusing to accept his own words, or those of their friends, or those of angels; they were rebuked for not believing the Old Testament. They had accepted it in part; as men often accept just so much as suits their prejudices and tastes and notions; but they failed to believe in all that the prophets had spoken, and particularly the predictions of Jesus' atoning death, and of his return to the heavenly glory which he would share when he ascended. They listened in wonder to his explanation of the Scriptures, and finally as they were sitting at meat with him they discovered that they were in the actual presence of their living Lord. As he disappeared from sight, they hastened back to the disciples in Jerusalem and found them already wondering at the news that earlier in the day Jesus had appeared to Peter.

No story tells us more impressively the truth that a divine Savior walks beside us all the way of our earthly journey. It is pathetic that our eyes are so often dimmed by unbelief that we fail to realize his presence. We walk and are sad while we might be rejoicing in his companionship. It may be as the Scriptures are opened to us, or as we meet to break bread in his name, that our blindness will be removed; and surely when the journey ends and we enter the home toward which we are moving, we shall see him face-to-face, and the vision will not fade in deepening twilight, but grow more glorious through the eternal day.

M. JESUS APPEARING TO THE APOSTLES
Ch. 24:36-43

36 And as they spake these things, he himself stood in the midst of them, and saith unto them, Peace be unto you.

37 But they were terrified and affrighted, and supposed that they beheld a spirit. 38 And he said unto them, Why are ye troubled? and wherefore do questionings arise in your heart? 39 See my hands and my feet, that it is I myself: handle me, and see; for a spirit hath not flesh and bones, as ye behold me having. 40 And when he had said this, he showed them his hands and his feet. 41 And while they still disbelieved for joy, and wondered, he said unto them, Have ye here anything to eat? 42 And they gave him a piece of a broiled fish. 43 And he took it, and ate before them.

The incidents of the day on which Jesus rose from the dead, as recorded by Luke, form not only a sequence in time, but also move in logical order. The empty tomb can be explained by no other theory than that of a resurrection; but this was only negative proof. To it was added the actual appearance of Jesus to two disciples on their way to Emmaus. Yet this was not evidence enough. Some persons might believe that such an appearance had been a mere vision, a phantom, a ghost; therefore, as Luke relates the appearance of Jesus to the eleven disciples in the upper room, after night had fallen, he lays stress upon the fact that Jesus appeared in bodily form. When the disciples saw him they thought that they did see a mere specter, an apparition, a spirit, just as many persons have thought, even to the present day; but to forever dispel such a false impression, Jesus, by every possible appeal to the senses, made it evident that he possessed not an "immaterial," or "spiritual," or "celestial" body, but the identical body of flesh and blood which on Friday had been crucified and laid in the tomb; in that actual body, scarred by the cruel nails, a body capable of eating food, a material body which could be touched and felt, he appeared to his disciples. Moreover, he solemnly declared that he was not a disembodied spirit; he showed them the wounds in his hands and feet; he declared that a spirit does not have flesh and bones which they saw he had; and finally, to remove every lingering doubt, he took "a piece of a broiled fish" and "ate before them." The appearances and disappearances of Jesus after his resurrection may have been mysterious or miraculous as was his walking upon the sea in the days of his previous ministry; but he gave his disciples to understand by every conceivable, sensible sign that he had risen from the dead in his actual, physical, human body. The theory that the resurrection can be explained as a hallucination, a vision, or an apparition is forever silenced by the testimony of Luke, the careful historian, the intelligent physician. Upon the foundation of the established fact of a literal, bodily resurrection, this superstructure of our Christian faith firmly stands.

N. THE LAST WORDS Ch. 24:44-49

44 And he said unto them, These are my words which I spake unto you, while I was yet with you, that all things must needs be fulfilled, which are written in the law of Moses, and the prophets, and the psalms, concerning me. 45 Then opened he their mind, that they might understand the scriptures; 46 and he said unto them, Thus it is written, that the Christ should suffer, and rise again from the dead the third day; 47 and that repentance and remission of sins should be preached in his name unto all the nations, beginning from Jerusalem. 48 Ye are witnesses of these things. 49 And behold, I send forth the promise of my Father upon you: but tarry ye in the city, until ye be clothed with power from on high.

It need not be supposed that the last words of Jesus as recorded by Luke were spoken on the day of the resurrection or at any one time or place. They more probably indicate the general substance of those teachings which are given by the risen Christ to his disciples during the forty days between his resurrection and his ascension.

They are luminous with truths which are needed by the disciples of Christ today. Among them are such facts as these: The Scriptures contain authoritative messages concerning Christ; these messages can be understood only by those who believe in Christ and are guided by him; the essential truths concerning Christ center in the facts of his death and resurrection; in virtue of the salvation thus secured, repentance and forgiveness of sins can be preached; this salvation is to be proclaimed in all the world; the followers of Christ are the messengers by whom this good news is to be made known; the power for such proclamation is imparted by the Spirit of Christ who was manifested in new power on the Day of Pentecost, and who is now an abiding Presence and a source of limitless strength to all who seek to do the will of Christ and to glorify his name.

O. THE ASCENSION Ch. 24:50-53

50 And he led them out until they were over against Bethany: and he lifted up his hands, and blessed them. 51 And it came to pass, while he blessed them, he parted from them, and was carried up into heaven. 52 And they worshipped him, and returned to Jerusalem with great joy: 53 and were continually in the temple, blessing God.

The ascension of our Lord was an event quite distinct from the resurrection; it occurred nearly six weeks later, and indicates a number of supremely important truths.

1. Jesus then withdrew from the sphere of the seen and physical to the sphere of the unseen and spiritual. He did not pass up or down through vast spaces of the skies. We are not to think of him as far away. He is an unseen, divine Presence, superior to the limitations of time and space, and capable of being manifest in any period or place. The ascension should make us feel that Jesus is near rather than far away.

2. Jesus then assumed universal power; not at the time of his resurrection but at the time of his ascension, he was seated "on the right hand of the Majesty on high." This

indicates divine omnipotence.   It is the continual repre-
sentation of the New Testament that Jesus Christ has all
authority in heaven and on earth.   The ascension should
therefore remind us of the limitless power of Christ.

3. It was therefore at the time of the ascension that
Jesus entered "into his glory."   Then it was that his body
was transformed, made deathless, "spiritual," celestial, immortal; and then he again began to share the divine glory
which he had with the Father "before the world was."
The ascension, therefore, is a pledge and type of the glory
which yet awaits his followers.   It is an assurance that he
yet will fulfill his promises and will again appear; emerg-
ing from the sphere of the unseen, he will be manifested
to all mankind both as the ideal Man and as the Savior
of the world.